NON-FICTION

355.1342 Sch78

Schubert, Frank N
Black valor :buffalo soldiers and t
he Medal of Honor, 1870-1898

10/97

9000804524

DISCARDED BY
MEAD PUBLIC LIBRARY

D1320266

BLACK VALOR

BLACK VALOR

Buffalo Soldiers and the Medal of Honor, 1870-1898

Frank N. Schubert

A Scholarly Resources Inc. Imprint
Wilmington, Delaware

© 1997 by Scholarly Resources Inc.
All rights reserved
First published 1997
Printed and bound in the United States of America

Scholarly Resources Inc.
104 Greenhill Avenue
Wilmington, DE 19805-1897

Frontispiece: Shown, left to right, are the 1862 and 1896 versions of the U.S. Army Medal of Honor. All twenty-three buffalo soldier recipients wore medals of one of these two designs. Photograph by Tony Skiscim. Medals courtesy of the U.S. Army Institute of Heraldry.

Jacket design: Ellen C. Dawson

Library of Congress Cataloging-in-Publication Data

Schubert, Frank N.
 Black valor : buffalo soldiers and the Medal of Honor, 1870–1898 / Frank N. Schubert.
  p. cm.
 Includes bibliographical references (p.   ) and index.
 ISBN 0-8420-2586-3
 1. Afro-Americans—West (U.S.)—History—19th century. 2. Afro-American soldiers—West (U.S.)—History—19th century. 3. United States. Army—Afro-American troops—History—19th century. 4. Medal of Honor. 5. Indians of North America—Wars—1886–1895. 6. West (U.S.)—History. 7. Spanish-American War, 1898—Participation, Afro-American. I. Title.
 E185.925.S43   1997
 355.1'342'08996073—dc21   96-29897
                                                        CIP

⊗The paper used in this publication meets the minimum requirements of the American National Standard for permanence of paper for printed library materials, Z39.48, 1984.

recycled paper

804524

To My Mother

Elizabeth Schubert

Contents

Preface

This book examines the lives and military experiences of twenty-three black American soldiers who were awarded the Medal of Honor for valor between the Civil War and World War I. Serving in the Army just after the era of slavery ended, they participated in some of the more grueling frontier campaigns and America's first overseas war in half a century. These buffalo soldiers, as they came to be called, made important contributions to the fighting ability of the small Army of which they were members. They also served as role models and as reminders that blacks may have lacked opportunity but not soldierly skill or commitment to the nation. Along the way these heroes kept alive a tradition of courage under fire established during the Civil War and carried on by their successors in the twentieth century.

The idea for this book came from Richard M. Hopper, editorial director of Scholarly Resources. Shortly after the company published my *On the Trail of the Buffalo Soldier*, he suggested that I take on this project. I accepted his proposal eagerly for two reasons. First, my research on the experience of the buffalo soldiers has always led me to find out as much as possible about these men as human beings—where they came from, who they were, and what happened to them. So now I would have an opportunity to look closely at the lives of these twenty-three soldiers—their role in the frontier drama, their relations with their white officers, and their views of the Indians who valiantly and futilely resisted the onslaught that the buffalo soldiers represented. Second, I was given the opportunity to deal once again with the fine people at Scholarly Resources, with whom I had thoroughly enjoyed working on my previous book. I was not disappointed. Again I thank Rick, Daniel C. Helmstadter, Carolyn J. Travers,

Linda Pote Musumeci, Ann M. Aydelotte, Sharon L. Beck, and James L. Preston for their help, support, and friendship.

Along the way many other friends and colleagues helped with my research. I thank Preston E. Amos, Jerald R. Anderson, Louise Arnold-Friend, Kathleen M. Brassell, Emmitt Brotherton, Thomas R. Buecker, John A. Cash, Roger Cunningham, Roger Daniels, William Dobak, Charles Endress, Patricia and Mark Erickson, Barry W. Fowle, Hal H. Hubener, Angela Lakweta, Pete McRae, Lawrence McSwain, D. J. Neary, Gordon L. Olson, R. Eli Paul, Jeffry M. Platt, David L. Riley, Lynne Schubert, Max Schubert, John Slonaker, and Houston D. Wedlock. I owe a special debt of gratitude to Tony Skiscim for his photographic skill and his tolerance of my strange ideas and absentmindedness. In addition, three dear friends—Professor John M. Gates, Dr. Erwin A. Schmidl, and Colonel Anita W. McMiller—read and commented on portions of the manuscript.

My wife Irene read the entire draft, made it easy for me to disappear for entire evenings and weekends, and tracked down obscure sources. For all of this, I thank her. More important, after twenty-eight years together, she is still my best friend. For that, I cannot thank her enough.

F.N.S
Fairfax County, Virginia

Buffalo Soldier Recipients of the Medal of Honor*

NAME, RANK, AND UNIT	CAMPAIGN OR ACTION
Baker, Edward L., Jr.	
Sergeant Major, 10th Cavalry	Spanish-American War, 1898
Bell, Dennis	
Private, H Troop/10th Cavalry	Spanish-American War, 1898
Boyne, Thomas	
Sergeant, C Troop/9th Cavalry	Victorio Campaign, 1879
Brown, Benjamin	
Sergeant, C Troop/24th Infantry	Paymaster Escort, 1889
Denny, John	
Private, C Troop/9th Cavalry	Victorio Campaign, 1879
Factor, Pompey	
Private, 24th Infantry	Staked Plains Expedition, 1875
Greaves, Clinton	
Corporal, C Troop/9th Cavalry	Apache Campaign, 1877
Johnson, Henry	
Private, K Troop/10th Cavalry	Ute Campaign, 1879
Jordan, George	
Sergeant, K Troop/ 9th Cavalry	Victorio Campaign, 1879
Lee, Fitz	
Private, M Troop/10th Cavalry	Spanish-American War, 1898
Mays, Isaiah	
Corporal, B Troop/24th Infantry	Paymaster Escort, 1889
McBryar, William	
Sergeant, K Troop/10th Cavalry	Apache Campaign, 1890
Payne, Adam	
Private, 24th Infantry	Comanche Campaign, 1874
Payne, Isaac	
Trumpeter, 24th Infantry	Staked Plains Expedition, 1875
Shaw, Thomas	
Sergeant, K Troop/10th Cavalry	Apache Campaign, 1881
Stance, Emanuel	
Sergeant, F Troop/9th Cavalry	Texas Raid, 1870
Thompkins, William H.	
Corporal, A Troop/10th Cavalry	Spanish-American War, 1898
Walley, Augustus	
Sergeant, E Troop/10th Cavalry	Apache Campaign, 1881
Wanton, George H.	
Private, M Troop/10th Cavalry	Spanish-American War, 1898
Ward, John	
Sergeant, 24th Infantry	Staked Plains Expedition, 1875
Williams, Moses	
Sergeant, I Troop/9th Cavalry	Apache Campaign, 1881
Wilson, William O.	
Corporal, I Troop/9th Cavalry	Pine Ridge Campaign, 1890
Woods, Brent	
Sergeant, B Troop/9th Cavalry	Apache Campaign, 1881

*Lists rank, unit, and campaign or action at the time the medal was earned.

~ 1 ~

Two Traditions: The Medal of Honor and Black Valor

𝕿 he Civil War spawned two enduring military traditions, the Medal of Honor and the continuous service of black Americans in the U.S. Army. Although the Medal of Honor came directly out of that war to become the nation's preeminent award for military valor, American precedents for such an award existed. The Purple Heart, now presented in recognition of wounds received in combat, had been created by General George Washington as the Badge of Military Merit near the end of the Revolutionary War in 1782 to acknowledge "singular meritorious action," but it never received official government approval in its original form. The Certificate of Merit, established in 1847 during the war with Mexico, also recognized gallantry but was only rarely issued.[1] The Civil War, which underscored the importance of the Army and Navy in preserving the nation, created the political climate in which the idea of a medal recognizing military valor found ready acceptance.

Congressional action was initiated during the first year of the war, when Senator James W. Grimes of Iowa, the Republican chairman of the Senate Naval Committee, introduced a bill to create a Navy medal. Both houses passed Grimes's bill, and President Abraham Lincoln signed it on December 21, 1861. The medal was the first decoration officially authorized by the national government as a badge of honor. Only a short time later, Senator Henry Wilson of Massachusetts introduced a proposal for an Army version. Wilson wanted "medals of

1

honor" to be presented to enlisted soldiers who "shall distin-guish themselves by their gallantry in action, and other soldier-like qualities." After Congress made officers eligible for the award as well, Lincoln approved the idea on July 12, 1862.[2]

The star-shaped designs of both the Army and the Navy versions of the medal featured in bas-relief an allegory of the Union, carrying a shield in her right hand and repelling an attacker crouched alongside with forked-tongued serpents that struck at the shield. In her hand, Union held the ancient Roman symbol of government authority, the fasces. The thirty-four stars around the figures represented the number of states at the time. The reverse was left blank for engraving the recipient's name and the date and place of the act of bravery for which the medal was awarded. The Navy medal was sus-pended from the ribbon by an anchor, while an eagle stand-ing on crossed cannon and cannonballs held the Army version. The Navy design stayed in use until World War I, but the design of the ribbon on the Army version changed slightly in 1896. The medal changed again in 1904, in a num-ber of significant ways, including the addition of a bar with the word "Valor" above the star. All buffalo soldier recipi-ents received either the 1862 or the 1896 Army version.[3]

Even before the Civil War ended, the traditions of the medal and black military service came together. On April 6, 1865, twelve black soldiers became the first African Ameri-cans to receive the medal. Members all of the five regiments of U.S. Colored Troops who had borne the brunt of the fight-ing at New Market Heights just seven miles outside Richmond on September 29, 1864, they had charged with their regiments three hundred yards across open fields and through enemy obstacles into heavy Confederate fire, proving their will and ability to fight for their country.[4] Major General Benjamin F. Butler, in whose Army of the James they served, thought that the troops had proved themselves, thus vindicating his faith in them; and he "felt in [his] inmost heart that the capacity of the negro race for soldiers had then and there been fully settled forever."[5]

These twelve soldiers did much more than validate Butler's faith in their ability to fight—they extended themselves beyond the call of duty to breach enemy works, rescue comrades under fire, and protect and advance the national and regimental colors. William E. Barnes of the Thirty-eighth U.S. Colored Troops, for example, was severely wounded but nevertheless "forged ahead and was among the first to enter the enemy's works and close with him."[6] Private James Gardiner of Company I, Thirty-sixth U.S. Colored Troops, was also among the first in the enemy's trenches, shooting a rebel officer who was on the parapet rallying his men and running him through with his bayonet.[7] Sergeant Major Christian Fleetwood of the Fourth U.S. Colored Troops also received the medal; he "seized the colors, after two color bearers had been shot down, and bore them nobly through the fight."[8] Sergeant Alfred Hilton of the Fourth U.S. Colored Troops, Corporal Miles James of the Thirty-sixth, First Sergeant Alexander Kelly of the Sixth, and Private Charles Veal of the Fourth all distinguished themselves in similar ways.[9]

They also showed that they could lead other men, even under the greatest pressure and in the face of extreme peril. First Sergeant Powhatan Beaty of Company G of the Fifth U.S. Colored Troops saw all of his officers fall to Confederate fire and "took control of his company, leading them gallantly throughout the battle,"[10] as did First Sergeant James H. Bronson of Company D. Three others—Sergeant Major Milton Holland and First Sergeant Robert Pinn of the Fifth and First Sergeant Edward Ratcliff of the Thirty-eighth—also received medals for their leadership, picking up the reins of command when their officers fell and leading their men through the fight.[11] Captain John McMurray, a white Pennsylvania newspaper editor who commanded a company in the Sixth U.S. Colored Troops, was extremely proud of serving with such men. "I want to say for the honor of our regiment and the whole brigade," he wrote after New Market Heights, "I believe not a man turned his back toward the enemy."[12] They proved themselves to be dedicated and courageous soldiers, to be sure, but they also showed that they were leaders.

In the years after the Civil War, the names of four more black soldiers went on the honor roll of those who held the Medal of Honor for gallantry during the conflict, bringing the total to sixteen. Two, Sergeant Major Thomas Hawkins of the Sixth and Sergeant James Harris of the Thirty-eighth, joined those who had already been recognized for distinguishing themselves at New Market Heights. In addition, Sergeant Decatur Dorsey of the Thirty-ninth received the medal for gallantry in the battle for Petersburg, after advancing ahead of his regiment in an assault and planting the colors on the Confederate works; and Sergeant William Carney of the fabled Fifty-fourth Massachusetts Infantry received the medal for similar action at the assault on Fort Wagner, South Carolina.[13] Overall, for the Civil War, sixteen black sailors joined the sixteen soldiers as recipients of thirty-two of the 1,196 medals that were awarded.[14]

Although recognition for gallantry came only to a few black soldiers, their contributions in general were impossible to ignore. The 180,000 blacks who fought for the Union alongside 2.5 million whites participated in over four hundred engagements. They made up nearly 7 percent of the men who wore Union blue through the war, but they made their presence felt particularly toward the end, when they comprised 12 percent of the one million men under arms. Furthermore, they faced perils that white soldiers never experienced. Between 2,700 and 2,900 died, partly because Confederates did not always take black prisoners, and capture frequently meant death rather than confinement.[15]

When the war ended and a peacetime force was reassembled from the remnants of the vast army that had saved the Republic, black soldiers made up part of the regular establishment for the first time. Some opposition to their inclusion developed in both houses of Congress; but with the formerly rebellious states not represented and the memory of the significant contributions of black soldiers in the late war still fresh, the issue was never in doubt. However, the bill that the House Committee on Military Affairs sent to the full chamber on March 7, 1866, did undergo important changes. The initial draft included only black infantrymen, but Senator Benjamin Wade of Ohio added a provision for two black cavalry regiments.[16] Another important amendment, proposed by Representative Halbert Paine of Wisconsin, added to the new black regiments chaplains who were responsible for "instruction of the enlisted men in the common branches of an English education." Aware of the grave lack of learning among freedmen, Paine claimed that his proposal would serve the public interest as well as the soldiers by raising their level of competence.[17] The law that President Andrew Johnson signed on July 28, 1866, contained both changes.[18] The issue of whether to include black commissioned officers never received serious consideration. The Army sought only black enlisted men and soon sent out white recruiting officers in search of soldiers for six new black regiments: the Ninth and Tenth Cavalry and the Thirty-eighth, Thirty-ninth, Fortieth, and Forty-first Infantry, which in the reduction of the force in 1869 were consolidated into the Twenty-fourth and Twenty-fifth Infantry.[19]

The new units made up a substantial proportion of the peacetime Army. The two infantry regiments were nearly 10 percent of the twenty-five in the service, and the cavalry units made up a full 20 percent of the ten mounted regiments. With the entire Army in 1870 consisting of only about 30,000 soldiers and officers and still declining, there were 2,700 blacks in the ranks. For the rest of the period up to the war with Spain in 1898, the total strength of the force hovered around 25,000. The black soldiers in the four regiments made up about 10 percent of the men in this small constabulary.[20]

While the black regiments matured and made names for themselves on the frontier, the Army took its first steps toward clarifying policies regarding the award of the Medal of Honor. The Army's senior administrator, the Adjutant General, announced in 1875 that the medal could be awarded "for special and distinguished service in Indian warfare," in recognition of "some act of conspicuous bravery or service *above the ordinary duty of a soldier*."[21] Brigadier General Alfred A. Terry, in whose Department of Dakota some of the heaviest fighting took place, echoed this standard and reinforced it vigorously. In 1876 he disapproved the large number of recommendations made on behalf of soldiers who had tried to reach Lieutenant Colonel George A. Custer's beleaguered command at the Little Big Horn. Terry wrote that "Medals of Honor are not intended for ordinary good conduct, but for conspicuous acts of gallantry."[22] Thus, even where all of the details of an action in which a soldier earned the medal have not survived, by the time of the Indian wars the standard for the award that had begun to take shape during the Civil War was becoming set.

In the early days of the Medal of Honor, standards were not always precisely stated or followed. Corps of Engineers Sergeant Major Frederick W. Gerber received the medal in 1871, not for any singular act of bravery but in recognition of twenty-five years of faithful service that included participation in many Mexican War and Civil War battles. A number of other awards could only be described as trivial and even frivolous. The most egregious example involved 864 soldiers of the Twenty-seventh Maine Volunteer Infantry who received the medal merely for reenlisting. In 1917 the Army rescinded these awards and a number of others, including one presented to William F. "Buffalo Bill" Cody, whose actions tended more toward conspicuous showmanship than bravery. None of the 910 recisions involved black recipients.[23]

In the twentieth century the concept of the Pyramid of Honor evolved to recognize acts of courage that did not merit the Medal of Honor. The Bronze Star, the Silver Star, the Distinguished Service Cross, and other awards came into use to acknowledge different levels of bravery. The Medal of Honor, at the apex of the pyramid, became the supreme award, its distribution limited strictly to the handful of those meeting the "most severe tests of heroism."[24]

During the period in which the medals were awarded to the buffalo soldiers, the Certificate of Merit continued in use as the only alternative to the Medal of Honor. The certificate was intended for private soldiers only, in "cases of extraordinary merit" in recognition of distinguished service. Verification by an eyewitness, preferably the soldier's immediate commander, was required, as was approval by every level of command all the way to Washington.[25] This standard overlapped with the criteria for the Medal of Honor, and in the 1890s the Army tried to separate the two, with the medal reserved for bravery and the certificate set aside for distinguished service in action or otherwise, involving such acts as life saving, preservation of public property, or rescuing public property from fire.[26] It was not always clear which of the two awards had precedence. The situation was especially clouded by the grant of an additional two dollars per month in pay to soldiers who earned the certificate. This financial incentive was significant to privates of the Indian wars, with their starting base pay of thirteen dollars per month. As a consequence, soldiers who received the Medal of Honor sometimes also sought the certificate for the same acts, occasionally but rarely with success.[27]

Frequently, soldiers initiated their own claims for either the certificate or the medal. Some buffalo soldiers submitted their own papers, and the Army did not reject any application because it was overdue or because a soldier initiated it. The practice, which clearly was not unusual, peaked in the early 1890s. In 1892 one soldier applied for a Medal of Honor based on a deed that he claimed had taken place in 1864. No supporting evidence could be found, and the Army rejected the application. Shortly afterward, procedures became more rigorous, and regulations published in June 1897 prohibited soldiers from filing for their own medals. From that point, only the individual's commander "or [a] soldier having personal cognizance of the act" could apply. Then, in 1901, Secretary of War Elihu Root required that an application be submitted within three years of the deed for which a medal was sought, to allow officials to make a determination while the facts were still ascertainable. Finally, in 1904 the establishment of the Pyramid of Honor and the granting of a patent on the design of the medal brought stability to the situation. The 1917 recision of frivolous early awards served to emphasize standards.[28]

All twenty-three of the buffalo soldier heroes who received the Medal of Honor for their bravery during the Indian wars and the Cuban campaign earned their recognition during the period of flux that occurred before 1904. A few of them sought

Certificates of Merit as well as medals for a single act of heroism, and some filed their papers themselves. Occasionally,
some of the soldiers received certificates for their courage in
action, while others who served alongside in the same opera-
tion earned the Medal of Honor.

Despite the ambiguity in procedures and standards and
the frustrating lack of detail to illuminate some of the actions
that led to awards, it is clear that all of these men stood out
from their fellow soldiers. Army officialdom, from the company and regimental commanders up to the Secretary of War,
agreed that these men took risks, served with valor, and merited recognition for exceptional service. Among the thousands
of buffalo soldiers who served so well in some of the harsh-
est fighting and in the face of frontier racism, these twenty-
three were remarkable. Like the sixteen Civil War soldiers
who preceded them and the black heroes who would emerge
later, they embodied the finest qualities of soldiers, placing
themselves in harm's way to save their fellows, pushing beyond normal limits of endurance to protect settlements, and
showing leadership that turned the tide of battle. Only a few
years after the abolition of slavery, these men grasped the
opportunity that the Army presented them and participated
in the quintessential American drama of the westward movement. They proved to a nation, which did not generally care
to notice, that black men could ride, shoot, fight, and lead.
They embodied black valor.

~ 2 ~

Emanuel Stance and the Emergence of the Black Professional Soldier

𝕰manuel Stance and the Ninth Cavalry grew up together. When Stance enlisted on October 2, 1866, the regiment was less than two months old, and neither the soldier nor his unit had a clear or certain future. Stance was an unprepossessing youth, barely nineteen and only slightly over five feet tall. The Ninth, one of the six Regular Army regiments set aside for black enlisted men in recognition of the significant military contribution of 180,000 black soldiers to the Union victory, was also immature. The recruits swelling the ranks of the nascent regiment were mainly former slaves, largely unschooled, and new to the ways of the Army and to citizenship but eager to learn both.

The first soldier to be accepted into the regiment, one George Washington, had been enrolled in New Orleans on August 5, 1866, and assigned to A Troop. Recruiting had started near New Orleans and Baton Rouge to tap into the concentration of veterans of Civil War black regiments. This source began to dry up in October, and recruiters cast their nets over a wider region, first spreading out to other towns in Louisiana, particularly Lake Providence, Alexandria, and Greenville, and then moving farther north early in 1867 to Louisville and Lexington, Kentucky. The total number of enlisted men at the end of October 1866 stood at 541, about 60 percent of the regiment's anticipated full strength of nine hundred.[1]

In October, Stance was among fifty recruits to sign up for five-year terms in Lake Providence, a Mississippi River town in his home parish of Carroll in the northeastern corner of the state.[2] Three other soldiers of later note enlisted at Lake Providence on October 1, the day before Stance himself joined. Moses Williams, also from Carroll Parish and only slightly older than Stance, later received a Medal of Honor for heroism against the Apaches and retired in 1897 as an ordnance sergeant. Another new recruit, Wesley Jefferds, already had three years of Civil War service behind him and made a career out of the Army before retiring from the Ninth Cavalry as a sergeant to Washington, DC, in 1892. A third man who joined the regiment that day, light-skinned, tall Harrison Bradford, also had a promising future. The twenty-four-year-old Civil War veteran from rural Scott County, just north of Lexington, became a sergeant in less than six months.[3]

The officer who administered the oath of enlistment noted Stance's civilian occupation as farmer, although that may very well have meant that he had been a field hand before Emancipation. Recruiters listed hundreds of new soldiers as farmers, but never as former slaves, field hands, or sharecroppers. More important than his status was the fact that he could read and write, an ability that made him a highly desirable recruit. The hundreds of men who first made up the regiment included only a few who could read and even fewer with useful administrative or clerical experience. The Army tried to compensate by appointing chaplains, who were ordinarily assigned to posts rather than units, to each of the new black regiments and directing them to look to the educational as well as religious needs of the troops. But until the schooling took hold, officers found themselves required to perform most of the administrative tasks while training the troops on hand and recruiting to fill the ranks. With only a handful of officers on duty, their ranks were stretched very thin. In October 1866, when Stance enlisted, only three officers of the usual complement of forty-five actually served with the regiment. By November, there were five. Some were elsewhere signing up soldiers for the Army or on staff duty at headquarters in Washington, while others declined assignments with black soldiers and lobbied for transfers or simply left the military. Not until February 1867 did the situation improve measurably and the number of regimental officers begin to increase significantly.[4]

Fortunately, some of the officers were extremely capable and committed to their work. Colonel Edward L. Hatch, the regimental commander, was in Washington on detached service through the autumn. He had entered the Army as a volunteer officer at the outset of the Civil War and served with distinction in numerous actions in the western theater of operations. He had ridden with his friend Benjamin Grierson, another volunteer cavalryman who now commanded the Tenth Cavalry, in the Vicksburg campaign of 1863. Although he was shot through the lungs and had a shoulder shattered at Moscow, Tennessee, in December 1863, Hatch was back in the saddle and chasing rebels less than one year later. He finished the war as a brevet major general and a colonel in the Regular Army. He and the Ninth Cavalry served together for twenty years.[5]

Although Hatch had never commanded black troops during the Civil War, at least seven of his officers had done so. Three who helped to organize the Ninth Cavalry had served together in the Eighty-first U.S. Colored Troops. A fourth, Captain James S. Brisbin, formerly commander of the Sixth U.S. Colored Cavalry, was one of the very few officers on duty with the regiment when Stance enlisted. He had been a staunch advocate of the abolition of slavery and came out of the Civil War with a high regard for the fighting ability of black troops.[6]

Organizing a new regiment under the conditions faced by the Ninth at New Orleans taxed even officers of Brisbin's ability and dedication. The city was still tense from the July 1866 race riot, which had started as a black demonstration in support of civil rights and ended with thirty-eight people, almost all black, dead. Ninth Cavalry recruits found themselves crowded into unsanitary and badly ventilated industrial buildings where steam engines run by slaves had once pressed cotton into five-hundred-pound fifty-inch bales for shipment by sea to textile mills. There the men slept and cooked their meals over open fires while a cholera epidemic raged around them. Nine soldiers died in October, fifteen more in November, and another five in December. Some of those who survived abandoned the regiment and their commitment to the Army. In a regiment that ultimately came to be known for its low rate of desertion, thirty men disappeared before the end of 1866. In the first three months of 1867, another sixteen vanished. New Orleans was not a healthy environment.[7]

This situation was not exactly conducive to training. When Hatch moved the Ninth out of New Orleans to Greenville until the epidemic subsided, he only added the complex, time-consuming change of station to the many obstacles to a proper training routine. And there was so much to cover. The soldiers had to be clothed, fed, and taught basic military subjects—skills of military courtesy, marching, and marksmanship as well as horsemanship and mounted drills. A cavalryman had to know how to stay on a horse, guide his mount with his legs, ride in formation, and handle his carbine, revolver, and saber. The soldiers were willing pupils, but the few officers on hand to teach them also had to do sergeants' work as clerks and disciplinarians. The long frustrating winter ended with the Ninth—873 enlisted men and still only eleven officers—boarding ship for Indianola, Texas, imperfectly trained and disciplined and not always well led. The regiment was not ready for active service.[8]

Although the Ninth was still raw, Stance was already making a name for himself. By March 1867 he had impressed his officers sufficiently that he joined Harrison Bradford among the soldiers who quickly became sergeants. At the end of the month, Stance also received a two-month leave of absence, so, unlike Bradford, he did not board one of the Morgan line of steamers that took the regiment, organized in twelve troops of about seventy men each, to Indianola, along the Gulf Coast, for assignment to frontier duty.[9]

The troop, as cavalry companies were frequently called, was the basic organizational unit of the mounted regiment. The designation "troop" was not officially adopted until 1883, but by then it had been used informally for a number of years to refer to cavalry companies.[10] At full strength, each had one captain and two lieutenants and anywhere from fifty to one hundred enlisted men, with the President as commander in chief empowered to fix the specific number at any given time. Rarely did a cavalry troop or infantry company ever have more than eighty men actually assigned. Soldiers lived, ate, and served in their troop, participated in social and athletic events as a troop, and went into action as a troop. The unit was small and cohesive, the basic social as well as administrative and organizational core of the regiment.[11] "A frontier soldier's first loyalty," Don Rickey accurately concluded, "was to his company."[12]

Because Stance was on leave when the Ninth left New Orleans for the frontier, he missed the violent confrontation between soldiers and officers at San Pedro Springs, near San Antonio, Texas. The regiment began disembarking from its steamers at Indianola on March 29, "suffering," historian Byron Price wrote, "from festering internal problems, poor morale, and questionable discipline." The troopers got their first taste of the frontier with a march of 150 miles or so inland to San Antonio. The trip, which represented valuable field training, was not accomplished without incident. Rumors flew about the perils of frontier service, control of the troops became difficult, and a disturbance in Lieutenant Fred Smith's K Troop was put down with force. Lieutenant Edward Heyl's E Troop also developed problems. The troopers feared the twenty-three-year-old Heyl, who had started as an enlisted man before serving as a captain in a Pennsylvania cavalry regiment. He was a hard drinker and a stern, sometimes vicious taskmaster who browbeat and terrorized his men and on occasion physically assaulted them. His fitness for command of any kind would be open to question today, but officers who brutalized their men were not uncommon in white or black regiments. In any case, no officer who would name his horse "Nigger," as Heyl later did, should have been in the Ninth Cavalry.[13]

The morning of April 9, 1867, started badly in E Troop, with Heyl trying to ride down Private Frank Handy while cursing him for being late to formation. Private Louis Brown

watched in amazement and alarm. "I never," he said, "saw
him [Heyl] go on as he did that morning, before in my life."
Then, after the men fed their horses, Heyl had three privates—
Fayette Hall, Alphonse Goodman, and Albert Bailey—strung
up by the wrists from a tree limb because they did not re-
spond promptly to his order to remove nosebags from the
horses. Afterward, he went drinking in a nearby saloon. Meanwhile, one soldier, apparently Private Hall, slipped his bonds
and escaped the tree to which he had been tied, and another
tried to reach a tree stump with his feet. Heyl returned and
beat the latter with his saber while most of the company
looked on. The senior noncommissioned officer, First Sergeant
Joseph Douglas, saw this performance. Despite his experience in the Civil War, Douglas may have been too confused
or fearful to react, so he did nothing.[14]

Orderly Sergeant Harrison Bradford was made of bolder
stuff. He knew that Heyl's behavior was unacceptable, decided that he had to protest, and started to march E Troop to
Lieutenant Colonel Wesley Merritt's tent. On the way, Heyl
with unholstered pistol and Bradford with drawn saber confronted each other. Heyl fired at Bradford and missed, then
fired again, shooting Bradford in the mouth as the latter struck
him with his saber. Lieutenant Seth E. Griffin rushed to Heyl's
aid and fired at Bradford twice, hitting him in the temple.
Bradford and another soldier cut Griffin severely before Lieutenant Smith killed Bradford with two shots. The fight spread,
with more of the soldiers attacking Smith before the entire
company finally dispersed.[15]

When the dust settled, Lieutenant Colonel Merritt dis-
armed the unit and assembled it for roll call. By that time, ten
soldiers had already deserted. Merritt assessed the situation,
concluding that Heyl's behavior and the shortage of officers
were responsible for the incident. General Ulysses Grant endorsed Merritt's report with the urgent recommendation that
the regiment receive its full complement of officers. Meanwhile, Lieutenant Griffin died of his wounds, and the military trial of the surviving miscreants in June confirmed
Merritt's analysis. Two soldiers, Corporal Charles Woods and
Private Irving Charles, were convicted and sentenced to death

but were later pardoned and restored to duty. In the chaotic conditions that the regiment had experienced in New Orleans, the cavalrymen had not even been introduced to the Articles of War and had no idea of the proper means of seeking redress. The other so-called mutineers were initially imprisoned but reinstated in March 1868. Clearly, the Ninth needed more (and better) officers and a distraction-free place to train.[16]

As for Heyl, there is no evidence that he was ever held accountable for his role in the ugly episode. He was charged with "brutal conduct to the prejudice of good order and military discipline," but apparently a court martial never convened to try the matter. He stayed in the Army and prospered there, even being allowed to remain in the Ninth for four more years. When he died in 1895, he was serving as a colonel in the Inspector General Department.[17]

The men of the Ninth soon found themselves too busy being soldiers to focus on their grievances. The regiment divided between Fort Brown on the Gulf Coast at Brownsville and two isolated frontier posts in the southwest corner of Texas, Camp (later Fort) Quitman on the Rio Grande and Fort Davis north of the Big Bend of the river. Here there was ample opportunity for training without the distractions of a big city. Here also were foes of many descriptions, "numerous bands of Comanche, Apache, Kickapoo, Navajo and Lipan Indians, and Mexican and white renegades," according to regimental historian George Hamilton. The regiment's first year in Texas mixed garrison duty and training with escorting the mail and protecting settlers from depredations of marauding Indians and bandits.[18]

The Ninth reached the Texas frontier just as the last chapter opened in the long intermittent war with America's native populations. On the plains and in the mountains beyond were the last groups that put up significant resistance to the United States in its spread across the continent. Comanche, Kiowa, Cheyenne, Arapaho, Sioux, and other plains tribes as well as the Apaches of the southwestern mountains and the Nez Percé in the north fought desperately to protect their homelands, occasionally defeating the troops in battle but ultimately overwhelmed by numbers and technology. These

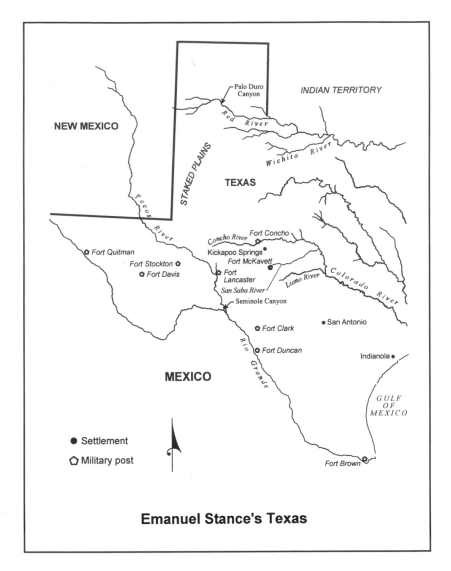

Emanuel Stance's Texas

tribes differed from each other in many ways and lacked political cohesion beyond small local groups, but for the Army
their similarities were at least as important as the differences.
All were fine horsemen, tough, self-reliant, and brave; and
they used a variety of weapons, including traditional bows
and lances as well as the firearms that they acquired by trade
or war. They also knew the terrain over which they fought,

and how to use it to their advantage, and excelled at the tactics of raiding and ambush. "Man for man," historian Robert Utley wrote, "the Indian warrior far surpassed his blue-clad adversary in virtually every test of military proficiency."[19]

The cost of training while in action against such formidable foes was high. Six men died in combat before the year ended. In October, Corporal Samuel Wright and Private Eldridge Jones, from D Troop at Fort Lancaster, were killed while escorting the mail. In December, Private Nathan Jones of Stance's troop, which was stationed at Fort Davis, also died while escorting the mail, about one hundred miles west of Davis at Eagle Springs. Then, on December 26, three more troopers—Privates Edward Bowers, William Sharp, and Anderson Trimble—fell in a massive attack on K Troop at pre-Civil War Fort Lancaster by an estimated force of nine hundred Indians and outlaws. Not until 1879 and 1880, when the regiment lost ten and eleven men against the Apaches, respectively, did the Ninth have higher casualties.[20]

While the Ninth Cavalry matured under the pressure of active service, Emanuel Stance also grew as a leader. He rejoined the regiment from his leave in May 1867. Stationed with F Troop at Fort Davis in the middle of Mescalero Apache country in far western Texas, he acquired considerable experience. From its perch about five thousand feet above sea level, Fort Davis looked downhill at the vast expanse of Texas to the east and guarded the southern stagecoach and emigrant route across New Mexico to California. Stance spent three months in the middle of 1868 in charge of a small detachment of soldiers on extra duty in the Quartermaster Department. Perhaps the detail involved the issue and inventory of the regiment's supplies, which would have put his valuable ability to read and write to good use, or it consisted of any one of a myriad of less cerebral small construction projects. The Texas posts were largely built by the troops who manned them, and Stance could have been running a sawmill, a stone quarry, or an adobe brickyard, tasks that took soldiers away from their primary duties and caused officers to complain that those forced into the construction trades were more likely to desert. Then in September he led his first patrol, a short reconnaissance in which he commanded eight privates. He also probably learned from the other noncommissioned officers of F Troop—men such as Sergeant Jacob Wilks, who had started life as a slave and escaped across the Ohio River with his parents while still an infant. Wilks had seen a lot more soldiering than Stance, having served almost four years in the 116th U.S. Colored Troops during the Civil War before witnessing, as a sergeant in the Army that brought about slavery's defeat, Robert E. Lee's surrender at Appomattox.[21]

While Stance learned from the old soldiers at Fort Davis, he ran afoul of the military justice system for the first time. An argument with Saddler John Graves over a misplaced currycomb escalated quickly to threats, with Stance warning Graves that he would "mash his mouth," and finally both men threw punches. Captain Henry Carroll defended Stance at the court martial, calling him "one of the best sergeants I have in my company" and adding that he had "always been attentive to duty . . . and shown a wish to improve himself in tactics." Responding to Carroll's plea for leniency, the court fined Stance ten dollars and Graves five dollars.[22]

Throughout his months at Fort Davis, Stance continued to show Captain Carroll that he deserved his stripes. He fought in the two major Indian battles of the autumn of 1869. In September he rode with Major John M. Bacon and a force of one hundred troopers who logged 637 tough miles. On September 16 on the Middle Brazos River they killed twenty-five warriors in a party of twice as many Kiowas and Comanches. Then on October 28 the same expedition, reinforced by a detachment of the Fourth Cavalry and some Indian scouts, battled five hundred Indians between the Clear Mountain Fork and Double Mountain Fork of the Middle Brazos, charging into the Indian camp, scattering the foe, and killing forty without losing a man. In November, Stance led a detachment of six privates on escort duty along the emigrant road. At the end of the year, when he moved east to Fort McKavett with his unit, he was a much more seasoned soldier.[23]

When 1870 dawned, the Ninth Cavalry was stretched across Texas at seven posts along a 630-mile line, anchored on the west at Fort Quitman and meandering east through Forts Davis and Stockton before turning south at Fort McKavett and ending back on the Rio Grande at Fort Duncan. The troops at this string of outposts faced Indian raiders from two directions, those coming south from Indian Territory (now Oklahoma) and others coming north from Mexico. Captain Carroll and F Troop, forty-nine strong after deducting the eighteen detailed to other duties, seven who were sick, and four in the guardhouse, occupied McKavett jointly with one company of the black Twenty-fourth Infantry.[24] The fort stood on a hill at the headwaters of the San Saba River, about 150 miles northwest of San Antonio along the road to El Paso and beyond to New Mexico and California. Established in the early 1850s, McKavett epitomized the isolated frontier post. In 1854, Albert Sidney Johnston derisively called it "prairie dog city." To break the monotony and loneliness there were only the mail and a visit to Scabtown, the nearby settlement that emerged after the Civil War and offered the garrison the usual array of vices. Scabtown could be as dangerous as Indian fighting, according to post historian Jerry Sullivan, sometimes resulting "in a hangover, a brawl, a visit to the post hospital, even a gunfight."[25]

About twenty-six miles directly north of the San Saba, the subpost at Kickapoo Springs surpassed even McKavett in isolation and boredom. At the tip of one of the many branches of Kickapoo Creek that resembled the frayed strands of a rope and flowed north into the Concho River, the base consisted of a single stone building. Garrisoned by from three to ten soldiers, sometimes with a sergeant, the little base guarded a mail and stage station along the route north from McKavett. For the first half of 1870, D Company provided the detachment; then it was F Troop's turn.[26]

On May 20, 1870, Captain Carroll sent two detachments of F Troop north toward Kickapoo Springs on a desperate mission, "to endeavor to the utmost to intercept the Indians that stole the two children of Phillip Buckmeier of Loyal Valley." Buckmeier's stepsons, eight-year-old Willie Lehmann and his ten-year-old brother Herman, had been abducted by Apaches four days earlier from their farm some forty miles east of McKavett in Mason County, and troops combed the country trying to find them. Lieutenant John L. Bullis of the Twenty-fourth Infantry led one of the ten-man patrols sent north with five days of rations. Sergeant Stance led the other, with orders to scout along Kickapoo Creek from its source at the spring north to where the strands started to come together. The assignment showed just how far Emanuel Stance had come. Only three and one-half years earlier, he had been a nineteen-year-old recruit. He had spent the intervening time on one of the rawest of frontiers, known the company of some older experienced Civil War veterans, supervised detachments on a variety of details, been out on scouts, and seen his share of combat.[27] He and the regiment had come a long way; and by 1870, William Leckie has written, the "proud tough, and confident [Ninth] was the equal of any similar combat unit in the country."[28] Now, Stance commanded his own independent little force of these campaign-hardened troopers, making their way north over the low divide separating the streams that formed the Concho from those that ran into the San Saba, in search of the kidnappers.

Stance's patrol might have been responsible for Willie Lehmann's escape.[29] On May 20 the buffalo soldiers were riding up the Kickapoo road toward the springs, about fourteen miles from Fort McKavett. At the same time, the Apaches were moving northwestward toward the Texas panhandle with their captives and some stolen horses. Stance discovered a party of Indians making its way across the hills with a herd of horses. "I charged them," Stance later reported, "and after slight skirmishing they abandoned the herd and took to the mountains." The troopers secured all nine horses and resumed the march to Kickapoo Springs, where they camped for the night. Near the Kickapoo road, soldiers did in fact stampede the Apache kidnappers and capture their horses. A warrior, fleeing the soldiers on a pony he shared with Willie and losing ground to the pursuers, pushed the boy off into the brush to make his escape. The bruised, cold, and very hungry boy found his way to the stage station at Kickapoo Springs the next day and was eventually reunited with his family. His older brother remained with the Indians for eight years before he came into Fort Sill, Indian Territory, with a Comanche band in 1878.[30]

Encumbered by the extra horses, Stance decided the next morning to take them back to Fort McKavett. His detail mounted and started back at sunrise. About ten miles out from Kickapoo Springs, he saw an attack about to unfold three miles ahead, with a party of around twenty Indians making for a small herd of government horses and their guard detail. Stance and his men spurred their own mounts into a charge. The enemy turned, trying to make a stand and protect the horses, but to no avail. "I set the Spencers [carbines] to talking and whistling about their ears so lively," Stance later reported, "that they broke in confusion and fled to the hills, leaving me their herd of five horses." He resumed his march toward the post, but he had company most of the way, with the same Indians staying on his left flank for several miles, determined, it seemed, to recover the horses. Wearying of the continuous skirmish, Stance "turned my little command loose on them." Near a waterhole known as Eight Mile, the buffalo soldiers charged again, firing away, and drove off the Indians. Finally, he said, "they left me to continue my march in peace." In midafternoon he reached camp with fifteen captured horses, one of his own horses slightly wounded, and all of his men uninjured.[31]

His commanding officer appreciated the decisive leadership that Stance had shown on May 20 and 21. "The gallantry," Captain Carroll wrote, "displayed by the sergeant and his party as well as good judgment used on both occasions, deserves much praise." While Carroll was impressed, he noted that Stance had previously distinguished himself as well. In fact, these fights were "the fourth and fifth encounter that Sergt. Stance has had with Indians within the past two years, on all of which occasions he has been mentioned for good behavior by his immediate commanding officer." Based on Carroll's recommendation, Stance received a Medal of Honor on June 20, 1870, and became the first black regular so recognized. "I will cherish the gift," he wrote, deeply moved, "as a thing of priceless value and endeavor by my future conduct to merit the high honor conferred upon me."[32]

The award of the medal to Stance less than four years after the regiment was organized showed just how far the Ninth had come. So recently a group of mostly illiterate former slaves, the Ninth was developing into a worthy regiment. Obscured by Stance's own celebrity as a leader and holder of

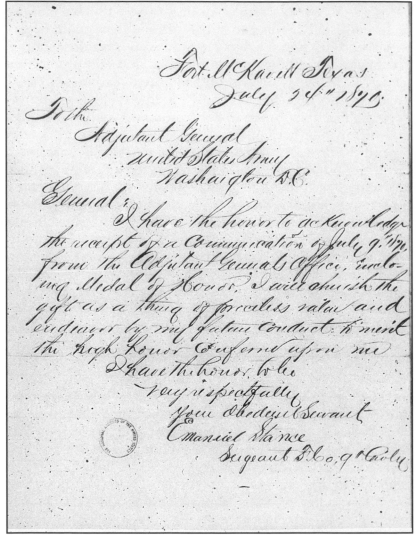

Emanuel Stance's signature appears on this letter acknowledging receipt of his Medal of Honor. The rest of the letter may have been written by a unit clerk. *Courtesy National Archives* (Microcopy M-929, roll 2)

the Medal of Honor, the performance of the men who rode with him also merits attention. Not only did the Ninth now have sergeants who could lead and earn recognition as heroes, but it also had soldiers who could obey and provide the support that such leaders could depend upon. A first-rate fighting organization had to have both, and the Ninth did.

Stance was one of the reasons for the emergence of the Ninth as an able regiment, but his behavior did not always meet the Army's standards. While still on his first enlistment, sometime between July 1870 and April 1871, he was reduced to private, and not for the last time. Like many soldiers, white as well as black, Stance at times found himself in trouble, either fighting, drinking too much, or failing to report for duty. Paydays brought drunkenness and brawls to every frontier post and regiment, and it was not unusual for troopers to find themselves brought up on charges and fined, jailed, and reduced to the ranks as a result. It was also not uncommon for competent noncommissioned officers to regain the rank that they had lost as a result of minor infractions. Stance made sergeant at least four additional times, twice in M Troop and twice after he returned to F Troop in October 1880.

When he completed his first enlistment on October 2, 1871, he was discharged as a private from F Troop of the Ninth Cavalry as Edmund Stance. He reenlisted under the same name in M Troop. We do not know why Stance experimented with the new name, but for some people the frontier was about reinventing themselves and carving out new lives, careers, identities, and futures. For the large numbers of former slaves, this reinvention was a new possibility, and the choice of a name was part of the new prospect. As Lerone Bennett wrote in *Before the Mayflower*, "Freedom . . . was a many-layered thing. . . . Freedom was two names. A man sat for a while and decided on a name, and if he didn't like it he could change it again tomorrow."[33]

There was more volatility to Emanuel Stance than merely moving from one name to another. His stormy personality was clearly evident when he got into a nasty brawl with First Sergeant Henry Green of his troop in December 1872. Green had reported him as drunk while on duty at the stables, and

Stance was furious. "If you reported that I was drunk," he told Green, in front of at least three soldier witnesses, "you reported a God-damned lie and God-damn you, you can't whip me." And with that challenge, the fight began. In the course of the fray, Stance bit off part of Green's lower lip. He lost his stripes and spent six months in the guardhouse.[34]

Whatever trouble he caused along the way, he must have been a remarkable soldier. Captain Carroll accepted him back into F Troop when he enlisted as a private in January 1882 for his fourth term, after a three-month break in service. By 1882, when Stance made sergeant for the fifth time, he had almost sixteen years of service and was approaching forty years of age, so he may have mellowed a little—at least enough to keep his stripes. He started smoking a pipe and even took his first furlough in the early summer of 1885, just after becoming first sergeant of F Troop and just before the unit left for Fort Robinson.

By the time he rode up to Fort Robinson in 1885, Sergeant Stance had battled Kiowa and Comanche foes on the southern plains, seen duty against the Apache chief Victorio in New Mexico, and chased Sooners (settlers so impatient to stake claims on Indian land that they dashed onto Oklahoma lands about to be ceded by the tribes sooner than the law allowed). He had survived an 1883 attempt to crush his skull by a soldier whom he had threatened with a saber. On his second Christmas at Fort Robinson, he celebrated twenty years in the Army with a dinner and dance given by his unit in his honor. But for all of his experience and age, he was still the Emanuel Stance, wiry, battle hardened, and belligerent, who had taken a bite out of a sergeant's lip. As first sergeant, he became the center of a series of disputes and brawls that hit F Troop during the last half of 1887.

Ten disturbances in that period involved eight of the forty-five or so privates and four of the ten noncommissioned officers. Stance, the senior sergeant in the troop, was himself involved in four confrontations. Twice, Private Louis Glenn ignored Stance's orders, once warning that he was "tired of you bulldozing me." Another soldier, Private Henry Royster, defied an order at stables; and a third, Blacksmith George

Waterford, responded to Stance's demand that he be quiet by growling back that "anyone who approaches me this morning is tired of living." In other incidents, privates complained sharply about their noncoms—Private Norbin Harris, for example, telling Corporal Robert McKeen that he was "tired of you God-damn niggers bulldozing me and I will not stand for it!" Overall, F Troop was a tense and volatile environment in which sergeants and privates were frequently at odds, sometimes violently so, while the troop commander, Captain Clarence Stedman, watched and at least tacitly approved a style of leadership that his sergeants and corporals could have learned from watching at work the likes of Edward Heyl and Captain Lee Humfreville, another Ninth Cavalry officer who brutalized the soldiers who served under him.[35]

Clearly, while Emanuel Stance had not changed from the days of his brawl with First Sergeant Green, the privates in the black regiments had. The style and personality that had made Stance an effective leader in 1870, followed willingly into battle by his troops, no longer worked. The new generation of cavalryman in the Ninth included men such as Sergeant Joseph Moore, who led a drive to buy John Brown's fort at Harper's Ferry, West Virginia, and preserve it as a historic site; Sergeant John Jackson, who killed a white soldier who had threatened his life; and Fort Robinson's intelligent and multitalented telegraph operator and post librarian, Private C. D. Dillard. These more articulate, assertive, and self-assured soldiers no longer tolerated leaders who browbeat and bullied them.[36]

Stance's behavior had tragic consequences. Just one year after sewing his fourth gold five-year chevron on his right sleeve, he was found by an officer on Christmas morning of 1887, shot dead with a service revolver on the road to Crawford. All of the circumstantial evidence pointed to privates in Stance's own troop. Private Glenn and Blacksmith Waterford had both threatened him, and the regiment's officers, Colonel Hatch included, believed that the soldiers were indeed responsible for Stance's death. Moreover, Private Simpson Mann, who joined the troop in 1888, told historian Don Rickey many years later that he had heard that the victim had been "dirty mean" and that the men of F Troop had done him in. Private Miller Milds of F Troop was charged with the homicide but ultimately freed because witnesses could not be found. No one was convicted of the crime, but Stance most likely was killed by one of his own men in the ultimate protest against the kind of leadership that he embodied and that Captain Stedman and the regimental officers condoned.[37] An anonymous obituary writer in the *Army and Navy Journal*, probably one of the officers at Fort Robinson, called him "a very strict disciplinarian" but considered Stance's severity justified: "His troop needed a strong hand, and it took a pretty nervy man to be first sergeant." The writer believed that Stance, who was highly regarded by his superiors, "was killed by one of his own men." In a tantalizing aside, he added that Stance "was a Congressional medal man and left it and a manuscript of his life, with drawings, which should go to the Army Museum." Although their fate is now unknown, these treasures were among Stance's personal effects, with other possessions—a gold watch and chain, an Indian bead necklace, and his pipes—that suggest that the mercurial tyrant sometimes transformed himself into a frontier dandy.[38]

Emanuel Stance left an ambivalent legacy. As the recipient of the first Medal of Honor awarded to a black regular, he was the original officially recognized hero in a new phase of the history of black soldiers in the service of the United States. His small physical stature and youth at the time of the award provide attractive material for modern motivational speakers to use with juvenile audiences, and at least one children's book celebrates his bravery.[39] The reason for this appeal is clear. Stance's decisive and bold behavior in the face of an armed enemy represents the finest tradition of the American soldier. But his leadership at other times, especially during the months leading to his death, showed serious shortcomings. He could not adjust to changes in the men under his charge. Stance was an imperfect, flawed hero, and the new buffalo soldier had left him behind.

~ 3 ~

The Seminole Negro Scouts

Ⓣhe facts of American history can be cruel to ideologues. Contradictions and paradoxes lurk to disappoint and frustrate those who try to fit the past into a modern view of how things should have been. In particular, the details of American race relations wait to confound those with fixed ideas about how people should have behaved and what relationships they should have formed. Late twentieth-century expectations that nonwhites can be expected to find common ground for cooperation in their skin pigmentation alone confront a baffling reality. In pre-Civil War America, some blacks owned other blacks and fought for the Confederacy, while some Indians caught black slaves and returned them to their white masters. After Emancipation, thousands of former black slaves wore the uniform of the U.S. Army and followed white officers against Indians. The descendants of still other black former slaves, who had fled their white masters and married into the Seminole tribe, became scouts for the Army and led black and white soldiers against western tribes. The Seminole Negro scouts, as this racially mixed group of warrior-trackers was called, reflect the complexity and anomaly that are inherent in race relations in the United States and, as much as any other of the ironies of the nation's history, confuse those with anachronistic expectations.

The Seminole Negro scouts followed a circuitous and difficult path from Florida to the borderlands overlapping Texas and Mexico. "Seminole" was the Creek word for runaway, so it was coincidental that in pre-Civil War days the tribe had offered a refuge to fugitive black slaves who had escaped bondage and fled to the roadless swamps of Florida. When the U.S. government removed the Seminoles from Florida before the Civil War, adopted black members of the tribe went west, too. Some then headed south across the border into Mexico, fleeing from the threat of confiscation of their weapons and even reenslavement. There they established settlements and in the early 1850s began to serve in the army of General Antonio López de Santa Anna.[1]

Conditions changed on both sides of the international boundary over the next two decades, and the U.S. Army moved to adjust to the new situation. The reduction of frontier garrisons during the Civil War created a military vacuum that resulted in increased Indian raiding north of the border. At the same time, the Seminole Negroes, under chief John Horse, became interested in returning to a United States that no longer tolerated slavery, and officers such as Major Zenas R. Bliss of the Twenty-fifth Infantry actively encouraged them by offering them employment as scouts.[2]

On July 4, 1870, the first Seminole Negroes to return to the United States and offer their services as scouts crossed over the Rio Grande to Fort Duncan, Texas. By then Secretary of War William W. Belknap had already authorized local commanders to hire as many as two hundred of "these Indian negroes" as scouts. Their reputation preceded them. Captain Frank W. Perry of the Twenty-fourth Infantry at Fort Duncan believed that they knew where the Kickapoos and Lipans, cattle-stealing scourges of the Texas frontier, hid in Mexico. Perry expected that they would be useful indeed as sources of intelligence and as trackers. Despite his anticipation, Perry was quite surprised by what he saw when they rode into his post. "The Seminoles whom I am directed to receive from Mexico," he reported with a trace of amazement, "turn out to be Negroes."[3]

The band that came over on Independence Day signed up six weeks later. John Kibbetts, leader of the group, was appointed sergeant. He and ten privates enlisted for six-month terms. Major Bliss, who replaced Perry as commander in July, shared his predecessor's view that the recruits did not look like Indians, but Kibbetts impressed Bliss as "a very smart and reliable negro." In appearance, as the late Kenneth Wiggins Porter, the distinguished pioneering student of the scouts, later wrote, "The scouts were hardly distinguishable . . . from the soldiers of the colored infantry and cavalry regiments with whom they frequently served." They shared more than appearance with the black troopers. They spoke English, albeit sometimes in a South Atlantic Sea-Islands Gullah dialect, as well as borderland Spanish; and most were, in Porter's words, "staunch Baptists."[4]

They may not have looked like Seminoles, but they certainly were not conventional soldiers. First and foremost, even if they did not know the area immediately surrounding Fort Duncan, they had patience, durability, and Indian skills in trailing, hunting, and fighting. As Captain Perry quickly discerned, they also knew where borderland rustlers had their hideaways. But there was more distinguishing them from the regulars than their ability and knowledge. They hated soldier work, the routines of camp and garrison that included inspections, cutting wood, standing guard, and police details, and they complained when they had to do such chores. Kibbetts made it plain to Bliss that his men were eager to serve as scouts, but they had no interest in enlisting in the Army. They were not readily awed by authority like normal recruits, and they did not take to military spit and polish. Some even wore warbonnets adorned with buffalo horns with their blue uniforms. The Army, not always tolerant of such individualism, accepted their quirks. Without doubt, the Seminole Negro scouts and the Army's officers stared at each other in wonder across a cultural chasm, but they came to terms with each other. The Seminoles needed employment and land; the Army needed scouts. And, as Major Bliss said, they were "excellent hunters, and trailers, and brave scouts . . . splendid fighters." He was pleased to offer the band a place to live and hunting privileges on the Fort Duncan military reservation in exchange for their service.[5]

During the early 1870s the Seminole Negro community grew larger and more important to the Army. In 1871, Elijah Daniel's band crossed the Rio Grande and settled at Fort Clark, near Brackettville and a little north of Fort Duncan.

Twenty men of that group enlisted. Back at Duncan, Major Henry C. Merriam of the Twenty-fourth, who had commanded the Seventy-third U.S. Colored Troops in battle during the Civil War, joined the chorus of officers who appreciated their work. "They are very faithful and efficient men," he wrote, "as trailers, guides, and for patrols." By 1873 the scouts numbered over fifty, with about half at Duncan and half at Clark. With wives, children, and old people, the scout communities at each fort totaled about one hundred people.[6]

Until the turn of the century, enlistments were only for six months. The brief terms reflected the apparent lack of interest among most recruits for long-term commitments as well as the Army's view that the need for scouts would be short-lived, but some of them served repeatedly over many years[7] —John Fay, for example, continuously from 1870 to 1888; Robert Payne from 1873 to 1879, 1882 to 1884, and 1890 to 1894 and perhaps at other times as well; and Isaac Payne served a number of enlistments between 1871 and 1901.

A few families came to dominate the ranks of the scouts. Certain surnames were clearly prominent among the 152 scouts who served between 1870 and 1914 and whose names are known. There were eight Julys, including Sampson July and all five of his sons. The ranks also included seven Factors and seven Bowlegs, two of whom had served in the Civil War in the Seventy-ninth U.S. Colored Troops. There were also seventeen Wilsons, eleven Paynes, and six named Washington, Daniels, and Bruner. These families were also connected by marriage. For example, Sergeant John Ward's daughter Dolly married scout Billy July, and scout Sergeant Sampson July's daughter married scout Bill Wilson. At least fourteen of these men ultimately received stipends from the government due to illnesses or injuries incurred in the line of duty, and five others who made careers of scouting qualified for retirement pensions.[8]

For about nine years, during their most active and important period, the scouts worked for Lieutenant John Lapham Bullis, a tough, unconventional soldier from a Quaker background who had married a Mexican woman. Bullis was, in the words of William Loren Katz, "clearly a man willing to charge uphill."[9] Slim, short, and wiry, he sported a black mustache across a face burned red by the sun. During the Civil War, he had seen service as a captain in the 118th U.S. Colored Troops; then he accepted a regular commission as a second lieutenant in the Forty-first Infantry, one of the original six black regiments established in 1866. Seven years later, he was promoted to first lieutenant and became commander of the scouts. He was brave—from 1873 to 1881 he received four separate citations for valor in battle—and faithful to his men. He and his scouts shared the perils of some twenty-five expeditions, ranging in duration from a few days to a month.[10]

Working together as a team, Bullis and the scouts quickly proved their worth. In May 1873, only two months after he took over the scouts, he and a detachment of twenty Seminole Negroes guided a massive expedition into Mexico. Colonel Ranald S. Mackenzie and six companies of his Fourth Cavalry followed Bullis on an all-night march that culminated in a huge surprise for a band of Lipans, Kickapoos, and Apaches, who had raided successfully into Texas and found safety in Mexico. Mackenzie scattered the Indians, killing at least nineteen, and took forty prisoners. In the years that followed, the scouts several times guided troops across the border, protests from the Mexican government notwithstanding. With the Seminole Negroes serving the Army, Mexico no longer provided a safe haven for raiders.[11]

Like his men, Bullis could endure hardship and eat sparingly. Scout Joseph Philips testified that Bullis shared the deprivations of campaigning: "That fella suffer just like we-all did out in de woods. He was a good man. He was an Injun fighter. He was tough." Like good leaders of any period, he motivated his subordinates by example. As Philips recalled, Bullis "didn't stand and say, 'Go yonder'; he would say, 'Come on, boys, let's go get 'em.' "[12]

Bullis and his scouts, according to Porter, were "more like a large patriarchal family than an ordinary cavalry troop," and Bullis came to be "more like a war chief than an officer of cavalry." His men expected him to examine and approve every newborn child in the Seminole Negro camp, and he even performed the marriage ceremony that united scout James Perryman and Teresita, the daughter of a Lipan chief captured in the 1873 raid into Mexico. Bullis also prized their talents highly and defended his scouts against the parsimony of the Army when, in one of its periodic spasms of sometimes misguided frugality, it cut their rations. The affection and trust that he shared with them only enhanced their effectiveness. They were so proficient a team that even enemy tribes came to respect Bullis no less than his own men, and he earned the nicknames "Whirlwind" and "Thunderbolt" from hostile Indians.[13]

Under Bullis's leadership, the scouts generally operated independently of regular troops or far to their front. They moved fast, ate little, and stayed on Indian trails for weeks at a time. They gave the Army a capability to track and locate elusive Indians whose hit-and-run tactics made them hard to find and bring to battle. Porter considered them "the most effective scouting organization in the United States army."[14] Other groups of scouts among the Tonkawa, the Pawnee, and the Apache had their admirers, but the dramatic impact of Bullis and his men on operations on the Texas frontier is beyond dispute. Recognition for their contributions to military success sooner or later had to come their way.[15]

Adam Payne was the first Seminole scout to be awarded a Medal of Honor. He was born in Florida, stood 5 ft. 7 in. tall, and as a child had traveled the Trail of Tears, as the expulsion and forced migration of the Indians westward was known. He was in his thirties when he enlisted on November 12, 1873, at Fort Duncan. He served two six-month enlistments and left the service in February 1875. Some of his fellow scouts called him "Bad Man."[16]

His act of heroism came during the Red River War of 1874–75. Colonel Mackenzie and the Fourth Cavalry played the leading role in this major conflict against an unusual coalition of the most warlike tribes of the southern plains, with the Comanches convincing some of their Kiowa, Cheyenne, and Arapaho neighbors to join in the fight. Members of all of these tribes, driven to war by the disappearance of the buffalo herds and the failure of the government to provide the rations that had been promised, left their reservations and began a series of raids that inevitably brought the Army in pursuit.[17]

On September 20, 1874, Mackenzie's main column left camp on Catfish Creek, moved north past the headwaters of the Wichita River, then through the valley of Quitaque Creek and up the bluffs to the Staked Plains, a treeless and dry table-land that straddled the Texas-New Mexico border and severely tested those bold enough to attempt a crossing. A party of four scouts, including Payne in a buffalo-horn headdress, rode in front, a day's march ahead of the main body. A group of twenty-five Comanches discovered them and attacked. The scouts put up a fight, with Payne calmly swinging out of his saddle to bring down with his rifle the horse of a charging Comanche. The fighting became intense, with Payne taking on as many as six of the enemy at one time before the small, outnumbered detachment managed to break contact and flee. All four reached camp safely. Mackenzie and his men were eating lunch when the scouts came back and reported their skirmish with the enemy. He increased the state of alert, sent scouts back out, picked up the trail, and followed it north.[18]

The big fight of the campaign came on September 26. Seminole Negroes helped Mackenzie track the Indians to their large camp in Palo Duro Canyon on the Red River, well up the panhandle of Texas and hundreds of miles from Payne's home base. Mackenzie discovered and struck a big Kiowa and Comanche camp in the canyon. The cavalry surprised the Indians and immobilized them by taking and destroying fourteen hundred horses as well as massive quantities of camp equipment and supplies. With winter coming on, this blow was devastating.[19]

When the dust cleared, Mackenzie recommended eight of his men for the Medal of Honor: seven white troopers of his regiment and Adam Payne. One of the Army's premier Indian fighters himself, Mackenzie highly appreciated the scouts' abilities and believed that as Christian English-speakers who tilled the soil, they had the potential to be strong role models on western Indian reservations.[20] He cited Payne "for gallantry on September 20th, when attacked by a largely superior party of Indians," and called him "a scout of great courage."[21] Moreover, Mackenzie later wrote, "this man has, I believe, more cool daring than any scout I have ever known."[22]

Among the scouts, Payne had no monopoly on boldness and courage. Three others, who rode with Bullis on a reconnaissance in April 1875, showed similar traits. On April 16 the commander at Fort Duncan sent Bullis out on a typical reconnaissance, seeking a large party of Indians thought to be camped with seventy-five stolen horses about eighty miles northwest of Duncan, near where the Pecos River emptied into the Rio Grande. Bullis took only the three scouts, "as I desired to leave but little or no trail and to not be seen," and headed north with Company A of the Twenty-fifth Infantry toward the Fort Stockton road.[23]

The senior man among the three, Sergeant John Ward, had been one of the original recruits who enlisted with John Kibbetts in August 1870 at Fort Duncan. A farmer who had been born John Warrior in Arkansas sometime around 1847 but whose name had been shortened on Army records by an enlisting officer, Ward was about 5 ft. 7 in. tall and black. He served until October 1894, with only short discontinuities caused by the brevity of enlistment periods. Twenty-one-year-old Trumpeter Isaac Payne, who was born in Mexico and was on his first enlistment, served intermittently for about twenty-five years. The third man, Private Pompey Factor, had been twenty-one when he joined the scouts with the Kibbetts group in 1870 and was himself the son of a scout. All three—Ward, Payne, and Factor—were assigned to the Twenty-fourth Infantry, and two had five years of experience as scouts when they set out with Bullis for the Pecos.[24] They traveled with the black foot soldiers for six days before Bullis cut loose on April 22 and headed west toward the Pecos. Soon, on a dry arroyo called Johnson's Run that ran into the Pecos from the east, they picked up Indian signs. They rode fifty miles that day and camped after dark "at a water hole in a rock, grass good."[25]

They spent April 23 and 24 searching for the Indians. On April 23 they left camp early, at about four-thirty in the morning. They rode southwest about twenty miles until they reached the Pecos at the mouth of Howard's Creek and rested for about four hours. From there, they crossed to the west side of the river and marched about twelve miles farther west before spending the night at a dry camp, where again there was good grass for the horses. On April 24 they set out even earlier, making a wide sweep that took them west toward the Rio Grande about forty miles, then southwest for fifteen miles, before they camped after dark near the river, once more without water. Luckily it had rained recently, so there was ample water standing in holes, for both the men and horses, along the way that day.

On the following morning, they left camp before sunrise, at four, and headed south down the Rio Grande toward the Pecos. Bullis and the three scouts crossed back to the east side of the Pecos about one mile above its mouth at an Indian crossing near the caves decorated by eight thousand-year-old native pictographs and rode southeast around six miles. (The area now honors the scouts with the name Seminole Canyon State Historical Park.) They camped six miles southeast of their crossing of the Pecos at a spring in Paint Cave. Although there were no fresh Indian signs, many old tracks pointed northwest toward a shallow ford of the Rio Grande known as Eagle's Nest Crossing.

Soon afterward they struck a fresh trail going in the same direction. "The trail was quite large," Bullis wrote, "came from the direction of the settlements, and was made, I judge, by seventy-five head or more of horses." Concluding that this was the herd that they were seeking, they immediately took up the trail. After following it for about an hour, they came up unobserved on a party of Indians and watched them cross to the west side of the Pecos.

Bullis and his scouts were on a reconnaissance, but they could not resist a fight. Dismounting quietly and tethering their horses, they crept up to within about seventy-five yards of the Indians. They too were dismounted when Bullis opened fire. He quickly discovered that he might as well have stirred a hornet's nest with a stick. The Comanches numbered between twenty-five and thirty and carried repeating

Winchesters, probably acquired in trade from border ruffi-
ans. A forty-five-minute fight ensued, with bullets flying as
Bullis and the scouts twice gained possession of the Indians'
herd of horses and twice had to withdraw. Although three
Indians fell dead, they kept up the pressure and forced the
scouts to pull back to avoid being surrounded and separated
from their own horses.

It was a narrow escape. Scout Charlie Daniels, who was
not there but heard from others what had happened, later
recalled the exciting details. With the Comanches advancing
closer, the scouts

> runned and went to de horses and de three scouts got on their
> horses, but Lieutenant Bullis could not; he horse were frighten
> and he could noe get on, and de Injuns were rushin' him. Well,
> he had to leave he horse, so this John Ward said to de other boys,
> said, "Boys, don't let us leave him," so they struck back and two
> commence to firin' to keep de Injuns back until they could get
> Lieutenant Bullis on with 'em. Well, this fella what took him up
> he was runned and de other two keep shootin' and so they made
> they escape. He got on with Isaac Payne; he tooks him up on he
> horse but dey would change about, you know, fust one horse then
> wid other.[26]

Plainly the loyalties that bound Bullis and the scouts ran
strong and deep.

Bullis confirmed Daniels's account. The lieutenant lost his
horse, saddle, and bridle and "just saved my hair by jumping
on my Sergeant's horse, back of him." Ward also barely escaped with his life. A bullet passed through his carbine sling
and shattered the weapon's stock before he picked up Bullis
and dashed through the Indians. As far as his scouts were
concerned, Bullis said, "they are brave and trustworthy, and
are each worthy of a medal." The return was uneventful. Two
days after the sharp fight, they pulled into Fort Clark with
their mission accomplished.

Lieutenant Bullis recommended that all three of his men
receive Medals of Honor. The awards were made one year
later, and Pompey Factor put his "X" on a letter that acknowledged receipt of his medal in March 1876. Without Bullis's

effort to see that they were given proper credit, they probably would have had none. The official roll of engagements with Indians listed the fight as having been between Bullis and three men of the Twenty-fourth Infantry on one side and a band of Comanches on the other and did not even mention that the soldiers were scouts.[27]

By the time that the medals came, the tenuous situation of the scout community at Fort Clark had deteriorated considerably. In April 1876, Brackettville whites petitioned for the removal of the scouts and their families, claiming that they were squatters on private property, indigents who preyed on local residents, and that except for those actually in the service of the United States the community was essentially out of control. Army officers believed that the complaints lacked substance, and Colonel Mackenzie called the scouts "hard working and industrious." Still, less than one month later, the opposition turned violent. On May 19 unknown parties shot at two Seminole Negroes on the Fort Clark reservation around five hundred yards south of the post hospital. The assailants wounded ninety-year-old Juan Caballo, who was also known as John Horse, in four places, killed former scout Titus Payne, and left no clues. The shooting of the old man must have been especially devastating because he was the chief who had led the people back to Texas. "The negroes seem to be very much alarmed," Colonel John I. Gregg reported from Fort Clark, "and I have been informed have made threats of retaliation, which has alarmed some of the whites residing in the vicinity of their camps."[28]

The shootings definitely had a profound effect on the scout community. Many among them began carrying arms wherever they went, and some feared going to their jobs in Brackettville. They even talked about returning to Mexico, a move that would have cost the Army a major asset and added to the number of potential enemies.[29] Colonel Hatch had warned earlier that space had to be found for the scouts on a reservation in Indian Territory or back in Florida so that they could support themselves without fear. Without some provision for their livelihood, they might return to Mexico and resume raiding north into the United States.[30]

It was clear to Brigadier General Edward O. C. Ord at Department of Texas headquarters, and perhaps to others as well, that the issue was not Seminole lawlessness or menace but rather that the citizens whom they protected from hostile Indians regarded them as flotsam. As the general wrote, the Seminole Negroes "are being badly used by the people around them, for the reason that they are in the way, and have nothing to pay."[31] Ord and other officers lobbied hard to convince the Indian Bureau to offer the Seminole Negroes land on a reservation in Indian Territory. Their motives were complex. Such a move would put the scouts out of harm's way and provide them with modest parcels of land for their support. It would also introduce a Christianizing influence among the reservation tribes. General Ord, who admired the scouts' "simple manners and religious tendency," thought that they would be "a real godsend . . . to some of the agencies where the . . . Sioux or Apaches defy the most earnest appeals of our missionaries." Some among the scouts had asked for such a transfer, and Colonel Edward Hatch of the Ninth Cavalry and Colonel Mackenzie of the Fourth had supported this solution, even before the troubles of the spring of 1876 added urgency to the matter. Lieutenant General Philip H. Sheridan lent his support as well.[32]

Nothing came of these suggestions or later efforts initiated by the Seminoles, and the situation worsened. Early on New Year's Day of 1877, just after midnight, former scout and Medal of Honor holder Adam Payne, who was wanted for allegedly knifing a black soldier, was at a dance in the Seminole camp at Fort Clark when a local deputy sheriff named Clarion Windus came looking for him. Instead of trying to arrest Payne, the sheriff "blasted him from behind" with a double-barreled shotgun. Shot from such close range that his clothes burst into flames, Payne died instantly.[33]

Within one day of his death, five scouts panicked and headed across the border for Mexico. Pompey Factor, another Medal of Honor hero, was among the deserters, although he returned and surrendered on May 25, 1879. The Army, in what was surely an unusual display of leniency but one that reflected an emerging understanding that the scouts could not be forced to march to a conventional military drum, forgave him and restored Factor to duty, provided that he make good the time owed and forfeit all pay and allowances that had accrued during his absence. He remained in the service only until 1880, after which he farmed in Mexico and Brackettville, where he died on March 28, 1928, a widower and, after a long struggle with the Veterans Administration, briefly a pensioner. He was buried in the Seminole Negro group's cemetery near Brackettville on Las Moras Creek.[34]

John Ward also managed to wrest a pension from the bureaucrats. He claimed that in January 1878 he had contracted rheumatism after spending a cold night on the ground while sergeant of the guard at Fort Clark. Finally, in 1895, he had to retire because his ailment became so severe that he could no longer mount his horse. He stayed in the Brackettville area, worked as a gardener, and received his pension until he died in 1911. His widow, Julia, continued to draw monthly payments until her death in 1926.[35]

Isaac Payne, who was the least experienced of the three scouts who had ridden with Bullis in April 1875, found the military bureaucracy a little confusing. Payne was out in the field with a detachment from Fort Clark in July 1875 when his first enlistment ended. Three days after his term of service expired, he went home, without permission. His detachment stayed in the field, and Payne went on the rolls as a deserter. He remained at Fort Clark until the others returned in December. The Army, which still found it worthwhile to learn to accommodate itself to the scouts, put him back on the rolls as returning from desertion and discharged him as of the scheduled end of his term. He later reenlisted many times, remaining active in the scouts until January 1901. Afterward, Payne lived with his family at the Brackettville camp, from which he applied for an invalid's pension in 1903, claiming that he had been completely incapacitated by service-connected rheumatism and was unable to work. He died in Mexico sometime in 1904.[36]

· After the period of the scouts' peak activity in the 1870s, their organization lingered on in gradual decline until the early years of the twentieth century. In 1884 there were only six on active duty, one sergeant and five privates. Finally, the scouts were abolished in 1914, and the remaining residents on the Fort Clark military reservation were evicted.[37] Lieutenant Bullis fared somewhat better, however. Widely recognized for his exploits with the scouts, he rose to the rank of brigadier general before he retired in 1904. He died in San Antonio seven years later, and a World War I military camp near the city was named in his honor.[38]

The scouts made a significant mark on Indian warfare in the borderlands, helping the Army find and fight an enemy that regular troops had difficulty locating and bringing to battle. Like more conventional black cavalry and infantry soldiers, they sought no more than a measure of respect, comfort, and dignity. But even while they actively risked their lives for the United States in war, it was clear that white Texans in the Rio Grande Valley would not willingly accept them as neighbors. Nevertheless, the scouts hung on, with a community anchored by the cemetery on Los Moras Creek, near which the offspring of the scouts still resided at the end of the twentieth century. The durable legacy of the scouts should not be surprising. As descendant Willie Warrior said, "Them suckers was tough."[39]

~ 4 ~

The Apache Wars,
1877–1879

he autumn of 1875 marked the start of a major transition for the Ninth Cavalry. In one of the periodic shuffles of regiments, the Army reassigned the Ninth to New Mexico—Apache country—where it would relieve the Eighth Cavalry. Slowly, the troops packed their equipment and pulled out of first one Texas post and then another, and the Ninth's eight years in the Lone Star State drew to a close. In September most of the companies and headquarters took up the long overland march to what Colonel George F. Hamilton, the regimental historian, called "new stations on the southeastern limits of civilization."[1] A new and harsh experience lay ahead for the Ninth, whose move to New Mexico was not quick or easy. For example, Captain Charles D. Beyer and the men of C Troop started out at Fort Brown, near the mouth of the Rio Grande. From Brown to Fort Clark, then through Pecos Station and Fort Selden, their long trek led to Fort Bayard near Silver City in southwestern New Mexico. After C Troop had spent the better part of three months on the march, its journey ended in mid-December, some 1,044 miles from where the unit had started.[2]

The complete transition took almost a year. By May 1876 the regiment was dispersed at seven posts, six in New Mexico and one in southern Colorado, with the headquarters at Fort Union in northeastern New Mexico. Only 370 of the 670 men on the rolls in June 1876 were available for duty. The rest were scattered all over the region on a variety of assignments, building barracks and stables and putting up firewood for the winter at their posts, inventorying and issuing supplies for the Quartermaster Department, and caring for herds of horses as well as scouting for hostile Indians and escorting the mail. Some also became involved in law enforcement and surveying uncharted areas as well as laying out and building primitive roads. For example, the forty-six men of C Troop cut trees, removed rocks, and graded the trail for the North Star road over the Continental Divide near the headwaters of the Gila River, on the west side of the mountains north of Fort Bayard. With many such assignments requiring attention, the regiment was at about half strength, and its soldiers and officers knew almost nothing about the country in which they found themselves.[3] Colonel Hatch did what he could to rectify the regiment's ignorance about New Mexico. He continuously kept detachments in the saddle, thereby curbing all but the most belligerent of the Indians and developing knowledge of the terrain and people at the same time. On almost constant patrol throughout 1876, the companies and detachments of the Ninth covered more than 8,800 miles and kept Apache raids to a minimum.[4]

Cavalry duty in New Mexico was tough. The Indian Department's policy of concentration of the Apaches at the huge San Carlos reservation in Arizona was proving to be a disaster. The adjustment to sedentary reservation life even in places that were familiar was extremely difficult for tribes accustomed to hunting for food, raiding their enemies, and roaming at will. But when the Indian Department decided to consolidate the Indians at San Carlos, they exacerbated the already serious problems by their choice of the remote and barren new site. The Indians loathed San Carlos, and some simply refused to go there.[5] They had good reason. San Carlos was a scalding earthly inferno. Novelist Owen Wister, author of *The Virginian*, claimed that "the creator did not make San Carlos. When He got around to it after dressing up Paradise with fruit trees, He just left it as He found it as a sample of the way they did jobs before He came along." According to Wister, San Carlos was the product of a simple recipe: "Take stones and ashes and thorns, with some scorpions and rattle-

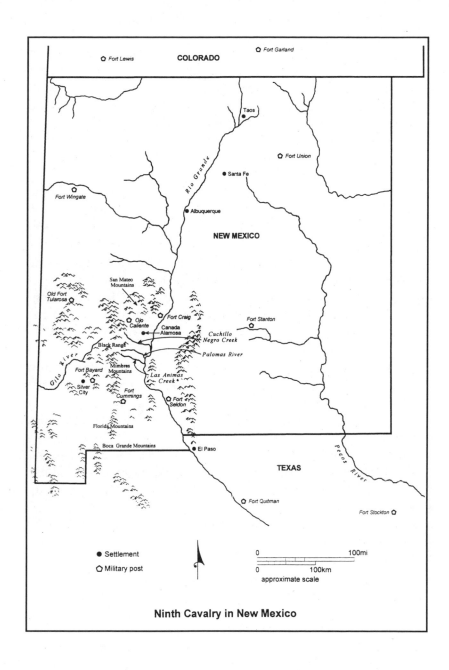

Ninth Cavalry in New Mexico

snakes thrown in, dump the outfit on stones red hot, set the United States Army after the Apaches, and you have San Carlos."[6]

Over time the Ninth's mission did not become easier. Among those who shunned the reservation, bands under Chiefs Juh and Geronimo roamed freely, raiding and coalescing with other Apaches who were seeking to avoid removal to the reservation. In 1877 the regiment again spent most of the year in the saddle, with both large and small detachments scouting and policing the border with Mexico and keeping the lid on the Indian situation.[7]

The activities of Captain Beyer's C Troop reflected the entire regiment's routine. His buffalo soldiers had stayed at Fort Bayard through 1876, an uneventful but rough year, and into 1877. With long, rigorous scouting, regardless of the weather, eventually the troopers began learning about the country. Occasionally, a fight with Indians broke the monotony.[8] Private Henry Bush, a cook in civilian life and a native of Ontario, Canada, soldiered with the unit through the entire period of service in New Mexico. He remembered being driven hard, "continuously on scouting service which subjected us to great exposure, such as sleeping in rains and snows in the mountains unprotected from the elements, sometimes no sleep for two days, sometimes subsisting on the most meager diet, sometimes marches of ninety miles . . . in a hot scorching sun."[9]

This was the situation when outlaw Chiricahua Apaches, reinforced by men from the Warm Springs and Mescalero bands that had fled the San Carlos reservation, stepped up their raids. In late January 1877 the Fort Bayard garrison learned that such a party had fought a small portion of the Sixth Cavalry in Arizona and had slipped eastward into New Mexico. Captain Beyer soon ordered his troops saddled and in the field to look for the raiders.[10] He sent a small separate detachment of only six troopers and three Navaho scouts under Lieutenant Henry Wright in search of the Indians' trail. Wright, still a second lieutenant after five years with the Ninth, found between forty and fifty Indians camped in the

Florida Mountains. The fighting men among them outnumbered his little command by at least two to one. With the odds clearly against him, he did not attack—but he did not withdraw, either. Instead, he and his troops rode straight into the Indian camp, and he called the chiefs to council. Through one of the Navaho scouts, Lieutenant Wright told the Apaches to give up their weapons and mounts and return to the reservation, where, he promised, they would find protection and provisions.

After about thirty minutes, it became obvious to Wright that he had wasted his time trying to negotiate. Looking around, he saw that the women and children had slipped out of the Indian camp. Just as quietly, eighteen Apache warriors had surrounded his detachment. Once he saw his predicament, he reacted quickly, ordering his small command to break through the tightening ring before it became too late. Then the firing started. For a while his men held off the Indians, who continued to press in on them.[11]

As Wright's troops tried to break free, the shooting dissolved into a vicious hand-to-hand fight. Corporal Clinton Greaves, in the center of the combat, fired his carbine until it was empty and then swung it like a club, knocking aside Apaches to bash a gap through the circle for his comrades. Meanwhile, the other troopers continued to shoot, and five Apaches fell dead before the detachment rode out of the opening that Greaves had cleared. Lieutenant Wright and Corporal Greaves each killed one Indian, while Privates Richard Epps and Dick Mackadoo dropped three more. The rest of the Apaches sought refuge in the surrounding cliffs and rocks. Once they reached the high ground, they opened fire on Wright and his troops. Now in an exposed and untenable position, Wright withdrew to Fort Cummings, taking eleven captured horses with him.[12]

The Indians had driven off Wright, but C Troop hit them again four days later in the Boca Grande Mountains. This time, Captain Beyer's men captured the whole camp, destroyed all of the Apaches' gear, and took four horses. But the warriors escaped, an outcome that was to be repeated over and over as the Ninth continued to battle and wear down the Apaches, who would get away, leaving their camp equipment to be confiscated and burned.[13]

After logging over two hundred tough miles, Wright and his men received immediate recognition for their bravery. Post orders cited everyone: "The conduct of Lieut. Wright and men under him is deserving of the highest praise and furnishes an example of gallantry and soldierly conduct worthy of emulation by all." But Wright clearly understood that his men had earned more than such perfunctory recognition. Their prompt action and ready obedience to orders had saved the entire detachment from annihilation, and he was extremely grateful, singling out four of his six troopers—Greaves, Epps, Mackadoo, and Private John Q. Adams—and scout José Chávez for recognition.[14]

His recommendations, sent up the chain of command for approval, showed both his appreciation for his men and the vagaries of a system of awards that was still in flux. The five had earned his gratitude, but clearly Greaves had made the most significant contribution. While Wright asked that Certificates of Merit be awarded to each soldier, for Greaves he sought both the certificate and a Medal of Honor. Colonel Hatch approved the Certificates of Merit, as did officers all the way up to Washington, where matters ground to a halt. Regulations blocked the awards that Wright wanted, for two reasons. First, Certificates of Merit were authorized only for private soldiers, and Greaves was a corporal—the lowest noncommissioned officer, but still a noncommissioned officer. And second, regulations required that each application be made on behalf of one person rather than a group. General William T. Sherman settled the matter by approving the medal for Greaves and rejecting the rest of Wright's recommendations. Clinton Greaves received his medal, the first awarded in the regiment since Emanuel Stance had been given his in 1870, on June 26, 1879.[15]

While the paperwork wended its way through the bureaucracy, there was still some hard riding ahead. Greaves and the men of C Troop were busy throughout 1877 with scouts and escorts of mail carriers between settlements and military posts. In April the unit rode 472 miles. The next year was a little different, with a detachment escorting military prisoners to Santa Fe to put them on a train for the prison at Fort Leavenworth, Kansas, and another chasing a gang that had robbed a mail coach near Fort Bayard, but life was no easier. Like the rest of the Ninth Cavalry, C Troop was still learning the country, but the skirmishes of these years were only a mild prelude to the bitter Apache wars to come.[16]

Meanwhile, Clinton Greaves reenlisted. Born in 1855 in Madison County, Virginia, on the eastern slopes of the Blue Ridge Mountains, Greaves had moved from there to Prince George's County, Maryland, on the fringe of Washington, DC, before joining the Army. He did not fare particularly well in Maryland, and when he enlisted in 1872 he was working as a laborer. His first five-year enlistment expired in November 1877, and he moved to H Troop. After he received the Medal of Honor in June 1879, he must have displayed it regularly. By early spring of 1881, he had worn out the ribbon and sent it to Philadelphia for repair. All told, he spent fifteen years in the Ninth Cavalry before he transferred to Columbus Barracks, Ohio, one of the depots where recruits received their first taste of soldiering before going to regiments. Described as "a big fine looking soldier" by fellow trooper Peter Watson, Greaves stayed for five years as part of the Colored Detachment. He left the service for good in 1893.[17]

The story of Greaves's heroism in the Florida Mountains followed him to Ohio, where the tale became a little bigger. By 1889, when Lieutenant Colonel William H. Jordan publicized Greaves's actions to his command at the depot, the fight had grown to involve thirteen buffalo soldiers against sixty-five hostile Apaches. Not only that, but the foe also had been led by Chief Victorio, later the scourge of the Ninth Cavalry, though in 1877 still not involved in the fighting.[18]

Greaves may have been the robust trooper described by his comrade Watson, but he seems to have become preoccupied with an assortment of real or imagined illnesses while at Columbus. Watson remembered that Greaves "was all the time talking about dying, thought he had heart disease and complained that he had asthma."[19] Another acquaintance,

Columbus police chief John O'Connor, had been in charge of the corral at the barracks when Greaves was post blacksmith. The trooper had told him around 1890 that he was going to quit the Army. O'Connor replied that "he was foolish to do so with his long service," but Greaves said that he was "compelled to do so on account of poor health."[20]

During most of his service years, Greaves was single, but by the time of his final discharge in 1893 he was married. Bertha Williams, whose first husband had deserted her, was also a Virginian, from Appomattox Court House. She was fifteen years younger than her new husband. They stayed together, Greaves working as a civilian for the Quartermaster Department at the barracks, until he died of heart disease in 1906. Bertha Greaves survived her husband by thirty years, supporting herself by doing housework. Both were buried in Columbus.[21]

When Greaves had earned his medal in the Florida Mountains early in 1877, the conflict with the Apaches was still in its long incubation period, but it soon evolved into a full-blown guerrilla war as difficult and bloody as any frontier conflict. Apacheria, the region that the six thousand or so Apaches called home, was a huge territory that stretched from the Colorado River on the west to the mountains on the east side of the Rio Grande in New Mexico and from the border with Mexico fully one thousand miles north to the great canyons. The country was as harsh and stark as it was big. And the Apaches—the word "Apache" meant enemy in the Zuni tongue—fit well. As historian Dan Thrapp wrote, "The tribes of Apacheria were a product of their habitat, harsh, cruel, and pitiless"; they were "the most implacable savages on the American continent." Joe Femler, a scout and blacksmith at old Camp Grant in Arizona, stated the first rule of war on the Apacheria frontier: "When you see Apache 'sign,' be *keerful*; 'n' when you don' see nary sign, be *more* keerful."[22]

When war actually broke out, replacing the long and uneasy period of tense quiet disrupted by skirmishes, ambushes, and atrocities, two significant elements were responsible. The first was the removal policy. The effort to force the Apaches and related tribes onto the hell-on-earth known as San Carlos met widespread and unanticipated resistance. The emergence of Victorio, "the triumphant one," as leader of the Warm Springs Apaches who refused removal to San Carlos was the second factor. Fifty-four years old in 1879, the "fierce-faced long-haired fighter of great ability" had deep-set penetrating eyes. He had followed the renowned warrior Mangas Coloradas, who had taught him how to set an ambush and wait for an enemy to move into the killing zone. White soldiers ultimately had captured Mangas Coloradas in 1863 and tortured, killed, and dismembered him. After his death, Victorio embodied Apache resistance to white encroachment. He was known for his self-control and intelligence as well as his tactical skills. With Victorio as its leader, the Apache resistance became what William Leckie has called "one of the bloodiest chapters in New Mexican history" and, for the officers and men of the Ninth Cavalry who bore the brunt of the pursuit, one of the most difficult campaigns that they ever faced.[23]

Victorio first struck out against the settlers of New Mexico in April 1879. He headed into the San Mateo Mountains and then west and south before surprising some herders near Silver City. From Forts Bayard, Cummings, and Stanton, Ninth Cavalry troops pursued Victorio in what Hamilton called an "almost constant campaign against him and his murderous band." Captain Beyer and his C Troop, which had spent much of its time in the saddle by May 1879, were in the field at Ojo Caliente. They covered a lot of ground during the month, including a grueling three-week scout in which they rode 280 miles. Overall, they marched more than 400 miles in May before catching up with Victorio.[24]

On May 25, Beyer, Lieutenant Wright, all thirty-one available men of C Troop plus fifteen men of I Troop, two Navaho scouts, and a local guide, John R. Foster, left Fort Bayard near Silver City.[25] Beyer's men included a number of veteran buffalo soldiers, but none had longer or more diverse service than Sergeant Thomas Boyne, a native of Prince George's County, Maryland, who had first enlisted in the artillery in 1864. During the Civil War he had served in B Battery of the Second Colored Light Artillery and had participated in the battles around Richmond, at Wilson's Wharf and City Point, Virginia, in May and June 1864. After the war, he went west with his unit and was discharged in March 1866 at Brownsville, Texas. Ten months later, he joined the new Fortieth Infantry, trying on a fresh identity and enlisting as Thomas Bowen of Norfolk, Virginia. He served in the Fortieth and then in the newly consolidated Twenty-fifth until 1875, when he joined the Ninth Cavalry. Among the enlisted men of the Ninth, not even Emanuel Stance had a more extensive or varied background than Boyne, with fifteen years of service in all three combat branches under his belt when he followed Victorio's trail with Captain Beyer.[26]

While there can be little doubt that the presence of this force of fifty men was well known to the Indians, Beyer had a harder time picking up his foe's trail. It took two days before the cavalry learned something of the Apaches' whereabouts from settlers near the junction of West Diamond Creek and the Gila River. A little to the north, Beyer struck two-day-old tracks made by around twenty Indians. Foster recognized the sign as that of Victorio's band, and the troopers set out in pursuit. The presence of the Indians became increasingly obvious as the party passed carcasses of cattle that had been slaughtered for food as well as the body of a dead stallion that Foster recognized as the property of a local rancher.[27]

By midafternoon on May 27 the trail became warmer. Beyer found a camp that had been abandoned by the Indians early that morning along with a cow and a mare that had been partly consumed. After time out to eat supper and graze their horses, Beyer pushed his men well into the evening and did not halt until almost midnight. He was in familiar country, camping near where the North Star road, which his men had built in 1877, crossed Diamond Creek. The next morning the cavalry broke camp early. At just after five o'clock they saddled up and followed the Indian trail east along Diamond Creek, stopping three hours later for breakfast and to rest their horses. They were closing in and found the camp used by Victorio the previous night. "Our march during the day," Beyer later explained, "having been a very hard one, most of the time on foot and through burning forest and underbrush (set on fire by the Indians to cover their trail), went into camp at 4:30 P.M."

On May 29, Beyer found Victorio. The large cavalry patrol picked its way over the summit of the Mimbres Mountains and entered a canyon "having on its left high ridges or rather mountains, [and] found small pools of water and fresh Indian signs." As the troopers emerged from the canyon, they deployed in a skirmish line. To their front, about one half-mile ahead, they saw two horses grazing. Minutes later they sighted the Indians in the distance, high up on a steep, rocky summit, building defensive positions out of rocks and brush. An Indian, whom Beyer later learned was Victorio, stood on the peak, called out in Apache for the soldiers to come near, and waved a white flag, indicating that he wanted to talk.

Beyer halted his troops. Moving about fifty yards in front of his skirmishers and carrying a white handkerchief on a stick, he directed his Navaho scout to tell Victorio that he would talk with him. But the Apache leader would speak with him only if Beyer came to his camp and breastworks, where the captain could see sixteen warriors. Beyer did not trust Victorio's promise of safe passage and tried to persuade him to meet halfway, which the chief declined. Victorio then launched into what Beyer called "a harangue . . . to the effect that he, Victorio, and his people were poor, that they did not want to fight my soldiers, and all they wanted was to be let alone." When he finished, Beyer watched him wave a lance over his head and take down his flag of truce.

As the talks went on, both sides improved their positions. Victorio moved his women and children out of harm's way while the men continued to strengthen their makeshift fortification. Beyer sent Lieutenant Wright and his skirmishers halfway up the mountain so that they were within two hundred yards of the Apaches. He also placed a small detachment of skirmishers between the Indians and their herd. Guide Foster and five cavalrymen captured all of the animals—ten horses, two mules, and two burros—without drawing any attention.

Just before noon, Beyer increased the pressure on the Indians by moving the skirmishers on his right under Sergeant

Delemar Penn of I Troop forward and to the right where they threatened the enemy's left. Penn carried out the order. Then Beyer signaled for the advance, and the shooting began, with the Apaches returning the fire from the cavalry. The line of buffalo soldiers kept advancing, the men moving from tree to tree, all the time climbing the mountain toward the Apaches. On the right, Penn got well around the rear of the Indians, forcing them to withdraw from their positions and to retreat down a ridge to their rear. Fleeing on foot, they scattered, leaving no trail and making futile any further pursuit. There was blood, but the Indians were able to remove their injured, making it impossible to count their losses. As so often happened, the cavalry managed to capture blankets, hides, baskets, meat, "and such other plunder as is usually found in an Indian camp" as well as supplies of mescal, the green desert staple that the Indians steamed and dried before carrying it with them on their travels. Beyer's men burned everything that they seized. However, the cost of such success was high. Private Frank Dorsey of C Troop was killed and buried near where he fell, and two other soldiers were wounded, Privates George H. Moore of C Troop and John Scott of I Troop. Beyer and his force stayed in the field another fourteen days before returning to Fort Bayard. They did not encounter Victorio again for several months.

This clash with Victorio was the second in which men of Beyer's troop had faced the Apaches, seen them disappear, and found themselves victors in possession of an abandoned camp. Wright, with a much smaller detachment, had achieved just such an outcome in January 1877 in the fight for which Clinton Greaves had received the Medal of Honor. For the second time, too, Beyer was careful to acknowledge the bravery of the men in his unit. With his troop often in the thick of the fighting, his soldiers had ample opportunity to display the gallant conduct that won attention and acclaim. Like Lieutenant Wright, Beyer did what he could to see that boldness under fire was recognized and rewarded, thereby perhaps ensuring that the men would be just as intrepid in future encounters. In addition to Lieutenant Wright, Captain Beyer singled out several enlisted men for special recognition for their gallantry in action—Sergeants Penn, Boyne, and George Lyman and Corporal Isom Mabry of C Troop, and Private Ridgely of I Troop. He also cited John Foster and the Navaho scout, Hostensorze.

After the fight of May 29, calm prevailed until August, when Victorio launched his war in earnest. He struck often and fast, primarily to acquire horses. On September 4 he killed two sheepherders in Temporal Canyon and took their horses. Then, on the same day, he killed five soldiers of E Troop, Ninth Cavalry, who were guarding the troop's horse herd at Ojo Caliente—Sergeant Silas Chapman and Privates Silas Graddon, Lafayette E. Hoke, William Murphy, and Abram Percival—and stole forty-six more horses, giving his band enough mounts to escape into the Black Mountains, along the way attacking isolated ranchers and settlers and causing panic wherever they went.[28]

Victorio chose the Black Range for good reason. The mountains were extremely rugged. The Ninth Cavalry's Colonel Hatch found it "impossible to describe the exceeding roughness of such mountains as the Black Range. . . . The well known Modoc Lava beds are a lawn compared with them."[29] But Victorio did more than flee to difficult terrain. With his trail marked by the bodies of soldiers and civilians and with a string of stolen horses in tow, he also was sending a message to the Army that there was going to be a long, costly, and severe war. Indeed, the situation seemed desperate to pioneer residents.[30] Nervous settlers constantly looked over their shoulders in alarm as Victorio and rumors of Victorio flashed through the Southwest.

The men of C Troop and other elements of the Ninth immediately pursued the Apaches. Relying on keen eyesight as well as knowledge of the terrain and Apache habits, along with sheer persistence, the Ninth's scouts picked up Victorio's track on September 16, less than two weeks after he had hit the warpath. Troops and scouts from several Arizona posts also took to the field, seeking to prevent him from going west into Arizona, but he was not interested in leaving New Mexico. Troops of the Ninth headed for the center of his haven near the headwaters of Las Animas Creek, a stream that flowed from the Continental Divide in the Black Range east to the Rio Grande, about forty miles south of Ojo Caliente. Turning his attention toward the cavalry, Victorio selected the ground on which he would fight. The Ninth did not catch up with him. He waited for them.[31]

A column made up of Captain Byron Dawson's B Troop and Captain Ambrose E. Hooker's E Troop followed the Apaches for two days to the canyons at the head of Las Animas Creek. Dawson's acting first sergeant, Sergeant John Denny, who was from the tiny town of Big Flats between Elmira and Corning in western New York, rode with his unit. The thirty-two-year-old Denny already had twelve years of service, five with the Tenth Cavalry and seven with the Ninth. Like the rest of B Troop, he had spent many days in the saddle since arriving in New Mexico.[32] On the morning of September 18, 1879, Denny was part of the long line of blue-clad troopers who followed Lieutenant Colonel Nathan A. M. Dudley into an ambush on the Las Animas, where Victorio's band crouched silently in well-protected positions. With about 150 men, the Apache chief waited while Dawson's troops rode right into his trap. From both sides of the canyon, Indians poured fire on the buffalo soldiers, pinning them in the valley.[33] Fortunately, the sounds of gunfire bouncing from one canyon wall to another reached Captain Beyer and Lieutenant William H. Hugo, who were searching with Companies C and G. But even all four companies were not enough to pry the Indians out of their positions. The reinforcements, Lieutenant Matthias Day later recalled, "made attack after attack to turn the flank of the Indians and release Dawson's command, but were as frequently repulsed, with loss, due to the precipitous nature of the country."[34]

Late in the afternoon, as the 9th was about to disengage, Lieutenant Day saw Private A. Freeland of B Troop lying wounded about four hundred yards from Beyer's position. Two unwounded soldiers were assisting Freeland, who was trying to walk toward the captain and his troops. The injured soldier and his comrades drew attention and fire from the Apaches. According to Day, "It seemed as if no one could pass this open rocky space alive," but neither Freeland nor Denny,

John Denny, from a collection of photographs assembled for the Colored Conference at the Paris (France) Exposition of 1900. The photographs of Isaiah Mays and Dennis Bell that appear later in this book are from the same collection. Christian A. Fleetwood Papers. *Courtesy Library of Congress*

who was helping him, faltered. As the shooting intensified, Denny picked up Freeland. Lieutenant Day, Sergeant Lyman, and Private James Jackson all saw Denny, with the help of another soldier, carry Freeland back to shelter among Beyer's soldiers. "The act," Day judged many years later, "was one of most conspicuous gallantry—and one deserving of a Certificate of Merit—more than simply a Medal of Honor." Private Freeland survived the fight and was back in action, scouting with B Troop, in October.[35]

At dusk, Colonel Dudley had to withdraw. Private Peter Haines of G Troop was dead, and Private Jeremiah Caump of B Troop was so severely wounded that he succumbed two days later. So precipitate was the withdrawal that the cavalry abandoned much of its camp gear to the Apaches. Victorio found himself in possession of the soldiers' hospital train as well as the personal baggage of most of the officers.[36] However, the situation could have been worse. Late in the fight, with ammunition running low, the troops were ordered to withdraw as well as they could. But Lieutenant Day refused to leave his wounded. He went forward alone under heavy fire and carried a disabled soldier from the field. Day infuriated Captain Beyer by this delay, but eleven years later the lieutenant received a Medal of Honor from his superiors to go with the gratitude and respect of his buffalo soldiers.[37]

With the help of Lieutenant Day and fellow troopers Lyman and Jackson, Sergeant Denny was awarded his medal almost sixteen years later, in 1895. According to Jackson, who had twenty-seven years of service (and whose wife was soon to be banished from her residence on Fort Robinson, Nebraska, for running rum), in 1894 the troopers were still talking about Denny's heroic act of fifteen years earlier against the Apaches. Captain Charles Taylor, Denny's commander at the time, assembled the documentation for the award and added his own recommendation, noting that "Captain Day performed similar service during this action and sometime since received a Medal of Honor in recognition of same. This man however seems to have been lost sight of."[38]

In January 1895, Colonel James Biddle, the Ninth's commander, formally rectified this oversight. Biddle presented the Medal of Honor to Denny, who had lost his stripes after at least two court martial convictions (one of which was for participating in a barracks fight with Blacksmith Lawrence

Galloway at Fort DuChesne, Utah) and was a private in C Troop at the time. Biddle told the regiment that "such acts of gallantry not only reflect credit upon the individual, but also on the organization to which he belongs, and the 9th Cavalry may well feel proud of having in its ranks a man so signally honored."[39]

Less than three years later, in September 1897, John Denny retired from the Army as a corporal. He had a pension of just over twenty-seven dollars per month, which he supplemented with a job at the Fort Robinson post exchange, where he made ten dollars more. He stayed in Nebraska at least until the spring of 1899 and soon afterward moved to the U.S. Soldiers' Home in Washington, DC. He died there on November 28, 1901, with his sister Maria Jenkins of Baltimore at his bedside. In addition to his medal, Denny owned only a silver watch and sixty-eight cents.[40]

After the debacle at Las Animas Creek, Colonel Hatch sent Major Albert B. Morrow, an able, hard-working officer, to replace Colonel Dudley in charge of operations in southern New Mexico.[41] Always seeking to force the enemy to stand and fight, Major Morrow constantly pushed his troops as he repeatedly fought Victorio. In the first clash, on September 24, 1879, along the Cuchillo Negro, the Indians surprised Lieutenant Wright while he and some of his troopers were bringing in a wounded man. Wright's horse fell dead under a hail of bullets, and the Apaches were closing in when Sergeant Boyne and a detachment came to the officer's assistance, flanked the Indians, charged, and drove them off.[42]

In another fight in the Mimbres Mountains near Ojo Caliente five days later, Morrow commanded a column of two hundred that also included Boyne. This time the fight lasted over six hours, until ten o'clock at night. The next morning the soldiers found three Apaches dead. With Victorio occupying the high ground, the battle started anew on the next day when an Apache sniper picked off a Ninth Cavalry sentry. Morrow succeeded in dislodging Victorio and then in the Apache camp found evidence of many killed and wounded. The major lost two men—Privates Woodward and John Johnson of L Troop—and captured about sixty horses.[43]

September had been a terrible month for the Ninth. Despite the heroics and hard work in the fights that punctuated the chase for Victorio, he remained on the loose. Pursuing his foe relentlessly, Morrow drove his tired troopers hard and rode his horses until they dropped. Still, he could not coerce his enemy into a decisive battle, although by the end of October he did force Victorio across the boundary into Mexico for the rest of the year. At least the Apache chief could no longer torment the settlers north of the border. But the tireless efforts of the Ninth notwithstanding, Major Morrow knew that a large share of the credit for even this small victory belonged to his Indian scouts: "Without the assistance of Indians the command would never have been able to follow Victorio's trail." The regiment, which saw forty-four men killed in action during the entire Indian war period, from 1867 until the Spanish-American War in 1898, lost nine in September alone.[44]

Sergeant Boyne, who had been in five battles against the Apaches by the end of September 1879 and took part in three more of his regiment's fourteen clashes with Victorio during 1880, started the paperwork needed for recognition by writing to Lieutenant Wright in January 1881, "asking the favor of your assistance in obtaining a Certificate of Merit."[45] Wright was only too happy to help, and so was Morrow. "I have seen him repeatedly in action," Morrow wrote, "and in every instance he has distinguished himself. . . . If any soldier deserves a Certificate of Merit or Medal of Honor, Sergt. Boyne does and I hope he may be so rewarded."[46]

On January 6, 1882, Boyne received a Medal of Honor rather than a Certificate of Merit because of the same legislative quirk that had denied the certificate to Clinton Greaves. The law authorized the certificate for privates, but Boyne was a sergeant when he had performed with such gallantry. Although Congress realized the error, it never got around to changing the law because of other, more pressing business. When issued, Boyne's medal was engraved with the following inscription: "The Congress to Sergeant Thomas Boyne, Troop C 9th Cavalry, for bravery in action at Mimbres Mountain, N. M., May 29th 1879 and at Cuchillo Negro, N.M., September 27th 1879."[47]

Boyne stayed in the Army, serving until 1889, but his health deteriorated gradually over the years. The winter of 1884–85 had been especially hard on him. His regiment was involved in keeping illegal settlers off tribal lands in Indian Territory, a thankless job made even worse by a severe winter. George Brown, who served with Boyne during the mid-1880s, said that "the cold was intense . . . , and over fifty men of the command were frost-bitten." According to Brown, "Thomas Boyne was among the number," and he finished the month of January in the post hospital at Fort Caldwell, Kansas.[48]

Boyne recovered enough to reenlist in July and transferred to the Twenty-fifth Infantry at Fort Meade, in the Black Hills of Dakota Territory. He took sick four times, finally developing a hernia while supervising a wood-gathering detail at Fort Missoula, Montana, in October 1888. The Army discharged him in January 1889, with a disability pension of eight dollars per month that increased to ten dollars at the end of 1893.[49] By that time he was already a resident of the U.S. Soldiers' Home. He had entered it shortly after he left the Army and was living among his old comrades, including George Brown and Alfred Ross, with whom he had chased Sooners out of Indian Territory. On April 21, 1896, he died of consumption; he was fifty years old.[50]

~ 5 ~

Henry Johnson and
the Ute War

𝕬 t the end of the 1870s, Colonel Hatch had more to worry
about than just the Apaches. He also had to keep one
eye on events to the north, where the seeds of a conflict with
the Utes were maturing. The trouble developing in Colorado
followed a standard script. White miners trespassed on lands
promised by treaty to the Indians, who resented the encroachment and the efforts of a zealous Indian Department agent to
turn them into farmers and enroll their children in school.
Weary of the constant pressure on their land and their way of
life, the Utes fought back, burning cabins and plundering livestock. This situation was just starting to evolve as the Ninth
Cavalry went from Texas to New Mexico in 1875 and 1876,
and D and L Troops of the regiment kept moving north to the
Ute country, where they were the only cavalry units. A disturbance in the early spring of 1878, on the southernmost of
the three Ute reservations on the La Plata River, required a
show of force and brought five troops of cavalrymen of the
Ninth under Hatch up from New Mexico.[1]

The trouble on the La Plata was resolved without blood-
shed, but an uprising in the autumn of 1879 on the White
River reservation in northwestern Colorado became more sig-
nificant. By then, most of the regiment focused on the Apache
trouble to the south. Only two troops remained in Colorado.
K Troop escorted the surveyors who marked the Colorado-
Utah border, and D Troop, which had alternated between
Forts Lewis and Garland in the south, moved north to patrol

Middle Park in the summer as tensions mounted on the White River reservation.[2]

In September, the Ute pot boiled over on the White River reservation. Agent Nathan C. Meeker, conscientious and well-intentioned but naive, had already aroused considerable resentment with his efforts to impose white ways. After a quarrel with a Ute called Johnson, the brother-in-law of Chief Ouray, over the amount of food issued to the Utes, Johnson gave Meeker a severe beating. The terrified agent called for troops. A courier carried Meeker's plea to Major Thomas T. Thornburgh, who had two hundred men at Fort Frederick Steele, near Rawlins, Wyoming. Another messenger also reached Captain Francis S. Dodge and D Troop at their camp on the Grand River.[3]

Thornburgh rushed to the rescue, dashing south as fast as he could with three troops of the Fifth Cavalry, one company of the Fourth Infantry, and a supply train of twenty-five wagons. The Utes, led by the obese and tactically astute Chief Colorow, watched him come. On September 29, 1879, Thornburgh reached the stream that the Utes knew as Little River but which the whites had called Milk River ever since a teamster overturned a wagonload of milk cans while crossing it. There the soldiers watered their horses. Minutes later, the Utes sprang their ambush. Several hundred Indians, well hidden on ridges that looked down on the trail, opened fire. The fight that followed was one of the sharpest and bloodiest of the Indian wars. Thirteen soldiers, including Major Thornburgh, fell dead within the first few minutes. The Army later counted thirty-seven dead Utes. At the nearby White River agency, Meeker and all of the white male employees were also killed. Thornburgh's command, now led by Captain J. Scott Payne of the Fifth Cavalry, circled the wagons, leaving only a small path through the defenses so that the men could get water from the river, and found safety inside. They also found themselves in a trap of their own making, which became more and more unpleasant as time went by.[4]

The Indians in the hills killed the soldiers' horses at their leisure. Sometimes they amused themselves by shooting to wound rather than to kill. This tactic caused its own special annoyance. "Soon," Robert Emmitt wrote, "the space inside the wagon circle was like a burning ant's nest, with horses screaming, kicking, plunging, and rolling all over the place." The soldiers improved their positions and reduced the stench by incorporating the carcasses in the breastwork and covering them with dirt. But the lack of horses meant a lack of mobility. There could be no breakout; the soldiers were going nowhere. After night fell on September 29, volunteer couriers went out for help. The situation was truly desperate.[5]

With the troopers encircled, the patient Utes were content to wait. "The soldiers," they recognized, "had made a good wall out of their dead ponies." The makeshift breastwork would stop bullets but would soon stink. Colorow, pondering the plight of the soldiers, found the situation comical. "This bad smell," Emmitt's Ute informants reported that he said, "will bring many flies—big, fat, blue flies. Those flies will get even fatter on those dead horses, and when the soldiers run out of food, they can roast them."[6] All told, the first day brought the Utes considerable satisfaction as well as amusement. The soldiers were surrounded by rotting horses and had their backs to the river. The Utes held the high ground on the other three sides and enjoyed taunting the troops. "Come out, you sons-of-bitches, and fight like men," they yelled. But the only soldiers who dared leave were the couriers. The rest of the command stayed in the improvised compound.[7]

On October 1, one of the couriers reached Captain Dodge. Already alerted by the message that Meeker had sent before the attack on Thornburgh, Dodge, Lieutenant Martin B. Hughes, and D Troop were on their way to the White River agency. After learning of the emergency, Dodge feigned preparations to camp for the night "to deceive any Indians near him," issued 225 rounds of ammunition to each of his thirty-five troopers, and waited for dark. When night fell, they picked up the pace, heading for the Milk River.[8]

Dodge led a veteran group of buffalo soldiers. First Sergeant Jasper Hope had only four years of experience, but others had been around considerably longer. Private John Q. Adams had served a five-year enlistment with C Troop and had been cited for bravery against the Apaches in January 1877, along with Clinton Greaves. He was in his second year with Dodge's unit. Another soldier, Madison Ingoman, was also in at least his seventh year of service. He later earned two citations for bravery against the Apaches in 1881. Even Private Caleb Benson, a young man from Jacksonville, Florida, who was only twenty years old, had four years under his belt. Benson had lied about his age to a recruiter and joined up when he was sixteen.[9]

Sergeant Henry Johnson was on his third enlistment, with twelve years of service behind him. He came from Boydton, in Mecklenburg County, Virginia, just north of the Dan River and the North Carolina line, and stood 5 ft. 5 in. tall. After enlisting in Detroit, Michigan, Johnson became an original member of F Troop of the Tenth Cavalry and fought the Cheyenne on the Republican River in one of the first engagements of buffalo soldiers against a hostile western tribe. A noncommissioned officer once before in the Tenth, where he had been a corporal from January 1868 to November 1869 and sergeant from that time until March 1871, he had been busted for some minor infraction, perhaps for a drunken brawl or for missing formation. Now he had earned back his stripes in the Ninth.[10]

When Johnson first joined D Troop from the Tenth Cavalry in June 1877, the unit was garrisoned at Fort Wallace, Kansas. The only element of the Ninth not directly involved in the Apache wars, D Troop soon went west to Fort Union, New Mexico, some 320 miles away. The rest of the year had the unit engaged in the usual rounds of scouting and patrolling. In the spring of 1878, Dodge's men went to Colorado as part of the Ute expedition, logging another 589 miles. In the autumn they escorted survey parties working on the Colorado-Utah line. As the year ended, they built their winter quarters at Pagosa Springs. The buffalo soldiers of D Troop had done a lot of traveling together by the time the courier from the Milk River arrived.[11]

They rode hard on the first of October, making seventy miles in twenty hours. Dodge's little command of just over forty buffalo soldiers reached Captain Payne's entrenchments before first light on October 2. They hit the main road a few miles from the besieged troops at about four in the morning, found the charred bodies of three whites, and reached Payne one-half hour later. According to Dodge's report, filed four weeks after his arrival on the Milk River, the embattled white troops cheered wildly when the buffalo soldiers arrived. Dodge's troops drew no fire from the surrounding warriors until they entered the circle of wagons and dead horses.

The lack of opposition surprised Dodge. With the noise of his horses and the cheering of the trapped cavalrymen, surely the Indians knew that they were there. "Singularly enough," he puzzled, "the Indians did not molest us in the least up to this time." He could surmise only that the Utes thought a stronger force was close behind, so they did not want to reveal their positions. His perception soon changed: "We were scarcely in the trenches when they commenced a fusillade which was kept up at intervals for the next three days."[12] When the bullets started to fly, Dodge's horses began to drop. "Captain Dodge was hardly inside the trenches," General Sheridan's headquarters reported later, "when the Indians opened fire, which was kept up at intervals for the next three days, killing all but four of Dodge's forty-two animals, and these four were wounded."[13]

In fact, while Dodge rode into view and through the entrenchments, not one Ute raised his rifle. They just watched with curiosity, according to Emmitt's informants, as the strange soldiers came. "The Buffalo Soldiers," Emmitt wrote, "were something to wonder about and to laugh about—perhaps, sometimes, to be a little angry with—but they were nothing to be afraid of." Several warriors called out at once: "To-Maricat'z! The black-whitemen! The Buffalo Soldiers!" After Dodge's men arrived, the Utes even sang songs that ridiculed them and showed an awareness of the impact of racism on the Maricat'z ("whitemen's") social structure:

> Soldiers with black faces,
> You ride into battle behind the white soldiers;
> But you can't take off your black faces,
> And the white-face soldiers make you ride behind them.[14]

The Utes may also have been just a little astonished. Captain Dodge, riding to the aid of the encircled troopers, had charged right into the trap. He did contribute fresh rifles to the defense and ultimately received a Medal of Honor for coming to the rescue, but the basic situation after his arrival remained unchanged.[15] The Utes still surrounded the soldiers, and the dead horses continued to pile up.

The Ute perception of his men meant little to Dodge, who was too preoccupied with the situation immediately in front of him: cut off from the outside, the enemy positioned on the high ground, and all of his horses dead. He counted forty-two wounded soldiers who could not be moved because of the lack of transportation and listed "the stench from the dead animals and distance from water" as his greatest problems. As far as the Utes were concerned, Dodge could not fathom their actions to that point: "It is impossible to anticipate their intentions, or give an idea of their next move."[16] The arrival of Dodge, however, had boosted morale and proved that at least one of the couriers had made it through. The captain settled into the defense and joined the rest of the command in waiting for help. The Utes still controlled the key terrain, from where they could observe everything that the soldiers did and had clear lines of fire.[17]

The battle reopened after sunrise and continued all day. Part of Dodge's troop provided a screen forward of the main entrenchment, where they drew unwelcome attention from Ute rifles. Henry Johnson, responsible for the outposts as sergeant of the guard, left his own position under heavy fire to make the rounds of the forward detachment and check on his men. As he remembered the situation years later, he "came out of the pit in which he had been fortified and went over to other pits to give necessary instructions to some of the members of his guard." While encouraging his troops, Johnson was "exposed to the fire from the Indians who were very near and at easy range."[18]

Throughout that day and the three that followed, Dodge's men helped keep the Utes at bay, while the trapped command waited to see whether the other couriers got through and found reinforcements. Dodge later wrote that "they endured

. . . loss of sleep, lack of food, and the deprivations attendant upon their situation without a murmur."[19] But the worst problem remained the lack of water. The Milk River was nearby, but the Utes were always watching. Only at night could soldiers risk sneaking down to the bank to fill canteens for the thirsty command, especially the wounded, some of whom suffered even more due to the scarcity of water. On October 4, Johnson played a significant role in making sure that there was enough for the injured men when he and a party of troopers were ordered by Dodge to go to the river. Johnson remembered that the Indians had fired on them, but they had fought their way to the river, filled their canteens, and returned safely to camp.[20]

At five o'clock in the morning of October 5, the notes of a bugle sounding Officer's Call rang out through the woods, announcing the end of the siege. By the time Colonel Wesley Merritt arrived with five troops of his Fifth Cavalry, the Utes had vanished. Merritt's horsemen, the advance element of a huge expedition of two thousand assembled at Rawlins in expectation of a general war with the Utes, had come by train from Fort D. A. Russell, outside Cheyenne, Wyoming, riding the rails to Rawlins and making an amazing 160-mile march in forty-eight hours. Another force, about half as large, also came up from New Mexico to discourage the southern Utes from getting involved. Merritt evacuated the wounded and prepared to pursue the fleeing enemy, but the Indian Department asked the Army to halt operations so negotiations could take place. Captain Dodge was proud of his men and their role in the standoff. They have, he wrote before the month was over, "proven themselves good soldiers and reliable men."[21]

Dodge's troops did not linger in Colorado. They rode north to Rawlins for a long, roundabout railroad journey that took them back south to Fort Union in New Mexico and subsequent duty in the Apache wars that remained the focus of Ninth Cavalry operations. For the next two years and the rest of Henry Johnson's term of service, D Troop saw action in the long and arduous campaign against Victorio and later against Nana.[22] After his enlistment expired, Johnson left the

Ninth. He accepted his discharge in January 1883 back at Fort Riley, Kansas, five and one-half years after his enlistment started instead of the usual five. The extra time in service came as a result of a court martial conviction in March 1881, when Johnson spent six months in confinement and again lost his stripes. He departed D Troop as a private. After a two-month break he reenlisted, joining the Tenth Cavalry and reporting for duty at Fort Grant, Arizona, where he was back in the saddle against the Apaches. He spent only one five-year term in the Tenth before he rejoined the Ninth.[23]

Private Johnson was in K Troop of the Ninth Cavalry at Fort Robinson, Nebraska, when he applied for a Medal of Honor in 1890 for his actions on the Milk River eleven years previously. By that time he might have had a reputation as something of a hell-raiser. He had risen back up to sergeant for the third time by 1889, but the promotion did not last this time, either. Johnson tangled with the bartender at the Fort Robinson post canteen after the latter refused to serve him more beer and lost his stripes again. After he had decided that he was entitled to a Medal of Honor for his efforts against the Utes, he wrote to Dodge, who was by then a major and a paymaster, and collected endorsements from him and from Hughes, who meanwhile had been promoted to captain. He also acquired affidavits from old soldiers Madison Ingoman and Lewis Fort, who were still in D Troop and supported his view that he had gone for water at great personal risk as well as shown considerable bravery in personally supervising his troops on picket duty earlier in the fight.[24]

Although Johnson's own version of his actions in supervising the pickets as sergeant of the guard went unchallenged, two alternative explanations of events emerged surrounding the dash for water. Caleb Benson, the young soldier of D Troop who had lied about his age to enlist, reminisced about the White River campaign fifty-five years later in an interview with a Nebraska newspaper. Benson remembered an affinity between the black cavalrymen and the Indians. He claimed— erroneously—that two white soldiers were killed while getting river water for coffee, although Ninth Cavalry cooks had done so without harm. According to Benson, a buffalo soldier had warned a white soldier that "before you go down there, you'd better black your hands and face." The white man scoffed at the idea, left for the river, and never returned. Another white trooper also went down to the stream and suffered the same fate. Benson concluded that "the Indians never shot a colored man unless it was necessary. They always wanted to win the friendship of the Negro race, and obtain their aid in campaigns against the white man."[25]

Another view, expressed by Emmitt, also held that the Utes did not expend much ammunition on the black troopers. However, he did not attribute this one-sided truce to racial empathy. Instead, he claimed that the Indians felt contempt for the buffalo soldiers who performed manual labor, such as carrying water, for the white soldiers. "All soldiers were funny" to the Utes, according to Emmitt, but these buffalo soldiers "were the funniest soldiers Colorow or any man had ever seen."[26]

According to this view, the Utes were not impressed with the water detail. They watched as two of the troopers came out of the impromptu fort and "began to wave and shout at them." To the amazement of the Utes, the buffalo soldiers carried buckets instead of rifles. They were going down to the river for water and did not wave back. In fact, they acted as though they did not even hear the shouting from the hills. "The Buffalo Soldiers," it seemed to the Utes, "had not come to fight; they had come to work for the white soldiers," thus making the young Ute warriors "very disappointed."[27] Whatever the Utes thought, the soldiers who went out for water felt threatened when they left the safety of their makeshift compound. Johnson convinced the War Department that his actions were indeed heroic, and he received his medal on September 22, 1890. According to the citation, he had voluntarily left fortified shelter and under heavy fire at close range made the rounds of the pits to instruct the guards, and he had fought his way to the creek and back to bring water to the wounded.[28]

Only a few weeks after joining George Jordan and Thomas Shaw as K Troop Medal of Honor holders, Johnson and the rest of the unit saddled up to answer the alarm that came from the government agent on the Pine Ridge Sioux reservation. The buffalo soldiers spent nearly four bitterly cold winter months patrolling the reservation before returning to Fort Robinson. Later in the spring of 1891, K Troop transferred to Fort Myer, Virginia, just across the Potomac River from the nation's capital.[29]

In the summer of 1893, K Troop finished its two-year tour of duty at Fort Myer and returned to Fort Robinson. Johnson, starting out on his sixth enlistment, served again under Captain Hughes, who now commanded K Troop. Certainly aware that a Certificate of Merit carried with it a bonus of two dollars per month while his Medal of Honor had no such benefit, Johnson initiated the paperwork to obtain a certificate in addition to the medal for his bravery at the Milk River. Captain Hughes knew that Johnson already had a Medal of Honor but remained sufficiently impressed with him to support the request for an additional award. The military bureaucracy turned them down, citing the unusual nature of the request for double recognition. The Adjutant General explained that Certificates of Merit should be awarded for distinguished service, in action or otherwise, that resulted in saving human life or rescuing public property from destruction or loss. "Simple heroism in battle," according to a War Department circular, "on the contrary, is fitly rewarded, by a Medal of Honor, although such act of heroism may not have resulted in any benefit to the United States."[30]

Henry Johnson served out his final enlistment at Fort Robinson as a private. In the spring of 1898, with the Ninth leaving for service in Cuba, the Army granted his request for a furlough, which he spent in Crawford, Nebraska, near the post. After his leave expired on July 26, he asked to be placed on the retired list. He was forty-nine years old.[31]

Johnson must have liked the Washington area while stationed at Fort Myer. He retired there and remained in the city for the rest of his life. Unfortunately, his time in Washington was neither long nor comfortable. He died at the end of January 1904, a public charge at what is described variously as the Washington Asylum and "the Work House, District of Columbia."[32] He had not exactly been a model soldier. Reduced to the ranks three times and disabled at least once with an illness that the Army did not think he contracted in the line of duty, Johnson had retired with a less than sterling character evaluation. Nevertheless, he had served his country long and well.[33] In death he found a measure of respect and dignity. As a retiree, he was entitled to a military funeral and interment in a national cemetery. The Army buried him at Arlington with full honors, a firing party to render a last salute, a trumpeter to sound taps, and bearers for his coffin.[34]

~ 6 ~

The Apache Wars
Continue, 1880–81

As the year 1880 began, the Ninth Cavalry focused all of its manpower and energy on the war against Victorio. With the Ute troubles to the north over, all of Colonel Hatch's regiment was concentrated in southern New Mexico, along with troops and scouts from Arizona. Hatch and the Ninth still bore the brunt of the Apache campaign in New Mexico when Victorio and his followers swept north out of the Mexican mountains, jabbing and dodging, and frustrating and exhausting the troops and their horses. By April the whole regiment, divided into three battalions under Major Morrow and Captains Hooker and Carroll, was in pursuit of its nemesis. Many hard days in the saddle and savage fighting awaited.[1]

In the spring, Colonel Benjamin H. Grierson and the Tenth Cavalry headed west from Fort Concho, Texas, to add their numbers to the fight against the Apaches. The Tenth played an increasingly important role in the chase as spring turned into summer. Black infantry units became involved, too. Elements of the Twenty-fourth and Twenty-fifth Infantry guarded Grierson's supply train, enabling him to employ all of his troops when he cut loose from his bases in search of the Apaches.[2] The campaign against Victorio marked an extremely unusual instance of involvement of troops of all four black regiments in the same campaign.

The Army harried the Apaches constantly. Soldiers stayed close on Victorio's trail in May, but he managed to dodge his pursuers in Arizona and circled back into New Mexico. The first word of his intentions came from a courier who alerted a detachment of twenty-five men of the Ninth under Sergeant George Jordan of K Troop. The breathless messenger said that Victorio was headed for the settlement at old Fort Tularosa, an abandoned post about fifty miles west of Ojo Caliente. The place was definitely in danger.[3]

Jordan was an old hand at frontier campaigning. He had left rural Williamson County, in central Tennessee, as a young man after the Civil War, enlisted in the Thirty-eighth Infantry at Nashville, and stayed in the service. Not an imposing figure at barely over 5 ft. 4 in., Jordan was a fine soldier. He made corporal during his first enlistment and retained his noncommissioned rank thereafter. A sergeant with over thirteen years' service in 1880, he had been in K Troop since January 1870. Some people could claim a town, a farm, or a county as home; K Troop of the Ninth Cavalry was George Jordan's home. His commander, Captain Charles Parker, clearly valued his service and trusted him with an independent command of almost half of his sixty men. When the courier came with word of Victorio's approach, Jordan showed why that trust was well placed.[4]

The rider from Tularosa found Jordan and his men escorting a wagon train of rations and bedding down for the night at a stage station. The messenger asked Jordan to "march the men the remainder of the distance to save the women and children from a horrible fate." The troopers were exhausted, and the settlement was a full day's march away, but Jordan explained the situation to them. "They all," he recalled, "said that they would go on as far as they could." So the troopers had supper, washed their feet, and at about eight o'clock set out for Tularosa.[5]

The men marched all night, picking their way over the rough terrain in the dark. One supply wagon tipped over while going down a steep hill, and they righted it before moving on. Finally, they came in sight of the settlement at about six in the morning on May 14, and Jordan deployed his men, in case Victorio had already arrived. But the troopers were first. They got within one-half mile of the town when the settlers saw them. "When they recognized us as troops," Jordan said, "they came out of their houses waving towels and handkerchiefs for joy."[6] After the soldiers had rested, Jordan built his defenses. His men reinforced an old corral and built a stockade fort near the tree line. Jordan, an experienced soldier, was smart and knew what he was doing. With no time to lose, he prepared his defenses, placed his men, set outposts in front of the stockade, and moved the civilians inside.[7]

The attack came that evening while Jordan was outside the fort talking with one of the civilians. The warriors charged the settlement, firing away. Jordan guessed one hundred shots were fired even before he gained the shelter of his makeshift stockade. Everyone reached safety except the teamsters and two soldiers herding the mules and cattle. According to Jordan, "The bloodthirsty savages tried time and again to enter our works, but we repulsed them each time, and when they finally saw that we were masters of the situation they turned their attention to the stock and tried to run it off."[8] When he saw that the herders were in great danger, he sent out a detail of ten men to help them. Keeping under cover of the timber, they made their way to the corral, drove the Indians away, and saved the men and livestock. "The whole action," Jordan summarized, "was short but exciting while it lasted, and after it was all over the townspeople congratulated us for having repulsed a band of more than 100 redskins." The settlers and soldiers suffered no casualties.[9]

Usually, Victorio picked his battlefield and surprised the Army, but this time it was his turn to be caught off guard. According to Jordan, the Indians concluded from the presence of a prepared defensive position that the rest of the regiment was nearby. The heavy fire from inside the fortification discouraged the attackers, and they broke contact. The remainder of the regiment arrived the next morning, and two battalions went in pursuit, but Victorio eluded them and once again sought safety in Mexico. When the smoke cleared, it was plain that Jordan's prompt action and able leadership had saved the settlers and his men.[10] The Medal of Honor, awarded one week short of ten years later while he still served in K Troop as its first sergeant, was granted "for gallantry in action against Hostile Apache Indians at Old Fort Tularosa, New Mexico, May 14, 1880, while commanding a detachment of 25 men repulsing a force of more than 100 Indians under Victoria [*sic*]."[11]

The moment of the Apache withdrawal from the attack on the Tularosa settlement was not the time to think about medals. Captain Parker's troop joined the pursuit and remained in the field, scouting for the enemy throughout the month. K Troop logged almost four hundred miles, and nine of its horses died from exhaustion and thirst.[12] Nine days after Jordan's defense of Tularosa, a unit of Apache scouts under civilian Henry K. Parker caught up with Victorio to the south on the Palomas River. Parker sprung a three-sided ambush that would have made Victorio proud, killed a large number of warriors (estimates range between ten and sixty), took over seventy horses, and sent Victorio fleeing toward Mexico, with Major Morrow hot on his trail. Although the Ninth had chased and harried the Apache chief for months, this was the decisive blow of the campaign.[13]

Throughout the summer, soldiers, local militiamen, and settlers kept up the pressure. Although they never caught up with Victorio, they made sure that he stayed south of the border. The Ninth became so preoccupied and distracted that the regiment fell behind on its paperwork, raising the hackles of the War Department bureaucrats in Washington. Hatch had to explain that "all the companies of the regiment have been engaged since about January 1st 1880, in active field service, and for [the] most part of the time in pursuit of Indians in sections of the country remote from all mail communication, and it has been almost impossible for them to forward company papers." He promised to do better, but Hatch had more important problems on his mind.[14]

In the meantime, Grierson and the Tenth Cavalry had blocked Victorio's way back north into the United States, garrisoning the springs and compelling him to fight his way to water. They had more success than Morrow in forcing decisive battles, weakened Victorio considerably, and pushed him back across the border, where Mexican troops took advantage of the deteriorating condition of the exhausted Indians to spring a successful attack. Surprised by General Joaquín Terrazas at Tres Castillos, Victorio was killed along with about sixty of his followers on October 14, 1880. Thirty Indians escaped the attack, including an old warrior named Nana.[15]

The survivors wasted no time in exacting revenge on the buffalo soldiers. On October 28, in Texas, they ambushed a cavalry patrol and killed five men of the Tenth Cavalry at Ojo Caliente, giving the regiment its single worst day until June 21, 1916, at Carrizal, Mexico.[16] The Apaches raided back and forth along the border until the summer of 1881, when Nana led fifteen survivors of Tres Castillos north across the Rio Grande. He was seventy years old, limped, and wore gold watch chains from both ears. But he rode hard and struck fast, and once again fear swept through the small settlements and ranches of New Mexico. Twenty-two Mescaleros from the reservation joined him on a rampage that sorely tested the Ninth Cavalry.[17]

Lieutenant John Guilfoyle's Indian scouts and I Troop of the Ninth bore the brunt of the initial pursuit, but before it was over Colonel Hatch set the whole regiment, about four hundred men, on Nana's trail. Eight companies of infantry, totaling nearly as many soldiers, and two companies of Indian scouts also joined the chase. The Ninth and the tough old warrior's small band clashed twelve times in one month, from July 17 to August 19, with the most intense fighting toward the end of the period. Captain Parker's K Troop, Ninth Cavalry, from Fort Wingate, headed for Carrizo Canyon on the west side of the Mimbres Mountains on August 5. One week later, on August 12, Parker and a detachment of nineteen engaged Nana in a sharp firefight.[18]

Sergeant Jordan accompanied Parker into the fray, but Sergeant Thomas Shaw was also there as acting first sergeant, the senior noncommissioned officer. Jordan commanded the right flank while Shaw rode next to the captain. Parker and his men came up on the Apaches and chased them into the canyon, where they turned, only one hundred yards away, and made a stand. Parker ordered his troopers from their horses and opened fire. Nana, with between forty and sixty warriors, outnumbered Parker's exposed force. The fight went on for over ninety minutes, with bullets flying and ricocheting all over the canyon, and the troops thwarted several attempts by the Indians to turn their flank and attack from the rear.

Shaw and Jordan were instrumental in assuring the detachment's survival. Shaw, an excellent shot, stubbornly held the point with a handful of cavalrymen and blunted frontal attacks. Jordan, in command on the right, kept the Indians from turning the cavalry's flank and surrounding the command. Five Apaches were known to have been killed; others were wounded. The Ninth lost Privates Guy Temple and Charles Perry, with three others wounded and nine horses

Thomas Shaw stands second from the right in this photograph of eight Ninth Cavalry noncommissioned officers that was taken in 1889 at Fort Robinson, Nebraska. Standing with Shaw, left to right, are Sergeant James Wilson of I Troop, First Sergeant David Badie of B Troop, and First Sergeant Nathan Fletcher, who succeeded the murdered Emanuel Stance in F Troop. Seated, left to right, are Chief Trumpeter Stephen Taylor, Sergeant Edward McKenzie of I Troop, Sergeant Robert Burley of D Troop, and Sergeant Zekiel Sykes of B Troop. *Courtesy Special Collections, U.S. Military Academy Library*

killed. Nana got away, and Parker, encumbered by his wounded men, could not follow immediately.[19] For their leadership in the fight, Shaw and Jordan both merited recognition. Jordan, who already had a Medal of Honor by the time that the Army got around to recognizing his bravery in Carrizo Canyon, earned a Certificate of Merit and the two dollars per month increase in pay that came with it. Shaw received the Medal of Honor. The awards were made in December 1890.[20]

Four days after the Carrizo Canyon fight, part of the Ninth collided with Nana again. This time, it was I Troop's turn. The company went out on patrol from Fort Craig on August 13, under the command of Prussian-born Lieutenant Gustavus Valois, who had come up through the ranks during the Civil War. The company rested at Canada Alamosa on August 16 when a distraught Mexican came into camp with the news that Nana had killed his family on a nearby ranch. Lieutenant George R. Burnett, just one year out of West Point, and fifteen of his men mounted their horses and set out westward in pursuit, while the rest of the unit prepared to follow. First Sergeant Moses Williams rode with Burnett. Since enlisting at Lake Providence, Louisiana, one day before Emanuel Stance signed up, Williams had more than eleven years in the regiment and at least five as first sergeant. He had the experience that Burnett lacked. Together, they found the mutilated bodies of the woman and her three children and then followed the Apache trail to the foothills of the Black Range along Cuchillo Negro Creek.[21]

At first sight of the Apaches, Burnett counted about forty warriors. Others in his detachment thought that they saw as many as sixty. Because the Indians, for the most part, were dressed as Mexicans with blankets on their shoulders and sombreros on their heads, the cavalrymen initially misidentified them. A group of Mexicans, similarly attired, already traveled with Burnett in pursuit of the killers. Nevertheless, Burnett approached with caution, his force deployed in three wings. He led the center, with First Sergeant Williams on the right and a group of Mexican volunteers on the left. Altogether he had about fifty men.[22]

When Burnett got within one thousand yards, the Indians opened fire. The troopers dismounted and returned the fire, sending the Indians back to the nearest ridge, where they tethered their horses and fought back. Burnett pursued, shooting as he maneuvered until he reached an intermediate rise where he and his men dismounted again. He then sent First Sergeant Williams with a few men to try and turn their right flank. At the same time he sent some of the Mexicans to make their way around on the other side. Meanwhile, he kept up the fire from the center. As soon as the Indians pulled back again, Sergeant Williams signaled Burnett, who hastily mounted and charged, pushing them back still farther into the hills while his cavalrymen took shelter behind the Apaches' former position. Repeating his tactic of fire and maneuver, Burnett drove the Indians eight to ten miles into the foothills of the Cuchillo Negro Mountains until they made a final and determined stand. Burnett seemed momentarily to have the upper hand. Nana had abandoned a large portion of his livestock and camp equipment and apparently had suffered many casualties. Burnett saw the Apaches dragging their wounded away and found a number of bodies concealed among the rocks as well as bloody bandages.[23]

By late afternoon, the situation began to favor the Apaches. Burnett found himself unable to dislodge them from the ridge and began to wonder if he could hold his own positions. He sent a volunteer courier, Trumpeter John Rogers, to Valois for help. Rogers made it through heavy fire, first crawling and finally sprinting for his horse and riding off in a hail of bullets. Burnett wanted Valois to take the hill to his right, which commanded the Indian position, while he went around the left flank to the Indians' rear. Valois received his message and moved into place.[24]

Meanwhile, the situation became even more desperate. Valois came fast to Burnett's right, but the Indians saw the threat and seized the high ground first. Shifting their fire, they killed ten of the troop's horses. Burnett charged from the left, drew heavy fire, and dismounted his men. Then his riderless horse bolted and started to the rear on a dead run. "Some one," Burnett later wrote, "started the cry, 'They've got the lieutenant, they've got the lieutenant,' and with this the whole outfit proceeded to follow suit." With the troopers now on the run, only Sergeant Williams and Private Augustus Walley remained with him. Burnett sent Williams after the fleeing soldiers, and the sergeant managed to rally them. Walley stayed with Burnett. Together the black soldier and the white officer found safety among the rocks and returned the Apache fire until Williams came back with the rest of the detachment.[25]

Soon it became clear that the Indians were concentrating their firepower on Valois and that he was in great danger. Burnett decided that he had no choice but to charge the Indians, attack, and drive them back to cover, holding them off long enough for Valois to collect his men and move his wounded to the rear. Then Valois, believing the Indians to be too strong for him, ordered his men to fall back and sent word to Burnett to follow.[26] Three troopers did not hear the order because they were cut off from the rest of the cavalry. When the main body started to leave, one of the three men called out, "For God's sake, Lieutenant, don't leave us; our lives depend on it." Valois was too far away to hear, but Burnett saw Privates Glasby, Wilson, and Burton crouched behind some prairie dog mounds about two hundred yards from the Indians. Burnett called for volunteers to go with him to rescue the stranded troopers. Sergeant Williams and Private Walley answered the call, and together the three, all of whom were crack shots, braved heavy enemy fire to reach the stragglers. Burton was hurt and could not walk, so Burnett told Walley to try to help him to the rear. Walley galloped under fire to Burton, dismounted, assisted him into the saddle, got back up on his horse behind him, and rode to the rear without further injury.[27]

Meanwhile, at a distance of less than four hundred yards, Burnett and Sergeant Williams endured the fire of twenty-five to thirty Indians, who aimed downhill and high over the two men. The Indians hit Burnett's horse and, seeing by his uniform and color that he was the commander, peppered the ground around him with bullets. He and Williams fired back with their carbines, and Burnett considered himself fortunate to be in the company of as skilled a marksman as Williams.

They kept up a steady fire while Glasby and Wilson crawled out of danger. While Williams and two other troopers covered their withdrawal, Burnett and Walley also guided to safety Private Martin, who had become disoriented and paralyzed with fear. The rescues took thirty nerve-wracking minutes. The fight went on until dark, when Nana broke contact and vanished into the hills.[28]

This fanciful depiction, first published in Beyer and Keydel, *Deeds of Valor*, shows three heroes of the clash with the Apache Nana on August 16, 1881. The figure of George Burnett, mounted and wielding his pistol, dwarfs those of Moses Williams firing his carbine in the right foreground and Augustus Walley in the background helping the wounded Burton onto a horse. Although ostensibly celebrating the bravery of buffalo soldiers, the artist placed a fourth man, the disoriented and terrified Martin, at the center.

With the exception of Private Martin, Burnett thought that the men of I Troop behaved splendidly and displayed considerable bravery. Even nine years after the fact, he remembered "the coolness and daring" of Walley, whom Burnett always found to be "a thoroughly reliable, trustworthy, and efficient soldier." He recommended Private Walley for a Medal of Honor for his rescue of Burton and urged that Trumpeter Rogers, who had carried the vital message to Valois while under great peril, receive a Certificate of Merit. But he saved most of his praise for Sergeant Williams, whom he singled out for a Medal of Honor:

> for his bravery in volunteering to come to my assistance, his skill in conducting the right flank in a running fight of three or four hours, his keensightedness in discerning the Indian in hiding and which probably prevented my command from falling into a trap, for the skill and ability displayed by him in rallying my men when I was dismounted and unable to reach them, and lastly for his coolness, bravery, and unflinching devotion to duty in standing by me in an open exposed position under a heavy fire from a large party of Indians, at a comparatively short range and thus enabling me to undoubtably save the lives of at least three of our men.[29]

In due course four awards were made. Walley received his medal in 1890; and in the following year, Rogers obtained a Certificate of Merit. In 1896, Williams was given his medal, and Lieutenant Burnett finally received one as well in 1897.[30]

On the morning after the Cuchillo Negro fight, the troop, which had suffered two men wounded and six horses killed, took up the chase again. They followed the Apaches' trail to the Mexican border but never caught up with them. The exhausted troopers returned to Fort Craig on August 26 after logging 878 miles.[31] Throughout the summer, the skirmishing continued with little respite. Only three days after I Troop's sharp clash, part of B Troop came in for a share of the fighting. A portion of the company under Sergeant David Badie had been in the field since early July and covered over one thousand miles before August ended. Badie was an excellent marksman and had been cited for valor by Major Morrow in 1879. His detachment included former Sergeant John Denny, now reduced to private but still a hero for his bravery against Victorio on Las Animas Creek.[32]

For most of the month, the whole company was in the field. Lieutenant George W. Smith headed north from Fort Cummings on August 17. Two days later, he encountered Nana in Gavilan Canyon, one of the intermittent streambeds leading from the Mimbres Mountains west to the Mimbres River, just south of Carrizo Canyon, where K Troop had fought the old Apache only one week earlier. The results of Smith's clash were disastrous. Although he knew better, he had followed a group of eager cowboys into the Gavilan Canyon without first reconnoitering. They rode right into the kind of trap that the Apaches had set many times for unsuspecting cavalrymen; the surprise was complete. Smith and three troopers—Saddler James Brown and Privates Thomas Golding and Monroe Overstreet—were killed immediately, along with ten horses. Among the living, chaos reigned. With the only officer gone and bullets flying from the guns of the well-positioned Apaches, the command became immobilized with fear and indecision. Then Sergeant Brent Woods took over. Private Henry Trout, a fourteen-year veteran, said that Woods "at once assumed command of the detachment and through his energy and skill defeated the Indians and saved the detachment from an entire massacre."[33]

Woods was midway through his second enlistment and therefore was less experienced than veterans like Trout. Nevertheless, he knew exactly what to do, and his response to the ambush would have made any officer proud. Rallying his men, he led them in a charge, scrambling up the rocky canyon wall toward the Apaches. The cavalrymen desperately fought their way to the high ground, driving the Indians before them. With Woods skillfully disposing his small force and leading the attack, the enemy was probably as surprised by the response as the soldiers had been by the ambush. Under the pressure of the counterattack, Nana pulled back.[34]

Lieutenant Charles Taylor, who was in the mountains with another detachment and some Indian scouts at the time, and Private Denny, who rode with Taylor, both heard stories that supported Trout's recollection of Woods's decisive role in the skirmish. Taylor and his men, alerted by the sounds of gunfire in the canyon, had dashed to the site of the fight and arrived shortly after Nana had broken contact. After Taylor arrived, the entire company under Captain Byron Dawson joined them at the scene. Soon they all took up Nana's trail, following it to Mexico. But, as usual, Nana had vanished.[35]

After the Gavilan Canyon ambush, even the white civilians spoke glowingly of Woods's leadership and energy. "That

Brent Woods, wearing his Medal of Honor. *Courtesy Cincinnati* Enquirer

Sergeant Woods is a son of a bitch to fight," one man said admiringly. "If it had not been for him, none of us could have come out of that canyon."[36] Private Denny heard similar praise from soldiers and civilians. "The general expression," he later affirmed, "was that it was owing to his skillful handling of his men and the exhibition of extreme coolness and daring that the detachment was drawn out of the canyon where it had been ambushed and moved to a good position."[37]

Woods did not receive proper credit for his leadership and bravery until many years later. The men with whom he served all expected that he would be awarded some kind of official recognition, but none was forthcoming. In 1894, Captain Dawson, his troop commander in 1881, finally submitted the paperwork from his retirement home in Indiana. Once started, the process, complete with the affidavits of Henry Trout and John Denny, progressed smoothly. Captain Taylor, Woods's commander in 1894, could only guess why a medal had not been awarded sooner. He suggested that the pressure of constant field duty, which kept the Ninth from filing its reports to Washington on time, might have combined with the turnover in commanding officers to allow the recognition to fall between the cracks. Whatever the reason for the oversight, Taylor believed that "no soldier of my acquaintance during my service deserves recognition for bravery and good conduct in the field more than Private Woods." He hoped "that tardy justice may be speedily accorded him."[38]

In considering the application, Major General John M. Schofield, the Army's commanding general, wondered why such bravery had not left a trace in official records. "It would seem," he observed, "that services of this character now (13 years after the action) made known in behalf of Sergeant Woods, should have been deemed worthy of official report or notation on rolls and returns, at the proper time." Despite the absence of such a record, the affidavits were persuasive. Schofield approved the award, and Woods received his Medal of Honor on July 12, 1894.[39]

The ambush at Gavilan Canyon was not the last encounter with Nana. Altogether the Army and Nana clashed ten times in less than a month before he disappeared into Mexico. The small band of Apache horsemen, led by an old man with rheumatism, drove the Army, and particularly the Ninth, to distraction. However, in a fierce firefight on October 4, Captain Carroll's F Troop and Captain Parker's K Troop scattered the last of Nana's band to linger north of the border. Still,

Nana lived to fight again, joining another old Apache campaigner, Geronimo, during his final rampage in 1886.[40]

The five buffalo soldiers of the Ninth who earned the Medal of Honor during the hard fighting of 1880 and 1881 shared a lot in common. They reacted quickly, made sound decisions under pressure, and were well respected by the men they led. George Jordan's exhausted soldiers had marched all night with him to reach Tularosa, and, even under fire, privates had followed Brent Woods toward the enemy. They also had the respect of their officers. Lieutenant Burnett had depended on First Sergeant Moses Williams to rally his men when they seemed ready to yield to confusion, and Captain Parker had trusted Sergeant Jordan with half of his troop. They also shared a long-term commitment to the Army. All five were thirty-year men and retired as noncommissioned officers. Denny and Woods both lost their stripes more than once along the way but regained sergeant's rank before leaving the service.

Of these five soldiers, Augustus Walley lived the longest after leaving the military. He retired from Fort Washakie, Wyoming, as first sergeant of E Troop of the Tenth Cavalry in 1907 and lived for a time in Butte, Montana, Prague, Oklahoma, and Cleveland, Ohio, before going home to Reisterstown, Maryland, where he had been born into slavery in 1856. With a citation for bravery for carrying wounded Major James M. Bell of the First Cavalry out of harm's way under heavy fire at Las Guásimas, Cuba, in June 1898, as well as his Apache war medal, Walley was twice a hero. In 1918, more than ten years after he retired, with the country at war in Europe, he volunteered for duty at Camp Beauregard, Louisiana, but was rejected for being too old. Nevertheless, he stayed at Beauregard, working there as a laborer for the Army and doing his part for the war effort. He died in Reisterstown in April 1938 at the age of eighty-two.[41]

For the other four, thirty years of hard frontier service took a severe toll. Thomas Shaw had started life as a slave in Covington, Kentucky, across the Ohio River from Cincinnati. His owner later moved him to Pike County, Missouri, where he walked away from her and bondage into a Union Army recruiting office. He enlisted in the Sixty-seventh U.S. Colored Troops in 1864 at the age of eighteen and stayed in the Army after the Civil War. He was new to K Troop in 1881, when he behaved so courageously at Carrizo Canyon, but had previously served as B Troop's first sergeant. His Civil War service made him the first of the five to become eligible to retire, and he left the Army from Fort Myer, Virginia, in 1894 to settle in nearby Rosslyn. He died one year later, leaving a widow and a daughter.[42] Moses Williams, who achieved the highest rank of the group (ordnance sergeant), retired in 1898. Although he was married when he last reenlisted in 1896, he died "alone and without friends" of heart failure at home in Vancouver, Washington, in 1899. He left behind only nine books, a pipe and a cigar holder, a handful of two-cent stamps, a pen and five pen points, his bed and four chairs, six neckties, and twenty-three dollars in cash.[43] Brent Woods, who retired to his native Kentucky with his wife Pearly at the end of 1902, died in the spring of 1906. He was only fifty-four.[44]

George Jordan lived a little longer than Shaw, Williams, and Woods. He stayed in K Troop, his home for twenty-seven years, until 1897, most of the time serving as first sergeant. In 1887 the commander at Fort Robinson, Nebraska, commended him for helping to apprehend an escaped prisoner, and he served with his troop on the Pine Ridge during the frigid Ghost Dance winter of 1890–91. Respected and liked by his men as well as by his superiors, he was chosen president of K Troop's Diamond Club by his fellow soldiers. After he retired from Fort Robinson, he eked out a living in the small but cohesive community of former buffalo soldiers that took hold in nearby Crawford.[45]

Jordan died in Crawford on October 24, 1904, under circumstances that did not reflect well on the Army that he had served so faithfully. Chaplain William T. Anderson of the Tenth Cavalry tersely summarized events, noting that "First Sergt. George Jordan, retired, died for the want of proper attention. He lived alone and had no one to attend to his wants. The doctor made two applications for his admittance into Fort Robinson Hospital and was refused."[46] Jordan had applied for admission to the hospital while the post commander, Colonel Jacob Augur of the Tenth Cavalry, was absent. The surgeon declined to admit him, claiming that the hospital was full and that Jordan should go to the U.S. Soldiers' Home in Washington, DC. Jordan declined because he had business in Crawford; he died shortly afterward. The Surgeon General of the Army supported the post surgeon's decision, stating that retired soldiers had no right to treatment in military hospitals, although post surgeons could grant the privilege on a case-by-case basis. His admonition that "surgeons should be careful to show all practicable consideration towards retired soldiers, especially when their records and services are as excellent as were those of 1st Sergeant George Jordan, Retired," came too late to matter.[47] In the end, Jordan's distinguished career availed him little.

~ 7 ~

The Wham
Paymaster Robbery

𝕱rontier service meant much more than Indian warfare. The wide variety of missions included mapping little-known regions, surveying and building roads, escorting the mail, protecting nascent communities from outlaws, and enforcing the law. "The wave of settlement," as Fairfax Downey wrote, "brought a tide of desperadoes, swindlers, and assorted bad men in its wake."[1] There was plenty to do, even without an active Indian conflict. Soldiers, with their meager pay and the more substantial government expenditures that sustained them with rations, forage, fuel, supplies, and construction, represented the cutting edge of the massive public outlays that breathed economic life into the frontier.[2] Their duties in establishing and encouraging settlement and transportation networks and their roles in stimulating commerce were all part of the drive to subjugate the Indians. In many ways, black and white soldiers alike contributed to the imposition on the region of an English-speaking social system and a market economy.

Like the patrolling and scouting that were the hallmarks of Indian warfare, the other duties that filled a soldier's day tended to be tedious and routine. Fighting the Indians usually meant dogged persistence and deprivation, braving the elements without enough food or water, and days, even weeks, in the saddle or on the march. Only rarely did the quiet explode into the violence and terror of a firefight. Similarly, survey and escort duty were usually the blandest and

most predictable of jobs, but every once in awhile a routine
mission became an extraordinarily dangerous and difficult
challenge. The following incident in southeastern Arizona,
on the road from Fort Grant to Fort Thomas in May 1889, was
such an exceptional case.

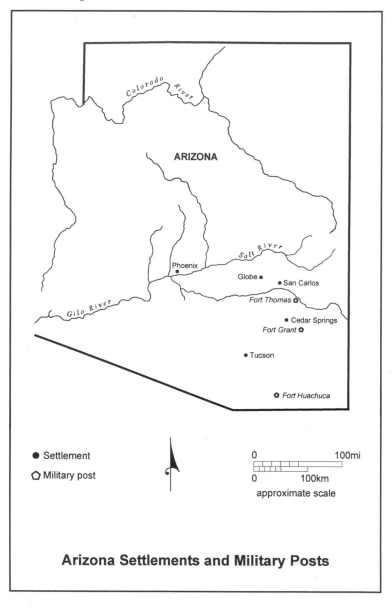

Arizona Settlements and Military Posts

Major Joseph W. Wham had been delivering payrolls to the troops for twelve years when he loaded his wagon at Fort Grant. Under his watchful eye, his clerk and the soldiers of his escort stacked the canvas sacks bulging with more than $28,000 in gold coins in the back of the Army ambulance. Wham and his assistant, with Private Hamilton Lewis of B Company, Twenty-fourth Infantry, at the reins, were about to drive their money wagon, powered by a team of twelve Army mules, to Fort Thomas to pay the garrison, made up of about 150 officers and men of both the Twenty-fourth and the Tenth Cavalry, and to settle other accounts on post. The paymaster had an escort of nine of the Twenty-fourth's infantrymen and two buffalo soldiers of the Tenth.[3]

Wham's escort was an experienced group of soldiers. Sergeant Benjamin Brown of the Twenty-fourth's C Company, from the river town of Platte City, Missouri, was the senior man. Married, childless, and a fine shot, Brown had eight years of service in Indian Territory and Arizona. The other noncommissioned officer, Corporal Isaiah Mays of B Company from Carter's Ridge, Virginia, also had eight years under his belt. Seven of the infantry privates who marched with them had a total of sixty-six years among them, more than nine years per man. Squire Williams of K Company had the most, with eighteen. Benjamin Burge of E Company and Julius Harrison of B Company both had fourteen, and Lewis, the wagon driver, had twelve. New Yorker Oscar Fox, one of the younger men with only three years, had not yet made a name for himself as one of the finest shots in the Army, but he would become a perennial member of the national infantry team when he matured. Although inexperienced, he must have seemed a good addition to the escort. The others were Privates George Arrington, George Short, and James Young of the Twenty-fourth and Privates Thornton Hams and James Wheeler of the Tenth.[4]

Fort Thomas was almost due north of Fort Grant, but the road did not follow a direct route. From Grant it ran northwest, skirting the western slopes of the Graham Mountains. About halfway to Thomas, it turned northeast and passed just south of the tip of the San Carlos Apache reservation.

Then it straightened and headed north to Fort Thomas. Just before the bend toward the northeast, near Cedar Springs, the road narrowed, went over a rise, and passed between some cliffs on the right and rocky hills on the left. Wham's two-vehicle convoy, his ambulance in the lead and followed by the wagon carrying the escort, was approaching this bottle-neck when the gang of white robbers sprung their ambush.[5]

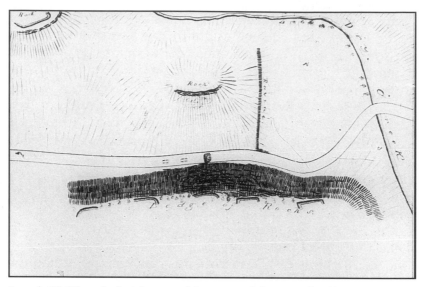

Joseph W. Wham's sketch map of the scene of the payroll robbery shows the boulder that blocked the road, the bandits on the right, and his own defensive positions. *Courtesy National Archives* (Microcopy M-929, roll 2).

When the ambulance came over the low hill, the paymaster saw the boulder in the middle of the road. As his wagon slowed and he turned to ask Sergeant Brown about the problem, Brown and his escort were already passing him to take the point; they approached the roadblock and prepared to clear a path. They had almost reached the obstacle when a shot rang out from the rocks, about fifty feet above the road and to the right. This signal shot was followed by a volley of fifteen to twenty more bullets. The bandits had planned well. Firing from six well-constructed and carefully selected stone emplacements with clear lines of fire, positions that might have made Victorio proud, they achieved complete surprise.

Wham's men, on the other hand, were out in the open. Brown, who became separated from the main body with Privates Young and Short, was entirely exposed. Wham and the rest of the escort managed to find some cover in a dry creek bed that ran perpendicular to the cliff line, but they remained perilously vulnerable. The outlaws, estimated to number at least twelve and perhaps as many as twenty, rained volley after volley onto the men huddled in the shallow depression. Wham guessed that they fired about 480 shots.[6]

The "sharp, short fight," Wham said, lasted more than thirty minutes. Eight of his men suffered wounds. Sergeant Brown was hit twice, first in the abdomen, but he did not give up the fight until he was wounded a second time, in the arm. Private Burge, fighting on Wham's immediate right, received a bad wound in the hand but gallantly remained at his post. Burge rested his rifle across his forearm and continued to fire without flinching, until he took another bullet through the thigh and two more through his hat. Arrington was shot through the shoulder while fighting alongside Burge. To Wham's left, Privates Hams, Wheeler, and Harrison were also wounded, Wham noted, "while bravely doing their duty under a murderous cross-fire."

Private Williams, who was near the ambulance when the shooting started, also fell, shot in the leg during the first volley. He crawled behind cover and continued to fire. Private Lewis, the driver, was with the vehicle when a bullet tore into his midsection. Blood gushed from his wound, but he took the injured Wheeler's rifle and fought on. Soon all but Wham, Corporal Mays, and Privates Fox and Short had been hit. As the bullets flew, Mays went to seek help. Without Wham's permission, he crawled to avoid detection and then ran the rest of the two miles north to the Cottonwood ranch to give the alarm.

Help came too late to save the payroll. The members of Wham's escort, pinned down in poor defensive positions with the majority severely wounded and unable to fight, could not stop the bandits from taking the sacks of gold. The Twenty-fourth immediately sent K Company from Fort Grant into the mountains in an effort to track down the thieves, and the soldiers spent three days patrolling and watching passes and trails. Their efforts were for naught, and they returned empty-handed.[7]

Nevertheless, Wham concentrated in his report not on the loss of the money but on the bravery and endurance of his black soldiers. He had fought his way through the Civil War as an enlisted man with future president Ulysses Grant's Twenty-first Illinois Infantry Regiment and participated in sixteen battles. Even with that experience, he wrote that he had "never witnessed better courage or better fighting than shown by these colored soldiers, on May 11th 1889, as the bullet marks on the robber positions to-day abundantly attest." A U.S. marshal who later investigated the defense agreed with Wham: "I am satisfied a braver or better defense could not have been made under like circumstances, and to have remained longer would have proven a useless sacrifice of life without a vestige of hope to succeed."[8]

The courage and tenacity of the escort so impressed Wham that he recommended ten of the men for awards. In a report filed in September 1889, he urged that Brown and Mays receive Medals of Honor and asked for Certificates of Merit for eight others. Two were deliberately left out. "In frequent conversations with the sergeant and other members of the escort," Wham wrote, "I have been convinced that two men did little or no fighting and almost immediately left the field."[9] Privates Fox and Short had not covered themselves with glory. In fact, their lack of involvement had seriously reduced the strength of the detachment and diminished its fighting ability while highlighting the courage of those who stayed and fought.

Wham's recommendations garnered strong support from the regiments in which his men served. The commander of the Twenty-fourth Infantry seconded the paymaster and so did the Tenth's commander. But while Lieutenant Colonel George G. Huntt of the Tenth merely passed the papers up through his chain of command, Colonel Zenas Bliss of the Twenty-fourth published a regimental order that expressed to the men of the escort "his high appreciation of their gallant conduct." He told them that he had "requested that a

Medal of Honor or Certificate of Merit for extraordinary gallantry in the presence of the enemy [be] awarded to each of them." Few commanders would risk making public their request for such recognition without some assurance that the decorations would be approved. And while Colonel Grierson, the former longtime leader of the Tenth and now head of the Department of Arizona, forwarded Wham's list to the Division of the Pacific headquarters in California and thence to Washington, there was nothing certain about the approval of these awards.[10]

While it was always true that recommendations did not automatically translate into awards, it was especially so in this case. Major Wham's nominations raised some eyebrows within the War Department. Colonel Robert H. Hall, the Department of Arizona's inspector general, dissented on two counts. He believed that the actions of the escort did not meet the standard of extraordinary gallantry established by regulations. In addition, as Hall observed, "the fact remains that the robbers drove them away from the funds they were detailed to protect." When General Schofield, the Army's senior officer, looked at the evidence, he tended to agree with Hall that the men of Wham's escort were properly recognized by mention in general orders rather than with medals or certificates.[11]

In spite of the dissenting views contained in the documentation, on February 1, 1890, Secretary of War Redfield Proctor approved the awards. Two weeks later the medals were shipped west, but by then the matter had already become politicized and began to receive journalistic attention.[12] The Chicago *Inter-Ocean*, a newspaper that supported the Republican administration of President Benjamin Harrison, accused the Army's professional soldiers of reluctance to recognize the gallantry of black soldiers and cast Secretary Proctor as a hero who overruled racist military bureaucrats. Proctor acted promptly, the paper complained, but the awards did not make their way west in time for presentation before some of the soldiers completed their enlistments and accepted their discharges. Nevertheless, the War Department processed two Medals of Honor and eight Certificates of Merit in less than six months from the date of Major Wham's original report.[13]

The *Inter-Ocean*'s claim that some of the soldiers had already left the Army was not correct. Most of them had spent some time in hospitals, but their wounds had healed and the men were back on duty. Of those honored, only Sergeant Brown, Corporal Mays, and Private Young had not been wounded. Young still required hospitalization while recovering from a venereal ailment. Arrington, Wheeler, Lewis, and Young did leave the Army before the end of 1890, but all ten were still wearing the blue uniform when the medals and certificates arrived in Arizona during February.[14]

Shortly after Corporal Mays received his medal, he began to have second thoughts about remaining in the Army. At first, he seemed to want to stay in the service. His enlistment expired in September 1891, and he reenlisted immediately, with a character evaluation of "excellent." Thereafter, his tenure turned stormy. He sought a discharge in February 1892, claiming that "my father and mother are now 70 years of age, and it is impossible for me to give to them the care and attention that they require at that age so far away from them." His company commander, Captain Henry Wygant, valued his services but supported his request. The War Department, however, rejected his application because he had just reenlisted, had taken a short furlough, and could not be discharged after honoring so little of his commitment.[15]

Within a few days of his application and its rejection, Mays got into a heated argument with his commander. Perhaps because of the rejection of his request for a discharge, he lost his temper in Wygant's office. "God damn it," he told his superior officer, with a witness in the room, "I will not be ordered about like a dog. By God, I will get out of here and I will fix you." Then he stormed out of Wygant's office, slamming the door, and, in the words of the court martial order, "intentionally behaving himself with disrespect toward his . . . commanding officer." The outburst cost him whatever chance he might still have had for a discharge under favorable conditions, his stripes, and ten dollars per month for six

Isaiah Mays, wearing his Medal of Honor on civilian clothes. *Courtesy Library of Congress*

months. He was reassigned in June to D Company, at Fort Bayard, New Mexico.[16]

In the summer of 1893, Mays gained his release from the rest of his obligation. He still insisted that he wanted to leave the Army to take care of his aged mother and father. His discharge was approved, with the proviso that he pay his own travel costs. Although he was free to leave the southwest and care for his parents, there is no evidence that he did so. Making his living as a laborer, he resided in Clifton, Arizona, east of San Carlos, in 1895 and 1896 and in nearby Guthrie in 1910. In 1922 he was still in the region.[17]

Sergeant Brown also stayed in the southwest, but with his regiment. He qualified as a distinguished marksman in 1889 and 1890 and represented his regiment in the Department of Arizona rifle competition three years later. When regimental Sergeant Major James W. Abbott received an appointment as a post ordnance sergeant, Brown was promoted into the regimental vacancy and became the Twenty-fourth's senior enlisted soldier. He remained on the job for one year and, for reasons that are not now known, was reduced to private. Still a valuable man, he served on special duty as a clerk in the Quartermaster Department at the regiment's Fort Douglas, Utah, headquarters.[18]

By 1904, at Fort Assiniboine, Montana, he was again a senior noncommissioned officer, serving as the Twenty-fourth's drum major. He was still an expert rifleman, ranked fifty-fourth in the entire Army. The same year, Brown had a serious stroke that disabled him permanently. He stayed in the post hospital until some time in 1905, when he was discharged and admitted to the U.S. Soldiers' Home in Washington, DC. Brown died there in 1910, the third buffalo soldier to be buried among the twenty-one Medal of Honor holders in the home's cemetery.[19]

~ 8 ~

William McBryar and the End of the Indian Wars in the South

illiam McBryar was an unusual soldier. The light-skinned recruit from Elizabethtown, North Carolina, was older than most enlistees, almost twenty-six, when he signed up in New York City at the beginning of 1887, and he was far from his home in the Carolina lake country about halfway between Wilmington on the coast and Fayetteville to the northwest. McBryar also had had three years of college in Tennessee, spoke Spanish, and even knew some Latin. The lack of civilian opportunity and the lure of the frontier may have combined to convince him to join the Army. When he signed up for the Tenth Cavalry, he embarked on a distinguished and frustrating career.[1]

McBryar soldiered for eight years with the Tenth. At the end of March 1887 he joined Captain Thomas C. Lebo's K Troop at Fort Grant, Arizona, just after the successful end of the Geronimo campaign. The Tenth had participated in the chase but not the capture of the legendary Apache leader. After the dust had settled, in October 1886, the Department of Arizona headquarters released an optimistic congratulatory order to the troops, announcing "the establishment of permanent peace and security." Nevertheless, the Tenth was occupied for much of 1887 in unsuccessfully chasing another Apache, a guerrilla called Kid. McBryar saw his first field service in this pursuit, spending almost all of June on mounted patrols around the San Carlos reservation. He soon had an ample supply of a cavalryman's occupational bruises and bumps. In addition to collecting the saddle sores that four hundred miles on horseback raised on a recruit, he took a severe battering the next spring when a horse fell on him, causing contusions all over his abdomen, left thigh, and leg. His eight years with K Troop, five in Arizona and later three in southern Montana at Fort Custer, exposed him to extremes of heat and cold that he probably never thought about during his North Carolina childhood. McBryar was a good soldier, rising to sergeant during his first enlistment and first sergeant during his second, with character ratings of "excellent" both times.[2]

While McBryar learned the cavalryman's trade, the Apache menace slowly diminished. The pronouncements from Department headquarters of the end of Indian hostilities did in fact reflect the actual fading away of resistance. Increasingly, the Apaches recognized the futility of their struggle. By 1890 they were beaten. As Major Edward L. N. Glass, the Tenth Cavalry's historian, disingenuously put it, they had "fairly well settled down to farming on their reservations."[3] Still, sporadic fighting against those who resisted removal to the reservation continued.

In March 1890, McBryar's troop was garrisoned at Fort Thomas, located in the Gila River valley east of San Carlos. Fort Thomas ranked among the more unpleasant of the Army's many frontier garden spots. Brigadier General Anson Mills, a former commander at Thomas who saw some of the Army's most primitive and isolated posts in thirty years of frontier service, called it "the hottest post in the republic and the most sickly, excepting none."[4] Given the heat and isolation, the post tended toward torpor, but it came alive on March 2 when word arrived that a small party of Apaches had ambushed and killed a freighter about ten miles to the west on the San Carlos reservation. General Grierson, who had turned over command of the Tenth to Colonel Huntt in 1888 and now presided over the Department of Arizona, ordered "every effort made to capture or destroy the murderers."[5] In response, ten men of K Troop under Lieutenant Powhatan Clarke went out immediately. Clarke, who had to

William McBryar in the uniform of a volunteer officer. *Courtesy National Archives*

leave the dinner table with his meal unfinished to lead the chase, was an officer whom a buffalo soldier could trust. During the pursuit of Geronimo in May 1886, he had risked his life under fire to save Edward Scott, a wounded corporal, and received a Medal of Honor for the rescue. McBryar and his fellow troopers knew that they rode with a leader who cared about them. For his part, Clarke felt comfortable with his men: "Many are old companions of many a trail, and their black faces have cheered you as you have watched them about the camp fire, when, homesick and discouraged, you were fresh from the Point."[6]

The cavalrymen linked up with the Tenth's Lieutenant James W. Watson and a detachment of Apache scouts and the white Fourth Cavalry from San Carlos at the scene of the shooting. They found the freighter's body, wrapped it in a sheet, and set it high up in a tree to protect it from coyotes. The combined expedition picked up the Indians' trail, following it overland from the Fort Thomas–San Carlos road. Finding and tracing signs of an Apache presence were never easy, and the Indian scouts frequently detected tracks where soldiers saw only hard, dry ground. They could also estimate the number of horses they followed and, from the dryness of horse dung along the way, guess the age of a trail. They were even able to tell whether women rode with a party by the position of urine in relation to the hoof prints of horses, because women tended to ride mares while warriors rode stallions.

In this case, the scouts and troopers followed five men, and the fugitives made the work of the scouts easier than usual by trying to take with them two large horses that they had stolen from the dead wagoner. Once the scouts found the route, they and the soldiers stuck to it, following the fleeing Indians—"bronchos," Lieutenant Clarke called them—over rugged mountains and plains for five days. The nights were cold and the days hot as they tracked their foe northwestward, passing abandoned Apache camps and even a stone breastwork filled with soft grass where the fugitives had only recently rested.[7]

Rations ran low as the pursuit continued, but a rancher contributed a cow, along with some coffee and salt. Then Sergeant Alexander Cheatham of I Troop, Tenth Cavalry, from San Carlos met the trackers with a wagon and several mules loaded with supplies for both men and horses. A Civil War veteran and an original member of the Tenth with almost twenty-three years in the regiment, Cheatham had led his detachment on a night march of forty-five miles, picking his way over a mountain trail in the dark with his reinforcements, to support his comrades. Despite the long, hard ride, he sat his horse, according to Clarke, "as if on review, sinewy and straight, the model of the non-commissioned officer."[8]

On March 7, after a two-hundred-mile pursuit, they caught up with the bronchos in the spectacular gorge of the Salt River, about thirty miles northwest of the settlement of Globe. With horses harder to use in the extremely rugged canyonlands, the fugitives killed their mounts and continued their flight on foot. Now the trail became very difficult to follow, and the scouts dropped down on all fours and scrutinized the canyon floor for traces of footprints. Just after noon, while Watson and Clarke and the cavalrymen watered their horses at the river, shots rang out and echoed through the canyon. The scouts had found their prey and forced a fight.[9]

There in the canyonlands, with the enemy cornered, the pursuit turned into a deadly business. Lieutenant Clarke felt "a calm chill about looking for a live Indian with a gun down in one of these great cañóns," an experience that he would have preferred to forego, but then a puff of smoke and the sound of the first bullet whizzing nearby ended the reflection. The outnumbered Indians put up a hard but futile resistance. The troops and scouts trapped their foe in the center of a three-sided tangle of boulders, firing and working their way ever closer, and forcing the hostiles from behind their rocks into a shallow cave where they were protected from direct fire. Then "one of the sergeants, an excellent shot," turned the cave from a haven into a trap by "firing against a rock almost in front of their cave, thereby spatter[ing] lead and splintered rock in their faces." With the soldiers closing to within fifty yards and preparing to make a final rush into the cave, the men inside surrendered. Four buffalo soldiers, one white trooper, and one scout received official recognition for their roles in the scrap. The Army commended the Indian Sergeant Rowdy of the scouts, Sergeant James T. Daniels of the white Fourth Cavalry, along with Privates William Turner and William Warrent of K Troop and Private Charles Taylor of I Troop, for "conspicuous bravery in action with Apache Indians on Salt River, Arizona." Sergeant McBryar was cited in general orders for "coolness, bravery and good marksmanship," suggesting that he was the sharpshooter who peppered the fugitives' cave with bullets and stone shards.[10]

General Grierson was proud of his old regiment and called the dogged pursuit "one of the most brilliant affairs of its kind that has occurred in recent years." He believed that the success "had a very quieting effect upon, and will no doubt prove a lasting lesson to the Indians at the San Carlos Agency . . . an excellent example of what promptness and indefatigable exertion may accomplish in the face of almost insurmountable obstacles." Two of the five Apaches were killed, while the other three were captured. McBryar's detachment returned to Fort Thomas on March 10, after covering more than 290 miles in nine days.[11]

McBryar also received a Medal of Honor for his role in the fight, as did Sergeants Rowdy and Daniels. The Army approved McBryar's medal with almost no delay, making him the first man in the Tenth Cavalry to be so honored. The speed with which the award was made suggests that McBryar did indeed distinguish himself. Frequently, years passed before officers got around to submitting recommendations for decorations, and sometimes the soldiers themselves had to start the process. Then months passed while officials collected statements and forwarded correspondence from one headquarters to another. As if to highlight the exceptional nature of McBryar's service, the Army issued his medal in only ten weeks, on May 15, 1890.[12]

By the time that McBryar received the Medal of Honor, the Tenth had spent more than twenty hard years in the remotest parts of the country. The regiment had served, according to Major Glass, "in the most undesirable stations known to any branch of the service, and with fewer accommodations as to quarters or barracks." Colonel Jacob K. Mizner therefore asked the War Department to give the regiment a well-earned respite. When the change of station came, it reflected what Major Glass sarcastically called Washington's "characteristic kindness." The Tenth boarded railroad cars for Montana during the southern spring and detrained in mid-winter—in a blizzard.[13] McBryar and K Troop rode their mounts to Fort Custer near the Little Big Horn battlefield where the Sioux and the Cheyenne had rubbed out the post's namesake, Lieutenant Colonel George A. Custer, in 1876.

In 1893, McBryar transferred from K Troop to H Company of the Twenty-fifth Infantry. When he did so, he did not go very far. His new company was also at Fort Custer and moved only as far as Fort Missoula later in the decade. The Indian wars were over, just as they were in Arizona, but there were some distractions from the monotony of garrison duty. In 1894, McBryar's company and most of the rest of the regiment became involved in the labor disputes that hit all of the western railroad lines, protecting the property of the Northern Pacific Railroad from striking workers. Three years later, he had a chance to watch Lieutenant James Moss and the Twenty-fifth's bicycle corps train at Fort Missoula and depart for St. Louis, Missouri.[14] McBryar stayed with the Twenty-fifth in Montana for five years and rose to the rank of quartermaster sergeant of his company. He participated in his share of the recreational activities that occupied the time of lesser soldiers and came down with gonorrhea in 1896. Nevertheless, his end-of-enlistment evaluations were "excellent," just as they had been in the Tenth; and his discharge in April 1898, just before another reenlistment in the company, referred to him as "an excellent soldier and man."[15]

He was still serving as his company's quartermaster sergeant in 1898 when war broke out with Spain after the American battleship *Maine* was sunk by an explosion in Havana harbor, and he went to Cuba with the Twenty-fifth in June. By then the Army was expanding and, after widespread black protests, even accepting black volunteer regiments. McBryar saw an opportunity to better himself. While at Tampa, Florida, waiting to board a troopship for Cuba in May, he applied for a commission in the black Third North Carolina Volunteer Infantry Regiment, which was being organized in his native state. Captain Eaton A. Edwards, an Irish immigrant who had nineteen years of enlisted service himself before earning a commission, had commanded McBryar's company for a time in Montana and wrote a glowing recommendation. He considered McBryar "thoroughly competent to Command a Company in such a regiment." He called the sergeant "intelligent, of good habits, unusual force, and more than average educational attainments" as well as courageous, as attested by his possession of a Medal of Honor. One week after Edwards wrote the letter, the Twenty-fifth boarded its ship for Cuba, and the Third North Carolina did not complete its organization until the end of July. McBryar's ambition had to wait.[16]

McBryar's unit saw combat very shortly after it arrived in Cuba. On the morning of July 1, 1898, with most of the U.S. Army tightening its siege around the key Spanish positions at the port city of Santiago, the Twenty-fifth clashed with the enemy. The regiment faced the Spanish Army at El Caney, a hill about four miles northeast of Santiago, where the Spaniards had built and occupied strongly fortified positions. Their stone blockhouse sat astride the road eastward to Guantánamo, where there was another important Spanish fort. The American firing line that formed at the western base of the hill included troops of the white Fourth Infantry and two companies of the Twenty-fifth, G and H.[17]

Company H had landed in Cuba under Lieutenant Vernon A. Caldwell, with no other commissioned officers. When the fight started at El Caney, McBryar commanded the second platoon. He brought his platoon onto the firing line and moved out with the general advance at around noon, under what Caldwell called "a very hot fire from the Spaniards." McBryar set a fine example for his men with his "coolness, bravery and soldierly bearing" that encouraged them throughout the day. The troops advanced until they were about five hundred yards from the fort, found cover, halted, and opened fire. At that point, the Fourth Infantry, blocked by impassable terrain, could go no farther but continued to fire into the fort. The Twenty-fifth continued the advance, breaking away from the Fourth on its left and bringing up C Company to fill the gap on the flank. As the black infantrymen came within fifty yards of their objective, they poured in a fire so effective that the Spaniards all sought cover, and in fifteen to twenty minutes they raised a white flag.[18]

Even though the men in the stone fort gave up, the Spanish cross fire from the village church and blockhouses to the left continued. Thus, no officer of the Twenty-fifth could traverse the last few yards to accept the surrender. A company of the Twelfth Infantry, which had been screened from the cross fire, managed to get inside.[19] One of Lieutenant Caldwell's men was among the first to enter the blockhouse. Private Thomas C. Butler of Baltimore, a former merchant seaman and a veteran of the Pine Ridge campaign with the Ninth Cavalry, went ahead of his company and seized the Spanish flag. "When the artillery blew that hole in the wall," he later told Lieutenant Caldwell, "I went in and got the flag." A man dressed like an officer—Caldwell later said that it was war correspondent James Creelman— made him give it up, but Butler tore a piece from it and gave it to Caldwell.[20]

The fight for El Caney lasted just over four hours. Along with buffalo soldiers at Las Guásimas a few days earlier and at San Juan Hill on the same day, the Twenty-fifth made a major contribution to the fall of Santiago and the American victory. A regimental general order, issued by Lieutenant Colonel Andrew S. Daggett in August, praised all members of the regiment for their intrepid advance against "a galling fire." The order singled out the skillful and brave leadership of "the officers in immediate command," who included Sergeant McBryar.[21]

McBryar continued to impress Lieutenant Caldwell with his leadership and technical knowledge. On the day after the fight at El Caney, with the company in reserve, McBryar still "displayed the same qualities of good judgment and coolness which have been noted in the El Caney fight." To fend off a possible night attack, he had his men dig entrenchments, "showing a sound theoretical and practical knowledge of this duty." He also properly handled advance, rear guard, and outpost duties and looked after the health and provisions of his men. Caldwell considered him "thoroughly competent in character and education to render the United States intelligent and valuable services as a commissioned officer."[22]

Colonel Daggett, the regimental commander, agreed. The government was creating ten new regiments of volunteers, made up of men from the South who were mistakenly thought to be immune from yellow fever, for occupation duty. Four of these regiments of "immunes" were set aside for black enlisted men and company officers. Even before the Twenty-fifth left Cuba, Daggett sent in his recommendations for commissions. He chose four, "in order named," with McBryar at the head of the list. Then came Sergeants Wyatt Huffman, Macon Russell, and Andrew J. Smith. Sergeant Smith, like McBryar and future regimental Sergeants Major Frank W. Pullen, Jr., and Anthony A. Marrow, was one of a number of excellent Twenty-fifth noncommissioned officers from North Carolina. All four men on Daggett's list received commissions.[23]

Shortly after the regiment returned to the United States in mid-August, McBryar was on his way to Fort Thomas, Kentucky, as a lieutenant in the Eighth Volunteer Infantry. McBryar's commissioning made him one of a new breed of badly needed black heroes. With violence against blacks and institutionalized segregation both on the rise, black soldiers who won lieutenant's bars in the volunteers for bravery in Cuba received wide recognition in the black press and in books that appeared soon after the Cuban campaign. "Negroes had little, at the turn of the century," historian Rayford Logan later observed, "to help sustain our faith in ourselves except the pride that we took in the Ninth and Tenth Cavalry, the Twenty-fourth and Twenty-fifth Infantry." Indeed, "many Negro homes had prints of the famous charge of the colored troops up San Juan Hill," Logan wrote. The soldiers "were our Ralph Bunche, Marian Anderson, Joe Louis and Jackie Robinson."[24]

The attention may have been satisfying to men such as McBryar, but he knew that the volunteer organizations were not likely to last very long past the end of the war. He looked beyond his service in the Eighth and sought Lieutenant Caldwell's help in getting a commission in the regular Army. Only three black men—Henry Flipper, John Alexander, and Charles Young, all of whom had graduated from the U.S. Military Academy—had received regular appointments in the thirty-four years since the end of the Civil War. Caldwell readily supported him, but the effort predictably came to naught. McBryar overcame an attack of malaria in November 1898 and served with the Eighth until it was mustered out in March 1899. Then he reenlisted as a private in the Twenty-fifth. He was soon a battalion sergeant major, on his way to the Philippines with the regiment.[25]

He kept trying to become an officer. Although his goal remained a regular commission, he also sought an appointment in either the Forty-eighth or Forty-ninth Infantry regiments, black volunteer units organized for duty in the Philippines. Colonel Andrew J. Burt, the Twenty-fifth's commander, supported his effort, as did regimental Chaplain Theophilus G. Steward. A distinguished scholar in his own right, Steward considered McBryar and Sergeant Major Edward L. Baker, Jr., of the Tenth Cavalry to be the cream of the crop among the black regulars. Both deserved to be captains. "These men were both First Lieutenants in the immunes, are old soldiers, highly intelligent, and gallant," he wrote; "I recommend them from personal knowledge." As far as Steward was concerned, McBryar "was a soldier distinguished by strength of character, prompt executiveness, quick decision, and courage." McBryar's mother even weighed in with a letter to President William McKinley: her son was "en route to the Philippines to do battle for the third time in defense of his country," had served with distinction, and deserved a commission in the regular Army. "Only one colored officer [Charles Young] represents our people in the U.S. Army," she reminded the president, "notwithstanding the deeds of daring performed by the colored troops in the Spanish war."[26]

With his eye still on a commission, McBryar nevertheless hedged his bets and applied for examination by a board of officers for the position of post ordnance sergeant. He was in fact selected for testing but soon lost interest. By the time that the Army published the list of candidates in early November, he had an appointment as a second lieutenant, assigned to M Company in the Forty-ninth U.S. Volunteer Infantry.[27] He found himself temporarily assigned as a lieutenant to his old outfit, the Twenty-fifth Infantry, on a long expedition on Luzon north of Manila Bay, from Tarlac Province westward to Zambales Province, in December 1899 and January 1900. Captain Joseph P. O'Neil commanded the battalion-size force that included McBryar's old company. McBryar went as O'Neil's commissary and quartermaster officer. His pack train fought off one Filipino attack and participated in the capture of the coastal town of Botolan and three other combat actions.[28]

McBryar spent almost two years in the Philippines with the Forty-ninth. In February 1900 he commanded the post at Cabagan for two weeks and in May led a detachment that captured a guerrilla band in Cagayan Province. In October he was promoted to first lieutenant, and for the first three months of 1901 commanded K Company. Those may have been satisfying days for McBryar, but they did not last long. The Forty-ninth mustered out in June, and he found himself out of the Army after more than fourteen years in uniform.[29]

McBryar's response to the situation was predictable. He was forty years old, a veteran of more than fourteen years of service, and an Indian-fighting hero. Plainly, he was committed to a military career. He tried to get back on active duty at the highest grade possible. Even before his discharge, he renewed his effort to get a regular commission. As usual, he had no trouble in garnering the support of his former superiors. Lieutenant Colonel Charles H. Noble, whom McBryar had served as battalion sergeant major, "heartily recommended" him for a regular commission. Noble knew McBryar "as a temperate, intelligent, honest and industrious man"; indeed, "few in the Army can equal his record," and he would "prove a credit to himself and the United States."[30] He also renewed his effort to become an ordnance sergeant or obtain a similar noncommissioned staff position. The Chief of Ordnance turned aside his request, since a number of eligible sergeants still awaited promotion. Moreover, McBryar was no longer in the Army. He would have to rejoin the service as a private and be promoted to sergeant before he could even be considered.[31]

These efforts to return to the Army at a suitable rank were complicated by an unresolved financial irregularity. In the Philippines, McBryar had signed for his company's payroll from a volunteer paymaster, Major George G. Arthur. Then he turned out to be $1,000 short. A War Department inspector investigated the affair without any help from Arthur, who had left the service in April 1901 and died in June of the same year. The auditor believed that McBryar was not responsible for the deficiency, and Major Arthur's estate was attached. Still, the affair added to McBryar's frustration as he tried to return to the service. In late August, sitting at home in Lincolnton, North Carolina, he learned that the War Department would not charge him with the deficiency, but by then he had dropped his sights even lower. He asked about whether he could reenlist in the Twenty-fifth and be assigned some Stateside duty until the regiment returned. McBryar had seen enough of the Philippines, as evidenced by his refusal to apply for a commission in the Philippine Scouts, an organization of native troops authorized by Congress in February 1901, and wanted to avoid another tour of duty there: "I do not care to go back there at present."[32]

McBryar's hopes and aspirations had traveled a downward arc, but the War Department would send them plunging still lower. The Adjutant General's Office told him only that if he intended to enlist, he would have to hurry: "With the exception of the 24th Infantry the colored regiments are full, and it is probable that the very few remaining vacancies in that regiment will be filled within a short time." There could be no exception for McBryar, regardless of his long and exemplary service. If he wished to rejoin the Twenty-fifth, he could do so—in the Philippines. At that point, McBryar stopped trying. He decided that he would remain in Lincolnton.[33]

After three and one-half years of trying to make a living as a civilian, he renewed his efforts to enlist. At his age (forty-four) and with the memory of once being battered by a horse that fell on him, the last move that he must have wanted was to join the cavalry as a private. Nevertheless, he applied for enlistment in the Ninth and was accepted. In March 1905 he reported for duty at Fort Leavenworth, Kansas, and soon made corporal.[34] Back in the Army, McBryar again tried to obtain a commission. He applied for an appointment in the

Philippine Scouts and even hired a civilian agent, one E. E. Cooper of Washington, DC, to plead his case with the War Department. This act must have been a desperate one, for McBryar had shown his dislike for Philippine service when he sought to negotiate a return to the Twenty-fifth without going back to the islands. Moreover, while Edward Baker and other black former noncommissioned officers had taken this route to a commission in 1902 and 1903, McBryar had tried every other approach first. In any case, this effort failed like all of the rest, apparently because of his age, and he was left contemplating legal action against Cooper, who McBryar believed had taken his money without making any effort on his behalf.[35]

McBryar did not last very long in the cavalry. His legs stiffened, and the ache turned out to be rheumatism. Within one year, he once again faced the civilian world, this time near Greensboro, in his home state. In December 1906 he married Sallie B. Waugh, a native North Carolinian like himself, and tried to make a living outside of town on their truck farm, where he stayed briefly before embarking on a series of short-lived jobs. In 1909 he worked as a watchman at Arlington National Cemetery in Washington, DC. He then returned to his farm for two years before spending one year as a military instructor at Saint Paul's Normal and Industrial School, a small black institution in Lawrenceville, Virginia, near the North Carolina border. In 1914 he traveled across the country to take a job with the Federal Penitentiary Service, at the federal prison on McNeil Island, Washington.[36] In that same year the fifty-three-year-old McBryar tried to return to the Army and offered his services to the government "if needed in connection with the present entanglement with the Mexican Republic." Two years later, he was back in Greensboro, and the war dragging on in Europe offered him another ray of hope. He applied for a commission as a major of infantry. Predictably the Army declined his services, claiming that he was too old.[37]

While the War Department's lack of interest was not surprising, McBryar's tenacity was remarkable. So was his willingness to serve the government that continued to reject his services except at the lowest grades. Again and again, for almost twenty years, he tried to obtain a commission, or at least an appointment to ordnance sergeant on the noncommissioned staff at some military post. Twice he endured the humiliating requirement to enlist as a private soldier. He moved from one unskilled job to another, still seeking the recognition and respect that came with the status of a commissioned officer. His unsuccessful quest raised the same questions brought up by the way in which George Jordan died: What were the Medal of Honor and a life of service worth to a black hero?

McBryar lived on beyond his last try for a commission during World War I for many more years. In his seventies, rheumatism plagued him and sometimes became painfully acute. In 1933, at the age of seventy-two, he was still able to work but feared that "as I grow older I may be disabled by it." Finally, unable to live without assistance, he moved in with his sister in Philadelphia, where he died in March 1941, just nine months before the Japanese attack on Pearl Harbor, at the age of eighty. He was buried in Arlington National Cemetery, where he had once worked as a watchman. The government provided a flag.[38]

~ 9 ~

William Wilson and
the End of the Indian
Wars in the North

𝕴 t was fitting that the Ninth Cavalry played a major part
in the Pine Ridge campaign of 1890–91. From its incep-
tion just after the Civil War, the regiment had spent twenty-
four years on the frontier and had been an active and effective
fighting unit. The Ninth had also been home for more than
twenty years to the first buffalo soldier recipient of the Medal
of Honor, Emanuel Stance, until his death at the end of 1887.
In the autumn of 1890, as the Ninth responded to the alarm
from the Indian agent on the Pine Ridge reservation, it still
boasted several officially recognized heroes in the ranks.
There were three in K Troop alone. In addition to First Sergeant George Jordan, Sergeant Thomas Shaw received his
Medal of Honor after the troop left Fort Robinson, Nebraska,
for the Pine Ridge; and Henry Johnson, again a private, had
just pinned his medal on his blue wool blouse in September.
John Denny, who was serving as a sergeant in H Troop at
Fort Duchesne, Utah, was not given his medal for heroism in
the Apache wars until 1891, but Augustus Walley, another
Apache war hero, was recognized in October 1890, just before he rode north from Fort Robinson to the Pine Ridge as
I Troop's farrier. After the smoke had cleared on the Pine Ridge
and the last major campaign of the Indian wars ended, one
more I Troop soldier would receive the medal: Corporal William O. Wilson.

This detail of a photograph of K Troop, 9th Cavalry, shows two Medal of Honor recipients wearing their medals: George Jordan, seated lower left, and Henry Johnson, standing upper right. *Courtesy Nebraska State Historical Society* (#R659-2599)

The Pine Ridge campaign took place in the winter of 1890–91, but the trouble that brought on the conflict had been brewing for at least ten years. The decade of the 1880s witnessed an assault on Indian culture and society on all fronts, with intertribal warfare forbidden, the buffalo herds gone, political confusion caused by the appointment of chiefs by whites, and the concerted attack on the Indian religion marked by the prohibition of the Sun Dance.[1] By 1890, Sioux culture and society had been devastated; and, as historian Robert Utley wrote, "a pervasive feeling of bitterness, helplessness, and futility gripped the Sioux."[2]

Added to the cultural disintegration (as if more problems were needed) were other difficulties—inexperienced and sometimes inept government agents, poor crops, and unfulfilled treaty agreements. The increasingly popular Ghost Dance, promoted by warriors such as Short Bull and Kicking Bear, who had fought alongside Crazy Horse in the glory days of the Custer fight, brought affairs to the brink of disaster by the late fall of 1890.[3] As for the unfulfilled treaty promises, an old Sioux quoted in the Indian Rights Association's annual report for 1891 probably said it best: "They made us many promises, more than I can remember, but they never kept but one; they promised to take our land and they took it."[4] The winter of the greatest discontent, 1889–90, was marked by starvation, disease, and the opening of Indian lands to settlement, all contributing to the hopeless situation. It was little wonder that the Ghost Dance religion found many adherents among the Sioux. The new theology spread from its Paiute founder, called Wovoka by the Indians and Jack Wilson by the whites, and blended traditional native rituals with the expectation that a messiah would come, bring the millennium, and restore the Indians to their lands and former glory. To the Sioux, miserable on their Dakota reservations, the Ghost Dance held out the promise of an end to white dominance and a return to the halcyon days when the tribes roamed at liberty and the buffalo were plentiful.[5]

Whites near the reservations saw the dancing as the harbinger of renewed Indian militance and another round of warfare. After panic struck and terrified Indian agents sounded the alarm, troopers from many posts converged on the Sioux reservations. The Ninth, stationed at nearby forts in Nebraska and Wyoming, arrived first. Units of the regiment departed their posts on November 19 and reached the reservations within five days. Two troops from Fort Niobrara, Nebraska, rode north to the Rosebud reservation, while one from Fort McKinney, Wyoming, went east to the Pine Ridge. There it joined three from Fort Robinson as part of a battalion commanded by Major Guy V. Henry, a tough old campaigner who had been shot in the face by Indians and had lost fingers to frostbite. Overall, the movement represented an impressive piece of military coordination that showed the influence of the railroad and telegraph on warfare. Troops from three posts, heading to the same area of operations at the same time, arrived almost simultaneously.[6]

Major Henry's battalion quickly settled into a training routine as part of an expanding military presence on the Pine

Ridge reservation. Each troop had three six-mule wagons, organized into a single pack train. Rain or shine, the battalion practiced loading the mules and wagons, marching with its supplies, and responding to whistle commands from the officers. By the end of November, Henry's men had ample military company on the reservation: over two-thirds of the Seventh Cavalry, the entire Second Infantry, one company of the Eighth Infantry, and a battery of light artillery. On the Pine Ridge, the Rosebud, and elsewhere, the Ghost Dance deployment played to a basic Army strength, its ability to fight in winter weather. The Indians, on the other hand, depended on grass-fed ponies and had their villages full of noncombatants to worry about, so they were at their most vulnerable in the cold months.[7]

As December unfolded, the general state of affairs on all of the Sioux reservations—Standing Rock and Cheyenne River to the north as well as the Rosebud and Pine Ridge—was tense and uncertain. Ultimately, over five thousand soldiers converged on the Sioux reservations. Everywhere the arrival of troops, intended to end the turbulence and bring stability, only led to increasingly fervent dancing and the departure of bands of dancers from the agencies into the hinterland, where they could avoid Army scrutiny and control. Never good, conditions deteriorated markedly after December 15, when an Indian policeman killed Sitting Bull, the chief who symbolized past glory and present resistance, at his Standing Rock home.[8]

The Army wanted to avoid conflict and induce as many of the Indians as possible to return quietly to their reservations. To encourage this development, units west and north of the Pine Ridge reservation formed a strong cordon intended to exert pressure back toward the agency. Into the latter days of December the soldiers gently but firmly tightened the ring, staying within coordinating distance of each other and occupying Indian camps as soon as the tribesmen vacated them and withdrew. The soldiers, who included Ninth Cavalrymen from Fort Leavenworth, Kansas, in a squadron commanded by the Ninth's Lieutenant Colonel George B. Sanford, all knew that an encounter could cause large numbers of Indian casualties and also take a toll on the soldiers.[9]

This concern proved to be well founded. Lieutenant Colonel Edwin V. Sumner, who had previously complained about the boredom and monotony of frontier service, found himself with too much excitement. With a force of three troops of cavalry and two companies of infantry, he had been closely following Big Foot's Miniconjou band. On December 24 he discovered to his chagrin and the Army leadership's extreme annoyance that he had lost contact with the Indians. They had slipped away in the night, and he feared that they might be heading toward the Badlands to join with other groups that refused to return to the reservations.[10]

Major Henry's battalion of the Ninth Cavalry left the Pine Ridge Agency and went into the field with orders to find Big Foot's band—"the gallant colored boys," reporter W. F. Kelley of a Lincoln, Nebraska, newspaper called them, as they set out to scour the country north and northeast of the agency in a slashing winter wind. Despite four days of hard riding, sometimes divided into troop-sized scouting parties, they never caught up with Big Foot. The Seventh Cavalry did, on Porcupine Creek, as the Indians moved peacefully in the direction of the Pine Ridge. On December 28 the Miniconjou camped for the night just eighteen miles from the agency, at Wounded Knee Creek.[11]

On the morning of December 29 the Seventh's attempt to disarm the Indians turned into a bloodbath. When the smoke cleared, 146 Sioux, children as well as adults, lay dead or dying. The Seventh lost thirty officers and men. As word of the massacre spread, the unrest that the Army had sought to contain and suppress moved beyond the control of the soldiers.[12]

Henry's battalion learned of the fighting at Wounded Knee on the evening of the 29th. The Ninth had spent the day scouting and was just finishing supper and preparing to bed down at a cold camp on the White River about fifty miles north of the agency. As the Seventh made its way toward the agency with its wounded, scouts brought the news of the fight to the

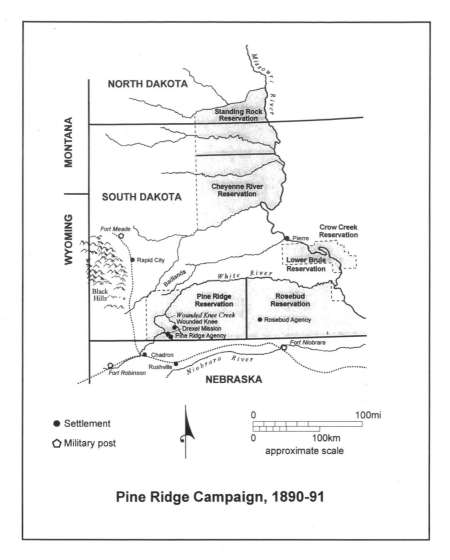

Pine Ridge Campaign, 1890-91

major along with orders to saddle up and hurry back to the
Pine Ridge. In thirty minutes the men struck camp, loaded
their wagons, and mounted. "We were in a hurry," Lieutenant Alexander Perry wrote, "and our gait was a rapid trot."
The men of F, I, and K Troops rode all night, with their wagon
train escorted by D Troop trailing behind them. They arrived
at five-thirty the next morning, just as reveille sounded.[13]

The battalion had covered over eighty miles in twenty-four hours, but the men would get little rest. Barely an hour later, at first light, they were tending their horses when their supply train, still making its way toward the agency, ran into trouble. About fifty warriors attacked the wagons, which were running about ninety minutes behind the main body under an escort provided by D Troop, just as they crossed Cheyenne Creek about two miles north of the agency. The Indians surprised the advance guard. One warrior, dressed in a cavalry uniform, shot and killed Private Charles Haywood of D Troop and his horse, taking the trooper's carbine and pistol along with his cartridge belt.[14]

Captain John S. Loud reacted quickly to the shooting to his front. He circled his wagons and called to his side his two lieutenants, Philip P. Powell and Philip A. Bettens, as the Indians turned their attention to the supply train itself. With the attackers numbering at least fifty and bullets flying all around them, the officers agreed that the situation was serious and decided to contact Major Henry for help. At Loud's request, Powell quickly scribbled a dispatch to Henry. He then turned to the two Indian scouts at his side and directed one of them to take the message to the agency. "Both scouts," Powell later said, "refused to go, stating that their horses were played out."[15]

Corporal Wilson was in a group of nearby soldiers who heard Powell's attempt to find a messenger. Wilson had been in the Army only sixteen months. A twenty-two-year-old native of Hagerstown, in western Maryland, he had done some traveling, enlisting from St. Paul, Minnesota, after supporting himself as an upholsterer. Already a corporal in December 1890 and experienced as the acting quartermaster sergeant of his troop, he could read and write. He was also one of the best marksmen in his unit. According to Lieutenant Powell, who served as the battalion quartermaster officer on the Pine Ridge and saw Wilson at work regularly, the young corporal took his responsibilities seriously and was "always active in the interest of his troop for which he drew rations and forage." Wilson also had an individualistic streak, which showed in the flamboyance of his attire. He liked to wear a black leather coat, a broad-brimmed white hat, and a big pair of spurs with his boots, even while on duty. And his officers, who tolerated his deviation from the standard soldier's uniform, must have agreed with Lieutenant Powell that he was "an intelligent, well-behaved non-commissioned officer."[16]

On the cold morning of December 30, with the Sioux threatening the wagon train, Wilson did not disappoint Powell. When the scouts declined to carry the note to Henry, Wilson stepped forward. "Lieutenant," he said, "I will carry that dispatch."[17] Powell understood the risk that was involved in dashing out of the circle of wagons and eluding the Indians. He told Wilson that he would not order him to undertake the mission. Wilson volunteered anyway, took the dispatch, and mounted his horse. The Indians spotted Wilson immediately as he spurred his horse out of the ring. He went only fifty yards before eight or ten of them left the main attack and started in pursuit, trying to cut him off and prevent his breakout. Inside the circle, the cavalrymen saw the attempt to block his way and opened fire, helping him to make his escape.[18]

Wilson outran his pursuers, made the short ride back to the agency, and spread the alarm. The battalion had been there less than two hours when he pulled into camp. Major Henry ordered the trumpeter to sound Boots and Saddles, the men mounted, and the battalion set off to relieve the besieged wagons. After a brief fight, the Sioux broke contact and withdrew, and Henry escorted the wagons safely into the agency. His troopers suffered no casualties, but they and their horses all badly needed a rest.[19]

December 30 proved to be a long and very unrestful day for the Ninth. The battalion had barely returned and dismounted when the order came to saddle up once more. Drexel Mission, three miles north of the agency, was in flames; and Colonel James Forsyth's Seventh Cavalry, still reeling from the previous day's debacle at Wounded Knee Creek, was in trouble again. The same Indians who had skirmished with Loud, a Brulé band under Two Strike, had gone north and set fire to a cabin near the Catholic mission school less than four miles from the agency, apparently as a ruse to draw troops into the narrow canyon that separated the bluffs just north of the school. The stratagem nearly worked.[20]

Despite his years of experience on the frontier, Colonel Forsyth almost fell into the Sioux trap. He led his men past the mission and dismounted just beyond the school. The valley was over one mile wide at that point; and, surmising that the Indians were in the hills on both sides, Forsyth sent his men up the slopes. As they advanced in a skirmish line, the Indians fell back, drawing the soldiers farther into the valley and up the slopes. As the cavalrymen picked their way up the wooded hills, hundreds of warriors appeared on the crests. Unlike at Wounded Knee, they had no women and children with them. Some among the Sioux thought that victory was at hand, but Forsyth, realizing his predicament, sent riders to the agency for help.[21]

Forsyth's courier reached the Ninth at noon with news that the Seventh faced serious trouble. Major Henry wasted no time in getting his troops back into the saddle. Although the horses were exhausted and the men needed rest almost as badly, Henry responded as quickly as he could. Trumpets sounded the charge as the Ninth rode into battle. At the mission, Henry's cavalrymen took the high ground and swept the foe from the hills, providing the cover that Forsyth needed to extricate his men. In thirty hours Henry's battalion had spent twenty-two hours in the saddle, marched 102 miles over rough terrain in bitterly cold weather, and engaged in two skirmishes with the Indians, all on mounts burdened by packs, blanket-lined horse covers, and two hundred rounds of ammunition.[22]

Major General Nelson A. Miles, just arrived on the scene from the Chicago headquarters of his Military Division of the Missouri, feared that the events of December 29 and 30 would seriously complicate the situation, thus making peace more difficult to achieve. A cruel blizzard from the north, the first of the year, roared down on the Pine Ridge just after the Drexel Mission fight. The soldiers of the Ninth, chilled to the bone in tents at the agency, increased their guard, but the snow made more fighting unlikely. It also brought added misery to the troopers. Private Charles Creek claimed that the men "ate out in the cold like a dog, [often] not in a tent," fearing that "the Indians gonna sneak up." It was so cold, Creek said, that "the spit froze when it left your mouth." When day broke on January 1, 1891, the storm had moved south, leaving a heavy blanket of snow to go with the frigid temperature. The conflict went unresolved for two more weeks as the troops gradually and cautiously pushed the Indians in toward the agency for the inevitable surrender, which took place on January 15. The Ninth had lost Private Haywood and gained a new hero in William Wilson.[23]

By the time of the surrender, Corporal Wilson's bold dash for help was known to all of his comrades. Major Henry saw to that. On New Year's Day, Henry's adjutant had described Wilson's bravery in Order No. 1, which called the ride "one involving much risk as the Indians knowing what was intended would endeavor to intercept the messenger, and overwhelmed by numbers certain death would follow"; thus, his "soldierlike conduct is worthy of emulation and reflects great credit not only upon Corpl. Wilson but also upon the 9th Cavalry." Henry had the order read to each troop of his command and sent a copy to regimental headquarters at Fort Robinson. Two weeks later, it appeared in the weekly *Army and Navy Journal*, a privately published newspaper that reported promotions, station changes, and a wide range of news relating to the military service. The civilian community beyond the Pine Ridge probably never heard of William Wilson, but the entire Army knew of his valor.[24]

Wilson's status as a regimental hero did not get him out of the cold. He and the regiment stayed on the Pine Ridge until the middle of March 1891. By that time, only the Ninth remained on the reservation. The first to arrive in November, it was the last to leave, "after spending the winter, the latter part of which," according to the Ninth's adjutant, Lieutenant Grote Hutcheson, "was terrible in its severity, under canvas."[25] All the other Army units had gone back to their posts, where potbellied stoves radiated heat in the barracks and family and friends spread their own special warmth.

Wilson may have been impatient for the warmth of companionship or merely for a snug room. Only a few days before Henry's battalion left the Pine Ridge for Fort Robinson, the hero made an unauthorized and unaccompanied trip south to Chadron, Nebraska. He stabled his horse and took a room at a hotel, but he did not remain at large for long. Sheriff James Dahlman spotted the soldier in his black leather coat and white hat and arrested him. The Army accused him of desertion. He also faced other charges: the theft of a rifle and forgery of a civilian's name to two hundred dollars in checks.[26]

Denying any intention of deserting, Corporal Wilson fought the charges. "My reason for being in Chadron," he explained, "was . . . a drinking spell and while I was under the influence of drink I found myself in Chadron." He sobered up during his twenty-three-mile ride from the Pine Ridge and realized that he had created a problem for himself. At that point, he fully meant to go on to Fort Robinson. Had he intended to desert, he argued, "I should not of stopped at a Hotel any way." The whole episode was the result of a winter's worth of intense stress: "Having been constantly on duty for about 4 months as acting commissary sergeant at Pine Ridge Agency and Battalion 9th Cavalry in the field which was the most mental strain to which I had been subjected to in my life."[27]

His rash departure from the Pine Ridge did finally bring him out of the cold, although the guardhouse at Fort Robinson was somewhat less comfortable than the Chadron hotel. His comrades returned to post less than one week later and suffered greatly on the way back. Their departure had been delayed by heavy snows; and when they finally left the Pine Ridge on March 24, they had to fight their way through five-foot snowdrifts in a new blizzard. "Many of the men," the regimental returns noted, "became snow blind and suffered otherwise incidental to the severity of the weather." But for the exhausted and freezing soldiers the winter campaign was finally over.[28]

Yet the memory lingered. Private W. H. Prather of the Ninth thought it significant that of all the troops who had served in the campaign, only his regiment and the Indians spent the slashing cold winter on the Pine Ridge. His verses, written while he was still in the field with I Troop, were tinged with bitterness:

> The Rest have gone home to meet the blizzard's wintry blast.
> The Ninth, the willing Ninth, is camped here till the last.
> We were the first to come, will be the last to leave.
> Why are we compelled to stay, why this reward receive?
> In warm barracks our recent comrades take their ease
> While we poor devils, and the Sioux are left to freeze
> And cuss our luck and wait till some one pulls the string
> And starts Short Bull with another ghost dance in the spring.[29]

Prather's caustic verses showed his awareness of a connection between the plight of the troopers and that of the Indians but did not necessarily indicate sympathy with the Sioux. As the concluding lines of the poem indicate, he was aware that there were operational reasons for troops to remain in the field. It was not clear to the soldiers that war would not erupt again when the weather warmed up. The Indians remained the enemy, the Ninth stayed on the alert, and Prather shared the prejudices of his time. Elsewhere in his writings, in the lyrics to a song called "The Indian Ghost Dance and War," he called adherents to the Ghost Dance religion "savage chieftains" and twice employed the dismissive epithet "Red Skins," which was popular among whites and was used by other buffalo soldiers.[30]

Nevertheless, Prather's sense of irony was unusual for the period. Few of the buffalo soldiers articulated any connection between the plight of the Indians and their own condition; and no buffalo soldier is known to have defected to any of the nomadic western tribes, although escaping slaves in the antebellum years had frequently sought refuge with more sedentary eastern tribes. When the buffalo soldiers referred to the Indians at all, they chose the same dismissive and contemptuous phrases employed by their white comrades —"painted red devils," "redskins," "savages," "murderous Indian bands," or "hostile tribes"—and indulged in racist caricatures, such as at a Twenty-fourth Infantry masquerade ball at Fort Bayard, New Mexico, in 1894, where "Robinson, of Co. D., was most admired by the spectators as an Idiotic

Indian Squaw."[31] Historian Kenneth Porter's observation about the post-Civil War Texas frontier, that "the only line was between the representatives of a sedentary, basically European civilization, whether white, Negro, or Mexican, and the hostile nomadic culture of the Comanche, Kiowa, and Apache," held true on the northern plains as well.[32] Astute as Prather may have been in finding some commonality between the respective plights of the soldiers and the Indians, it is not clear that this perception was widely held in the Ninth Cavalry.

While most of the Ninth reacclimated itself to the comforts of garrison life, Wilson stayed in the lockup at Fort Robinson. In May a court martial convened to hear the charges against him. The officers who sat on the court believed his explanation and convicted him of absence without leave rather than the more serious charge of desertion. They found him guilty of forgery as well. Both infractions carried stiff penalties, and the court sentenced him to reduction in rank to private, forfeiture of all pay, and four years' confinement at hard labor. However, Brigadier General John R. Brooke, the reviewing authority, did not believe that the forgery charge had been proved, so he rejected the entire sentence except for the reduction to private. Wilson's misadventures did not cost him as dearly as they might have.[33]

His brush with military law also did not keep him from asking for a Medal of Honor. He was, of course, not the only buffalo soldier to apply on his own behalf. Some of the Apache war heroes had initiated their own requests for the recognition; and, just as happened with them, once Wilson started the paperwork, his officers eagerly supported him. Captain Loud, whose letter to his family about the December fighting referred to "a brave little Corpl. Wilson of Troop I," endorsed the request with a recitation of Wilson's daring act. Lieutenant Powell, too, supported him. "It is with pleasure," Powell wrote, "that I commend the very gallant conduct of the within named applicant and invoke the bestowal upon him of a 'Medal of Honor' to which in my judgment he is unquestionably entitled." Along with his letter and this backing, Wilson also submitted a copy of the order with which Major Henry had publicized his bold ride. Within one month, he had a positive response from Washington, and his medal was on its way to Fort Robinson. Wilson was the last black soldier to earn the medal for heroism on American soil.[34]

He soon also became the only black holder of the Medal of Honor ever to desert from the Army. At the beginning of August 1893, Wilson was still a private, serving in H Troop at Fort Duchesne. He left his post to represent the regiment in the annual marksmanship contests held at the rifle range at Bellevue, just outside Omaha, Nebraska. After he attended the competition, he started back to Utah but only made it as far as Denver. There he seemed to run out of money and interest in completing the return trip. Claiming that he had lost his train fare, he asked for and received a duplicate ticket from Denver to Duchesne and money to pay for his meals during the rest of the trip. Then he disappeared, with thirty dollars worth of government property, primarily his Springfield carbine and Colt revolver. The Army never saw him again.[35]

The Army's failure to apprehend Wilson was due more to its own indifference than to Wilson's elusiveness. He did not hide indefinitely or take on a new identity but simply went home. Once back in Hagerstown, he married, fathered four daughters and three sons, and worked at many jobs, including teaching as well as cooking and carpentry. Residents of Hagerstown apparently knew him as "the penman" because he wrote elegant calling cards as a sideline. He remained in town until his death in Washington County Hospital on January 18, 1928, never speaking about his Medal of Honor. His daughter, Anna V. Jones, attributed his reticence to his humility, but his desertion may have had something to do with his reluctance to call attention to his military service. According to his daughter, he was laid to rest in the Jewish Cemetery in nearby Halfway, Maryland. Much later, in an Armed Forces Day ceremony in 1990, a small grassy area at the intersection of Jonathan Street and Pennsylvania Avenue in Hagerstown was named Medal of Honor Triangle and dedicated to Wilson's memory.[36]

By the time that Wilson died, the Pine Ridge campaign in which he had distinguished himself had faded from many memories. But the war had left its mark on the Army, the Sioux, and the buffalo soldiers. Thirty-one officers and men died in the fighting, the great majority on December 29 at Wounded Knee Creek. Forty others were wounded. The Army continued to consolidate its western garrisons, with an increasing number of regimental posts and very strong garrisons near the Sioux reservations, at Fort Meade, South Dakota, and Forts Robinson and Niobrara in Nebraska. Sioux fatalities, according to an estimate by Lieutenant Colonel Sanford of the Ninth Cavalry, numbered almost five hundred. Even more important, the disastrous winter ended the long period of war between the Plains Indians and the Army and brought home to the Sioux the magnitude of their defeat. The confidence of white settlers, only one of whom actually died as a result of the winter's warfare, returned; and the surviving Indians, in the delicate phrase of General Miles, "resumed their accustomed occupations."[37]

For the buffalo soldiers, the end of the Pine Ridge campaign also meant a symbolic end to a generation of isolation on the remotest edges of the frontier. Major Henry, alive to the opportunity to gain some recognition for his hardworking troopers, convinced General Oliver O. Howard, who commanded the Department of the East, to try to have part of the Ninth assigned to Fort Myer, Virginia, just outside of Washington, DC. Henry claimed that such an assignment "would be a most gracious way of admitting their deserts." Howard, a sympathetic officer who had headed the Freedmen's Bureau after the Civil War, agreed; and Secretary of War Redfield Proctor's annual announcement of spring transfers included the movement of K Troop, with its three Medal of Honor holders, to Fort Myer. The men served in a composite battalion with white troopers, all under Major Henry. They were the first black troops since Reconstruction to serve east of the Mississippi River. The *Army and Navy Journal*, which spoke glowingly of "the spirit of true comradeship between the white and black soldiers" during the fighting on the Pine Ridge, proclaimed the death of prejudice against blacks in the regular Army.[38] The declaration was premature, however, and the arrival of K Troop on the south bank of the Potomac was the only concrete manifestation of the new military brotherhood. The age of Jim Crow was just around the corner.

~ 10 ~

Four Cavalrymen in Cuba

The U.S. declaration of war against Spain in 1898 set almost the entire Army in motion toward Florida in anticipation of combat operations in Cuba. American opposition to Spanish rule of the nearby island, nurtured by extravagant newspaper reports of colonialist atrocities, had escalated into war fever after the American battleship *Maine* had mysteriously exploded and sunk in Havana harbor in February. Newspapers vied with each other in whipping up passions, and the Navy rushed to judgment, blaming a Spanish mine for the blast. (It proved to have been caused by a spontaneous fire that ignited ammunition aboard the ship.) Although Spain was conciliatory and apologetic and President William McKinley lacked enthusiasm for battle, everywhere the cry of "Remember the *Maine*! To hell with Spain!" rang out. Congress voted for war, and the United States stood on the brink of its first foreign conflict in fifty years.[1]

As a result, in April the decade-long process of consolidating frontier garrisons came to an immediate halt. Leaving only their families and housekeeping detachments behind them, soldiers of many regiments, including all four of the black units, boarded troop trains for the long trip east and watched from the cars as their loved ones and their old posts faded into the distance. Sergeant Frank Banks of the Twenty-fourth Infantry, a fourteen-year veteran, left a new wife at Fort Douglas, near Salt Lake City, Utah. Trumpeter Lewis Fort of the Ninth Cavalry, who had nineteen years of service, bid farewell to his wife of fourteen years at Fort Robinson, Nebraska. Their regiments, joined by the Tenth Cavalry and

Twenty-fifth Infantry from Montana posts, headed for a conflict that brought nationwide fame to the buffalo soldiers but took the lives of twenty-nine of them, including Banks and Fort.[2]

The Tenth Cavalry's week-long train ride from the far northern plains brought numerous transitions. The soldiers went from the comforts and routines of garrison duty with their families in the relatively calm post-Indian war West to the threshold of combat with a European power. As they went east and south, they noted other changes. Cheering crowds of black and white patriots greeted the regiment along the way until the train crossed into Kentucky. Then, at Hopkinsville, Corporal John E. Lewis of E Troop observed that whites stayed on one side of the railroad tracks and blacks on the other.[3] Gradually, the signs of segregation became more pronounced until the Tenth reached its final Stateside bivouac at Lakeland, Florida, "the hotbed of the rebels, a beautiful little town [but] a hell for the colored people who live here, and they live in dread at all times."[4] There, with a foreign war looming in the days ahead, nearly one thousand troopers camped on the gentle slopes along the eastern shore of Lake Wire, on the edge of the business district. After gaining renown as horse soldiers over the course of thirty years of frontier service, the men of the Tenth reluctantly turned in their mounts to the quartermaster and prepared to depart as infantry for the port of embarkation at Tampa thirty miles away.[5] Meanwhile, the Jim Crow South and the buffalo soldiers confronted each other, in Lakeland and in other Florida cities and towns. The showdown in Lakeland started when a white barber, angry because black soldiers had had the audacity to seek refreshment at a downtown drugstore, threatened several troopers and went for his pistols. It ended with the barber dead on the street, shot and killed by the soldiers he had menaced.[6]

When two-thirds of the Tenth left on June 7 after three tense weeks in the small Citrus Belt town, neither the departing soldiers nor the local whites had any regrets. Only the troopers who remained to care for the horses and regimental baggage were disappointed. However, while the first men to leave town spent seven miserable days on board their ships in Tampa harbor waiting for the order to sail, the number remaining in Lakeland dwindled, with some becoming involved in the fighting just as quickly as those who had gone with the main body of troops.[7]

Lieutenant Carter P. Johnson, a former enlisted man with twenty-two years in the Army and experience with special operations as the head of the regiment's Apache scouts during the last days of the fighting in the southwest, chose fifty of the men who remained at Lakeland for a special assignment. While the bulk of the American expeditionary force set out to confront the Spanish Army near Santiago de Cuba at the eastern end of the island's south coast, Johnson was on his way to reinforce and resupply Cuban insurgents to the west of the main effort. His cargo included a small group of American volunteers led by Winthrop Chandler and about 375 Cuban soldiers under Brigadier General Emilio Núñez as well as a sixty-five-mule pack train and rations, clothing, and ammunition to support the Cuban war effort. Such maneuvers to aid rebels behind the Spanish lines had been on the minds of American naval planners since early in the spring. As soon as hostilities commenced, support of military operations by the Cubans became an integral part of American strategy, and expeditions were organized to supply them with whatever they needed to participate in the war. The Army's commander, Major General Nelson A. Miles, expected that Cuban forces would provide substantial support to the overall war effort and that they would ultimately occupy major portions of the island.[8]

About half of Johnson's Tenth Cavalry detachment came from M Troop, with the rest consisting of men from A and H Troops. His four sergeants—Lewis M. Smith, James L. Minar, Robert J. Noal, and William H. Thompkins—had nearly sixty years of experience between them. Sergeant Smith, the senior man of the group with twenty-three years of service, was M Troop's acting first sergeant. He also boasted a long string of marksmanship awards earned with the pistol as well as the carbine. Even Thompkins, the youngest and least experienced, had been in the service for almost ten years and had served with the Ninth Cavalry during the Pine Ridge campaign of the winter of 1890–91. He had also shown a willingness to confront frontier racism directly. After a white civilian had insulted and threatened a fellow Ninth Cavalry soldier at Suggs, Wyoming, in June 1892, Thompkins had been among those who had sneaked out of their camp for a retaliatory raid on the settlement. While at Lakeland, Lieutenant Johnson had recommended that Thompkins be given a sergeant's stripes. In addition to the cavalrymen, one regular officer, Lieutenant George P. Ahern of the Twenty-fifth Infantry, also went along.[9]

Johnson and his little party left Lakeland on June 21, joined the much larger group of Cuban insurgents in Tampa, and prepared for their amphibious assault. Four days later, the combined force set sail on the transports *Florida* and *Fanita*, both of which were equipped with small landing boats. The U.S. Navy's gunboat *Peoria*, commanded by Lieutenant Thomas W. Ryan, accompanied the transports to provide covering fire for the attack. On June 29, General Núñez picked the landing place, at the mouth of the San Juan River east of Cienfuegos, and Lieutenant Johnson led the landing party that rowed quietly toward the shore. They never established a beachhead. The Spaniards, aided by the coral reef that kept the small boats from reaching shore, turned back the landing party with heavy gunfire.

Núñez was not easily deterred. On the next afternoon, he convinced Johnson to try again, arguing that the Cuban insurgent leader, General Maximo Gómez, would surely send immediate reinforcements. So Johnson agreed to try again at Tayabacao, a tiny settlement at the mouth of the Tayabacao River, just west of the town of Tunas. Núñez sent three hundred of his men ashore along with twenty-eight American volunteers in the face of "a strong force occupying a strong blockhouse" that overlooked the beach. Despite a preliminary shelling from the *Peoria's* four three-pound Hotchkiss guns, the defenders again drove off the invaders, sinking two of the small boats and inflicting some casualties. The attackers withdrew after nightfall; but with too few boats for everyone and the heavy enemy fire adding urgency to the departure, they left at least one man dead and several wounded ashore. The injured men hid at the edge of the surf.[10]

The wounded, including Chandler and another American, had to be brought back. They were in constant danger of being killed or captured, and because they were not uniformed regular soldiers of any army, they were not entitled to protection under the rules of war. As guerrillas or partisans—filibusters, in the term of the day—they were in danger of being summarily executed if caught. Rescue efforts began immediately. Friends of the wounded took some of the small boats back to shore, only to be driven off by the foe without even managing to land. Four times they tried, but with the enemy on the constant alert, the Cubans could not bring back their injured comrades. "The difficulties and dangers attending the rescue," Lieutenant Johnson later wrote, "proved too great for their courage, [so] all of these parties returned unsuccessful not having attempted to land." Throughout the day, only the constant firing of the *Peoria's* guns kept the Spaniards at bay and prevented the capture of the wounded.[11]

With every attempt at rescue turned back, Johnson finally considered committing his cavalrymen to the effort. He was very reluctant to do so, knowing that the well-armed enemy lay in wait, ready for the next attempt. But he was also aware that the wounded had little chance of survival if they were left on the beach. "Had I not known this fate awaited them," he explained, "I should not have permitted my men to run so great a risk, as this undertaking exposed them to." Johnson asked for volunteers for the hazardous mission, and several offered to go. He chose five: Lieutenant Ahern, Sergeant Thompkins, Corporal George Wanton, and two privates, Dennis Bell and Fitz Lee.[12]

None of the three cavalrymen chosen to go with Ahern and Thompkins had backgrounds that promised exceptional dedication or ability. Bell, a Washingtonian whose brother Arthur was also a member of the Tenth, had served one enlistment with the regiment in Montana. He had received his discharge with a middling character rating of "good," lower than the "excellent" and "very good" awarded to Fitz Lee,

who had been born in ru-
ral Dinwiddie County
south of Petersburg, Vir-
ginia, just after the Civil
War, moved to Philadel-
phia, and worked as a
manual laborer before en-
listing in 1889. Lee was
starting his third enlistment.[13] Compared to Lee
and Bell, Wanton had had
a stormy career. Like Sergeant Thompkins, Wanton
came from Paterson, New
Jersey. As a teenager, he
had gone to sea but left the
Navy after serving for almost five years. Then he
joined the Army in 1889,
and some difficult years
ensued, with eight court
martial convictions for of-
fenses that ranged from
sleeping on guard duty to
absence without leave and
a bout with "a loathsome
disease," as his troop com-

George Wanton wearing numerous decora-
tions, including a modern version of the
Medal of Honor around his neck. *Negro
History Bulletin* 41, no. 1 (January 1941): 87.
© by and reprinted by permission of the
Association for the Study of Afro-American
Life and History (ASALH) Inc.

mander delicately called gonorrhea, that put him in the Fort
Leavenworth hospital for twenty days.

Wanton's performance became so bad in 1892 that a board
of officers rejected his application for an early discharge because he had not served honestly and faithfully. He was also
refused a furlough for the same reason. While plainly far from
a model soldier, by 1898 Wanton was maturing. He had earned
the two stripes of a corporal and must have shown some trait
that prompted Lieutenant Johnson, who had been a member
of the board that took such a dim view of his service in 1892,
to accept his offer to join the rescue party.[14] All told, Johnson
saw the group of volunteers as a single unit, not a white West

Point graduate and four buffalo soldiers but what he called "this party of five regulars."[15]

With the Spanish garrison still alert and waiting to see what the Cubans and Americans off the coast would do next, Johnson watched the small rescue party lowered into a boat. They pulled on their oars and made their noiseless approach toward the beach, moving through the night under the glow of a full moon. Once they made it to shore, it did not take them long to find the wounded men at the water's edge, near where they had fallen and well within range of the Spanish blockhouse. Working quickly as Spanish bullets churned up the water around them, the cavalrymen completed the rescue, helping the wounded into their boat and making their escape without incident. When they returned safely, Wanton even offered to go in again and recover the body of General Núñez's son, who had died in the first assault. However, with the Spaniards fully alert, Núñez decided against the effort. Trumpeter Frank Henry and Private William Porter, both of whom watched and waited aboard ship, called the mission "one of exceeding danger, and more than ordinarily hazardous duty." Lieutenant Johnson agreed, noting that "the rescue was pronounced by all who witnessed it, as a brave and gallant deed, and deserving of reward."[16]

Meanwhile, there remained a mission to accomplish. The two successive attempts had brought Spanish reinforcements rushing to the coast in anticipation of what now appeared to be a major American landing. Lieutenant Johnson encouraged this misapprehension by directing the *Peoria* and the just arrived *Helena* to concentrate their guns on the landing sites near Tunas, while he steamed forty miles east to Palo Alto and put ashore the Cubans, who linked up with General Gómez there. Starting on July 3 and working for the next week, Johnson unloaded his cargo of supplies without enemy interference. When the task was complete, he was pleased, both with the bravery of his buffalo soldiers at Tayabacao and with the successful landing at Palo Alto. "The Cubans," he reported, "are greatly encouraged by the timely assistance." He was ready to go back to Florida, refit and supply his ships, and lead another expedition, but Spanish resistance lasted only a few more days. The fighting in Cuba ended on July 18.[17]

With the war over and with part of the Tenth Cavalry assigned to garrison duty in Cuba and the rest back in Texas, Johnson set about making sure that his men received the recognition that they deserved. Early in 1899 he asked "that proper recognition may be officially acknowledged by the bestowal of a medal of honor to the four enlisted men named in my letter of recommendation herewith enclosed."[18] The War Department responded quickly, and in June all four buffalo soldiers were given the Medal of Honor.[19]

Fitz Lee received his award while he was in the hospital at Fort Bliss, Texas. Then serving as a private in I Troop, his general health had badly deteriorated, and he had been bedridden for almost three months when the medal came. The problem started on the very day that he joined his comrades in the rescue of the wounded at Tayabacao, when he first noticed the dramatic change in his vision. Everything became dark before his eyes, and the alarming condition did not improve for two months. Other ailments also beset Lee, including abdominal pains and swollen limbs. Although only thirty-three years old, he clearly could no longer function as a soldier. The Army discharged him at Fort Bliss on July 5, 1899, just days after he received his medal.[20]

Lee returned to Leavenworth, Kansas, where he had been stationed in 1892–1894. Like impoverished former buffalo soldiers in other towns, the old troopers in Leavenworth formed a cohesive and supportive community, so Lee found assistance and a place to live among his former comrades in arms. He resided with old soldier Charles Taylor, a college-educated North Carolinian who later spent eighteen years managing teams in the Negro baseball leagues, and Taylor's wife, Cora. Taylor paid the doctor who looked after Lee, and other veterans also contributed to his support. Charles Giles, for example, purchased his medicines while his application for an invalid's pension made its way through a bureaucracy then wrestling with about 19,000 such applications. In constant pain, totally blind, and utterly dependent on his friends, Lee died at the Taylor residence on September 14, without ever recovering from his many ailments. His comrades arranged his funeral with the help of the local chapter of the Regular Army and Navy Union, which paid for a suit of clothes and the coffin and informed Fort Leavenworth that a holder of the Medal of Honor had died. The commander of the post saw to it that he was buried with full military honors.[21]

Dennis Bell obtained his medal while serving in Cuba on occupation duty at Manzanillo. He had recovered from a severe case of malaria that he had contracted during his first tour of duty on the island; gone on furlough to his home in Washington, DC; and then returned to his regiment and went back to Cuba. He later received a promotion to corporal and served with his regiment in Texas and the Philippines. From wearing his medal regularly, by 1902 the ribbon had become threadbare and he obtained another. Four years later, after leaving the Army and returning to Washington, he and another veteran, G. H. Robinson, visited their old first sergeant, Lewis Smith, who was living in retirement with his wife in Alexandria, Virginia. Bell pinned the Medal of Honor on his coat and boarded a trolley. On the next morning, when he left Smith's place, he noticed that the medal was gone. The War Department issued another one and sent it to him at his home.[22]

Like Dennis Bell, William Thompkins pinned on his medal while serving with the army of occupation in Cuba. He lost his decoration in 1900, an occurrence that seemed fairly common, but was issued a replacement. Unlike Bell, Thompkins stayed in the Army and made it his career. He succeeded in his profession, retiring in 1914 as a first sergeant in the Twenty-fifth Infantry, but he had to survive some rough spots to do so, notably the accidental shooting of a Filipino woman in 1902. Then a corporal in the Twenty-fifth Infantry, Thompkins was in charge of a detachment of two white Signal Corpsmen and their black infantry escort, probably out to string some communications wire on the military reservation at Subic Bay, when a flock of cranes flew overhead. Unable to resist such inviting targets, he and one of his soldiers unholstered their pistols and started to fire at the birds. One

Dennis Bell. *Courtesy Library of Congress*

of the bullets lodged in the thigh of a woman who was fishing nearby. The ensuing investigation absolved Thompkins of everything but carelessness, and the Army dropped the matter. In the last two months of the same year, military courts fined Thompkins three times, and his mother later begged the Army to release him so that he could take care of her. Still, he stayed; and at the end of 1914 he retired at Schofield Barracks near Honolulu, Hawaii, with twenty-five years of service and double credit for five years of overseas service. He was forty-four. In addition to his Medal of Honor, he wore the Spanish War and Indian War campaign badges. Although he told the War Department that he planned to return to Paterson, he stayed in Hawaii for at least part of the next year.[23]

George Wanton also made a career in the Army, overcoming his rocky early years and an ambivalent attitude toward the military to attain high noncommissioned rank. Soldiering was clearly not his first choice. He left the Army after the war with Spain, went back to Paterson, and tried to make a life as a civilian. He received some favorable attention from a hometown newspaper, which wrote about him as one of "the four gallant negroes [who] under cover of darkness landed and successfully carried down to a waiting boat thirteen badly wounded men." At least for a time he also had a job as a driver for the owner of a local hardware store, but the position led nowhere and he ultimately found himself out of work. After three frustrating years, he reenlisted, telling the recruiter in 1902 that "he is unable to get any kind of employment in that city, and his medal of honor and former service in the Army and Navy are of no benefit to him in getting a position of any kind, and thinks they should be of some benefit to him, at least in getting back into the Army."[24]

The Army took Wanton back, but he remained uncertain about staying in the service. When his enlistment expired in 1904, he found work as a chauffeur and coachman, but five years later he enlisted as a private for service with the Tenth Cavalry at Fort Ethan Allen in Vermont. This time, he stayed. He served with the regiment for six years, including a tour of duty on the Mexican border during the troubles with Pancho Villa. Before he left the Tenth for duty in the Quartermaster

Department in 1915, his troop commander called Wanton, who was then married and the father of three children, "a desirable man and . . . an excellent soldier." He retired as a master sergeant in 1925 at the age of fifty-eight and went home to Paterson, able to face civilian life with a pension.[25]

Unlike most of the buffalo soldiers who earned the Medal of Honor, Wanton enjoyed a fairly long retirement and even got the chance to savor some public recognition. He was an honorary pall bearer at the burial of the Unknown Soldier at Arlington National Cemetery in 1921 and later was invited by President Herbert Hoover to a White House reception acknowledging the Medal of Honor recipients. In 1930, during the American Legion convention in Boston, he attended a luncheon honoring Hoover and several Medal of Honor men as a distinguished guest. He died on November 24, 1940, and was interred in Arlington Cemetery.[26]

~ 11 ~

Edward Baker and the
Limits of Upward Mobility

While the four buffalo soldiers who rescued their wounded comrades in the surf at Tayabacao brought glory to themselves and the Tenth Cavalry, their fight was nevertheless a sideshow, an attempt to distract and annoy the enemy. The main event unfolded about two hundred miles to the east in the hills around the port city of Santiago. There, Major General William R. Shafter, known as "Pecos Bill" since his days as colonel of the Twenty-fourth Infantry, commanded a massive expeditionary force numbering over 17,000 men, including nearly 3,000 black regulars. By the end of June, Shafter had already established a beachhead east of Santiago and started tightening a ring around the 12,000 or so soldiers who were cut off in the city from the rest of the Spanish Army by harsh terrain, poor roads, and bands of Cuban insurgents.[1]

The Tenth Cavalry had been among the first of Shafter's troops to hit the beach. They came ashore on June 22 at Daiquiri, a small port town east of Santiago, unopposed but not without casualties. Two soldiers, Corporal Edward Cobb and Private George English, drowned when their landing craft overturned. Sergeant Major Edward L. Baker, Jr., the regiment's senior enlisted man, recorded their deaths in the journal that he had kept since the regiment left Montana. An exceptionally intelligent and literate noncommissioned officer, Baker kept track of the events and experiences of the campaign in Cuba. He noted in Daiquiri that "the few

half-clothed and hungry-looking natives" seemed pleased to
see the Americans, but that the town and railroad station were
smoldering ruins, put to the torch by the retreating Spanish
Army.[2]

Edward L. Baker, Jr., of the 49th Infantry. *Courtesy National Archives*

A keen observer, the thirty-two-year-old Baker had spent much of his life on the high plains frontier. He was born in an emigrant wagon on the Platte River road near Fort Laramie, Wyoming, in late December 1865, the son of a white French father and a black American mother. His family stayed in eastern Wyoming, and the young Baker grew up with a cowboy's toughness and skills in riding and roping. As Chaplain Cephas C. Bateman later wrote, Baker matured "accustomed to privations and hardships incident to life on the frontier"; he was "by instinct and training a horseman, a plainsman and a mountaineer." He also developed a fondness for education. As a youth, he learned French from his father, studied Spanish, and dabbled in Russian and Chinese. Bright and ambitious, he left the northern plains and enlisted in the Ninth Cavalry in 1882, midway between his sixteenth and seventeenth birthdays. He served one five-year term with the Ninth, transferred to the Tenth, and remained with the latter regiment from 1887 until the war with Spain.[3]

Although Baker advanced steadily through the ranks, his career showed evidence of tension between his professional goals and a craving for a stable family life. He met and married Mary Elizabeth Hawley in Santa Fe, New Mexico, in 1887, just as his career was taking off. He became regimental clerk in 1888 and moved with the headquarters to Fort Apache, Arizona, leaving his wife at East Las Vegas, New Mexico, "the nearest and least expensive point at which she can be to me." He found the separation difficult and tried to get out of the Army at the end of 1889. Considering himself a citizen of Wyoming Territory despite his years in the southwest, he asked Delegate Joseph M. Carey (later senator, at statehood) to intercede with the Army on his behalf. Carey took up Baker's request, but the soldier changed his mind when he arranged to move his Mary closer to him. The Army would not have been inclined to grant him an early discharge merely because he had taken a wife.[4]

Baker still searched for a combination of professional success and a stable family life within the Army. On the very day in January 1891 that he was promoted from chief trumpeter to regimental quartermaster sergeant, he applied to become a post quartermaster sergeant. This position, on a post noncommissioned staff, would have enabled him to stay in one place rather than move with the regiment when it changed stations. The regimental adjutant, First Lieutenant Thaddeus W. Jones, supported his application, as did Colonel Jacob K. Mizner, the Tenth's commander. Jones said that Baker's "character is exemplary" and added that "he has first-rate intelligence, and is well fitted for the position he seeks." The Army rejected his application because regulations required that applicants be chosen from sergeants of the line, but Baker served on the regimental noncommissioned staff.[5]

Four months before Baker's enlistment expired in August 1892, Regimental Sergeant Major Henry Briciño left the service. Colonel Mizner had already decided that he would appoint Baker in Briciño's place. On April 27 the War Department sent Baker his warrant appointing him to the top enlisted position in his regiment, a capacity in which he remained through the Tenth's six years in Montana.[6] By the time that he went to Cuba in 1898, he had compiled and published a valuable roster of Tenth Cavalry noncommissioned officers, complete with reminiscences and anecdotes about the regiment's history.[7] With his Cuban journal of 1898 and an article in 1899, this compilation was the first of at least three publications.[8] He had also, as his wife later wrote, "served in Arizona, New Mexico, Texas, Colorado, Kansas, Indian Territory, Nebraska, Wyoming, [and] Montana" and "took part in numerous scouts, arduous marches, and expeditions against isolated bands of Indians and other marauders from 1882 to 1898 on our western frontier."[9]

Baker's ambition never left him. In 1896–97 he tried unsuccessfully to enter the French cavalry school at Saumur, the Ecole d'Application de Cavalerie. Although he failed, the effort generated a correspondence that left ample proof of his methodical and thorough approach to problems, his dedication to his profession, and the high regard in which he was held by his officers. When he first broached the subject through official channels in November 1896, he had already taken steps to facilitate the process, contacting the French military attaché in Washington, Major C. de Grandprey, about the possibility of attending the school. The French officer assured Baker that although the request was unusual, he would forward it to his government if the War Department approved it first. Baker reminded his superiors that he spoke and read French. Moreover, he had not taken a furlough in all of his fourteen years of service, so he felt fully justified in asking now for a one-year leave of absence. He also expected to pay all of his expenses. "I am particularly anxious to enter this French School because there is no other country, that I know of, where a man in my position can seek instruction in the military profession such as can be obtained there," he explained in his application. Considering the forethought and planning that went into his request, there can be no doubt about his claim that he had "been preparing myself for some time for the above undertaking."[10]

The endorsements on his application showed that the officers of the Tenth had a very high regard for him. First Lieutenant Malvern Hill Barnum, the regimental adjutant, called Baker "a hard worker, [who] never touches intoxicating liquors, is ambitious to improve himself in his profession and always avails himself of any opportunities to do so; he is a young active man and a good horseman." Barnum's condescending view of Baker as "a man of unusual mental ability for one of his nationality" did not keep him from concluding that "should he be given the opportunity to take the course which he desires, he will prove himself fully equal to it."[11] Colonel Mizner was more effusive in his praise, calling Baker "a man of refinement, most excellent character, temper, and disposition." "As a soldier," Mizner considered Baker "zealous, ambitious and efficient, as well as very capable and intelligent." The opportunity to attend the school would fittingly reward his professional dedication and zeal. Mizner was confident that "he will do credit to his country and will fully appreciate any privileges or courtesies extended to him."[12] As Baker's request was passed up the chain of command, it continued to attract favorable comment and support. All seemed to agree with Chaplain Bateman that Baker was "a fine type of the true American Soldier, and a credit to the enlisted force of the United States Army."[13] Major

General Nelson Miles, commander of the Army, promised to approve the application if Baker were in fact admitted to the school.[14] But the approvals ended there, just short of success. Assistant Secretary of War Joseph B. Doe rejected the request without explanation, writing only that "This application is not approved."[15]

Baker was not easily deterred. In May 1897 he tried again from Fort Assiniboine, Montana, noting that he had never been told that the French government disapproved. This time, the War Department endorsed his application favorably and even sought the State Department's assistance in bringing Baker's request to the attention of the French government. State must have recommended against pressing the matter, because the Secretary of War reversed his department's earlier approval: "In view of the fact that since 1889 the French Government will not permit U.S. Officers to enter said school, the Secretary of War has decided not to ask for permission in the case of Sergeant Major Baker." Baker was caught in a double bind. The French would only consider his request if he had American approval; the Americans would not approve because they thought the French would reject his application.[16] Despite his "excellent record, both as a soldier and a scholar, and his determination . . . to make himself proficient in his profession," he would not go to Saumur.[17]

Thus, when the main drive on Santiago started on July 1, 1898, Baker was with his regiment in Cuba. Units of General Shafter's force attacked the Spaniards north and east of the city at two places: the blockhouse at El Caney, where William McBryar fought in the vanguard with the Twenty-fifth Infantry, and the San Juan Heights, where the Tenth Cavalry and the other two black regiments took their places in line alongside white regular and volunteer units.[18] The troops of Colonel Leonard Wood's division, made up of the First and Tenth Cavalry regiments and Wood's own First Volunteer Cavalry (the Rough Riders), whose lieutenant colonel was none other than the nearsighted and toothy Theodore Roosevelt, held the far right of the American line. They crouched in the early morning heat, their regulation blue wool and flannel uniforms soaked with sweat, and looked west through the dense matted grass, across the fordable San Juan River to the small promontory called Kettle Hill and the larger San Juan Hill behind it. The Spanish soldiers on the hills had already started to get the range of the approaching Americans well before they came near the river. There, in the thick high grass, the enemy fire began to take a serious toll. "The Dons," as Sergeant Major Baker called the Spanish soldiers, seemed to have zeroed in on the Tenth. From the blockhouse on top of San Juan Hill and the entrenchments around it as well as from positions on the Tenth's left, the enemy used the high ground to good effect. Baker wrote in his diary that "the atmosphere seemed perfectly alive with flying missiles from bursting shells overhead, and rifle bullets, which seemed to have an explosive effect."[19]

To make matters worse, the Signal Corps had sent up an observation balloon and anchored it and its hapless occupants, Lieutenant Colonel George M. Derby and Lieutenant Joseph Maxfield, about fifty feet above the waiting troops. The balloon drew constant fire from the Spaniards, Baker claimed; "every gun, both great and small, was playing on it." For the soldiers trying to make themselves as inconspicuous as possible in the grass, this attention was extremely unwelcome. For some, it was fatal.[20]

Baker seemed to lead a charmed life. He made several trips along the regimental position with his commander, Lieutenant Colonel Theodore A. Baldwin, to check on the troops. Each pass along the line took them directly under the despised balloon. On the last visit, an exploding artillery round knocked off Baldwin's hat, crippled his horse, and sprayed sand on both of them. Still, Baker escaped unscathed to seek cover with the rest of the regiment near the river. While he crouched behind a clump of brush, he "heard someone groan." He looked up and saw Private Lewis Marshall of C Troop face down and struggling in the waist-deep river. "The atmosphere," Sergeant Jacob Clay Smith remembered, "seemed perfectly alive with flying missiles from bursting shells and musketry."

Baker started up out of the grass toward Marshall, despite the advice of Blacksmith Charles Parker of G Troop, a twenty-year man with service against the Apaches, who joined other soldiers around Baker in trying to dissuade him from attempting the rescue. Baker ignored their pleas as well as the enemy shells that "passed so close as to cause me to feel the heat" and dashed to the wounded soldier's assistance. He pulled Marshall from the water, dragged him to safety, and went for the surgeon. Within a few minutes, to the delight of Baker and the rest of the regiment, the enemy shredded and shot down the balloon, leaving Lieutenant Colonel Derby dazed but unhurt, and the volume of incoming gunfire abated. By then the crossing of the San Juan was already known as Bloody Ford, and Baker took shrapnel in his left side and arm. In any case, the respite that followed the downing of the balloon was short. Less than thirty minutes later, after Baker had helped the officers cut some of the barbed wire that the Spaniards had strung around their positions, he and the regiment joined the advance that drove the defenders from San Juan Heights.[21]

The attack on the Spanish positions on the high ground started with the infantry units in the center and left of the American line. The enemy responded with heavy fire from the positions atop Kettle Hill as well as San Juan Hill, and soon the dismounted cavalry regiments on the American right joined the fray. The First, Ninth, and Tenth regulars and the Rough Riders came on line and moved forward toward Kettle Hill in the bright sunshine. The Tenth picked its way through barbed wire entanglements, across a clearing in plain view of the enemy. According to Baker, the troopers "advanced rapidly . . . under a galling, converging fire from the enemy's artillery and infantry." Occasionally, a trooper, felled by a bullet from a Spanish Mauser, disappeared quietly into the high grass; but the buffalo soldiers never wavered, drove the enemy off, and took over the blockhouse and entrenchments. They continued their advance, along with the other regiments in the American attack, clear to San Juan Hill. Along the way, Sergeant George Berry, the regiment's color sergeant, picked up the fallen colors of the Third Cavalry and carried them as well as the Tenth's to the top of the hill.[22]

Although the fighting around Santiago continued inter-mittently for ten days, the battles of July 1 represented major milestones for the black regiments. Compared to even the worst years of the Apache wars, the casualties that day were horrific. Twenty-six buffalo soldiers died as a result of the day's fighting—eight at El Caney, and eighteen at San Juan. Many received official recognition in general orders for dis-tinguishing themselves in battle—eleven from the Tenth Cav-alry, fifteen in the Ninth, eight in the Twenty-fourth Infantry, and two in the Twenty-fifth, with others also mentioned for bravery at Las Guásimas on June 24. Five Tenth Cavalrymen ultimately were awarded the Medal of Honor. The whole country woke up to the existence of the black regiments, and they became heroes overnight. Newspapermen and military officers lavished praise on the troopers, and magazines and newspapers recounted and dramatized their exploits. They returned to celebrations in their honor and the cheers of thousands.[23]

When the Twenty-fourth Infantry went back in triumph to Salt Lake City, Utah, the entire town took notice. Schools closed, and a big parade honored the heroes of Cuba, with bands and singing groups, the Utah state militia, veterans' and fraternal groups, citizens in carriages, and banners that proclaimed: "You fought a good fight," "You exalted your race," "Welcome," and "You have remembered the *Maine*." The festivities ended at Fort Douglas, with a banquet served to the troops by Red Cross ladies. A *Deseret Evening News* editorial claimed that the bravery of black troops in Cuba "went a long way towards eliminating the color line."[24]

The Tenth Cavalry went south to a different kind of re-ception. First at Camp Forse near Huntsville, Alabama, and later at several Texas posts, the Tenth encountered a wide range of racist hostility, including refusal of service by busi-ness establishments and even sniper fire from outside their camps. Two conflicting currents were at work, with the re-spect and acceptance won by the soldiers for their contribu-tion in Cuba clashing directly with the emergence of Jim Crow segregation. Only the departure of the Tenth for occupation duty in Cuba midway through 1899 brought a respite from southern animosity.[25]

Edward Baker did not see much of his old regiment during the months that followed the war. He came back from Cuba with a variety of maladies (dysentery and rheumatism as well as his gunshot wounds), and the Army's doctors decided not to let him join his regiment in the South. Instead, he was allowed to convalesce, first at Montauk Point, New York, the port of entry and quarantine camp for most of the returning soldiers, and then back at Fort Assiniboine with his family. Baker's health gradually improved, and by October he declared himself ready for active duty. When he returned, he did so as a commissioned officer, a first lieutenant in the Tenth Infantry, United States Volunteers, one of the four regiments of "immunes" set aside for black enlisted men and ninety-six black lieutenants. Overall, the postwar environment that he faced might have given him cause for optimism about his future. Montauk and Montana both welcomed the returning buffalo soldiers with open arms, the surgeons at Montauk had treated him as well as any other soldier— "*everyone* was *treated alike*," Baker had appreciatively written to the Adjutant General—and now he wore the silver bars of an officer in the United States Army, a tribute, Chaplain Steward wrote, to "his fidelity and efficiency."[26]

After about five months with the volunteer regiment at Camp Haskell, near Macon, Georgia, Baker returned to the Tenth Cavalry at Fort Sam Houston, Texas. The volunteer regiments recruited for the war with Spain were mustered out of the service, and he regained his old position as sergeant major.[27] He was at the post near San Antonio when the recommendation that he be awarded a Medal of Honor for his daring rescue of Private Marshall in Cuba started to make its way through military channels. Such proposals tended to come from commissioned officers who personally witnessed and appreciated the bravery of their men, or from the men who themselves had performed the acts of bravery but believed that they had been neglected, a practice that had just been prohibited by the Army in 1897. Baker's came from neither category but rather from an outspoken comrade in arms,

Jacob Clay Smith, who was serving in 1899 as a second lieutenant with the Ninth "Immune" Infantry in Cuba. Smith had never been afraid to speak his mind. In 1886 at Fort Elliott, Texas, he had called a meeting and participated in the drafting of a resolution condemning the behavior of a fellow sergeant who had allowed a military prisoner to escape. Now he presented a lucid exposition of Baker's heroic action, accompanied by the proper citation to general orders and referring to the appropriate muster rolls for documentation. Smith explained that he took the liberty of initiating the request because he saw Baker come to Marshall's rescue and because no commissioned officer was present at the time. Lieutenant Colonel Baldwin, for whom Baker had for three days "carried orders under the heaviest fire," agreed that he had "displayed a bravery and fearlessness that was wonderful." As far as Baldwin was concerned, "there is no man more worthy of a medal than he [Baker] and I do not hesitate to recommend him for one."[28]

Meanwhile, Baker again received a volunteer commission, this time as a captain in the Forty-ninth U.S. Infantry. He joined the new regiment, which was organized for service against the Filipino resistance to American rule, at Jefferson Barracks, near St. Louis, Missouri, in October 1899. As usual, he carried with him the high praise of his former commanders. Lieutenant Colonel Thaddeus Jones of the Tenth Volunteers, once before Baker's commander as adjutant of the Tenth Cavalry, called him the finest of the lieutenants in his regiment.[29] Chaplain Steward considered him and William McBryar to be the best candidates for commissions, both "old soldiers, highly intelligent, and gallant."[30] Chaplain Bateman endorsed Baker for his captaincy as " honest, frank, prompt, intelligent, sober, and a thoroughly capable soldier."[31]

After a short stint as a recruiting officer for the Forty-ninth in San Antonio, he joined his new regiment at the Presidio of San Francisco for the month-long voyage to the Philippines. He commanded Company L, with two frontier veterans— seventeen-year man Macon Russell, who had served in both the Twenty-fourth and Twenty-fifth Infantry, and Alfred Ray,

a "tall, fine-looking cavalryman" with sixteen years in the
Tenth Cavalry—now serving under him as lieutenants.[32]

Baker thrived in the Philippines. For most of his eighteen
months in the islands, he commanded his company and three
outposts on the northern tip of Luzon, where he made a name
for himself both as a leader and as a goodwill ambassador.
Four hundred miles from Manila, with his headquarters at

Jacob Clay Smith, who recommended Baker for the Medal of Honor, served as a
volunteer officer in the Philippines. Cashin, *Under Fire with the Tenth Cavalry*

Claveria and twenty-man detachments under Lieutenant Russell at Sánchez Mira and Lieutenant Ray at Pamplona, Baker was far from the fighting that took place in central Luzon. He sent out patrols, superintended municipal elections, built roads between his detachments, and even successfully brokered a dispute between local civil and church officials. Meanwhile, his men stayed out of trouble, regularly sent money home to their families, and kept off the sick lists. In the process he attracted favorable attention from senior officers and the new English-language newspapers that had set up operations in the Philippines. Clearly suited for command, Baker made a superb emissary for American rule in the Philippines. As his regimental commander, Colonel William H. Beck, wrote, "Captain Baker has managed affairs civil and military at his station with more pronounced success than usual. He is indefatigable in his efforts to pacificate [sic] the natives and at the same time to keep them disciplined. His time is given to his duties."[33]

Service in the islands must have represented a heady experience for Baker and others like him. In command of both units and stations, men who had served long and hard as private soldiers and noncommissioned officers achieved in the volunteer regiments what had once seemed beyond them. Monthly, Lieutenant Horace Wheaton, the Second Battalion of the Forty-ninth's acting quartermaster and a former volunteer private in a black Massachusetts unit, made his rounds, checking the supply situation at the regimental outposts and socializing with Baker, his lieutenants, and Surgeon William Wormsley of the Forty-ninth, who had once been a private in the Ninth Cavalry before attending medical school. These must have been halcyon days for the former enlisted men, now meeting as officers, enjoying their rank and status, and generally thriving as they faced the challenges and responsibilities of command.[34]

At the same time, they must have known or at least thought about the possibility that the situation might not last. Baker plainly knew, and he did his best to plan for the time when he would no longer be a captain in the Forty-ninth. His efforts to achieve commissioned status and respectability, which gave focus to his entire career after the war with Spain, had so far borne at least some fruit. Moreover, in February 1901, Major General Elwell S. Otis, commander of the Division of the Philippines, recommended that he and forty-one other black officers of the Forty-eighth and Forty-ninth be appointed second lieutenants in the regular Army. Nevertheless, the odds were heavily stacked against him: between December 31, 1898, and June 30, 1902, some 1,464 men received regular Army commissions from civilian life, the ranks, and volunteer units; of these, only two—Corporal John E. Green of the Twenty-fourth Infantry and Squadron Sergeant Major Benjamin O. Davis of the Ninth Cavalry—were black.[35] Baker saw the handwriting on the wall. Unlike William McBryar, who had the same goals but had seen enough of Philippine service, Baker applied in March 1901 for an appointment as an officer in the newly created Philippine Scouts.[36]

In spite of his planning and foresight, and his universally recognized ability and achievement, Baker returned to the United States unsure of his military status or future. He pulled out all of the stops in accumulating recommendations and testimonials, with Brigadier General Joseph Wheeler, the former Confederate who had commanded the cavalry in Cuba in 1898, Senator Francis E. Warren of Wyoming, and artist Frederic Remington all writing to the War Department on his behalf. Despite the illustrious and powerful support, the bureaucracy worked at a leisurely pace. Finally, a letter from Baker to President Roosevelt in January 1902 did the trick, and he won his commission in the Scouts in March. But when Baker went back to the Philippines in February, he did not know that he already had the appointment; he had waited eleven months and heard nothing. So, joining a number of black veterans who mustered out in the Philippines or emigrated there, he decided to return to the islands, find a farm, and send for his wife.[37] As it turned out, he succeeded in maintaining his commissioned status, but at the cost of his family life. Mary remained in the States; by 1905 she moved to Paris and lived with his French relatives for a while before returning to Los Angeles. By that time, at least one of his five children, his first-born son Edward Lee, was studying at Wilber-force University in Ohio.[38]

Baker stayed in the Philippines for seven years, serving at several obscure posts on the islands of Luzon and Samar. Shortly after his arrival, he received the Medal of Honor for his gallantry at Santiago, Cuba, on July 1, 1898; the citation noted that he had left cover and, under fire, saved a wounded comrade from drowning.[39] He had little opportunity to savor the award; almost overwhelmed with work as a second lieu-tenant in the Scouts, he was trying to run a company by him-self. At one point, higher headquarters complained about errors in the way that he processed two enlistment papers. Alone at his outpost in Albay Province on the long peninsula that juts south and east off the main portion of Luzon, Baker defended himself, pointing out that he spent much of his time with his men in the field. In addition, "I found myself alone in a new company on native service almost swamped with correspondence, with incomplete and incoherent records, without blanks, or clerical assistance; in fact everything a company commander ought to have except patience."[40]

Generally, he did not fare well physically or mentally during his long service in the Scouts. His language skills de-teriorated badly, until in 1906, the year of his promotion to first lieutenant, he reported only an ability to speak Spanish, where once he had claimed some familiarity with four for-eign languages.[41] Finally, even his capability as a commander, so highly lauded during his tenure with the Forty-ninth, also came under scrutiny. In 1908, Baker, who had so immersed himself in his profession that he gave two of his children—Dexter Murat and Eugenia Sheridan—middle names that re-called legendary cavalrymen, was actually found wanting by a board of five officers. According to the board, who thought Baker deficient in drill and most professional subjects, duty in the Scouts had been very hard on him: "Baker ap-pears . . . to be much older than his years indicate, and is considered unsuited to the scout service." It concluded that he should not be promoted or reappointed at the expiration of his current appointment early in 1910: "After an impar-tial consideration of the facts before it, the board considers

First Lieutenant Edward L. Baker, Philippine Scouts, not qualified for promotion, and recommends he be not promoted or
re-appointed upon expiration of his present provisional
appointment."[42]

The board's recommendation did not survive its trip up
the chain of command. At higher levels, Baker's long years
of service apparently counted. The Adjutant General in Washington bluntly threw out the report, kept Baker on active duty,
and even authorized his promotion: "The report of the board
that Lieutenant Baker is professionally disqualified for the
duties of Captain in the Philippine Scouts is not approved,
and the officer will be regarded as qualified for promotion."[43]
He was in fact promoted to captain in November 1908 while
stationed at Barongan on the east coast of Samar.[44]

What had happened to this superb soldier during his long
stay in the Philippines that convinced the board to recommend his elimination from the service? What was life like as
the only officer, the only American, at isolated stations in the
islands? His medical history recorded treatment for "alcoholism acute, not in line of duty," in June 1909, but surely this
notation only reflected the superficial manifestation of serious problems that overtook this highly effective officer in his
early forties.[45] We can only begin to guess at the strains and
the frustrations that beset Baker in such an environment. The
record shows only that within one month of his treatment for
an alcohol problem, he gave up. He tendered his resignation
from the Scouts and asked that he be allowed to enlist in the
Army as a post quartermaster sergeant or the equivalent and
that he then be permitted to retire. Baker's once elaborate and
firm signature now trailed off into a weak scrawl.[46]

At this juncture, the same Army that had made it so difficult for him to achieve respectability and commissioned status came to his rescue, making sure that he received the
retirement pay of a member of a post noncommissioned staff.
Major General William Duvall in the Philippines supported
his application, noting Baker's history of "efficient service"
but observing that "his age and his present physical and
mental condition unfit him for further service as an officer of
Philippine Scouts."[47] The Secretary of War ordered the Quar-

termaster General to hold a vacancy for him, and the Adjutant General told Baker how to secure it: he was to enlist for "colored infantry" in Los Angeles and report to Fort McDowell, accept an appointment as quartermaster sergeant, and submit his retirement papers.[48] At the same time, the Adjutant General instructed the recruiter in Los Angeles to ignore "any disqualification that may be found in his case."

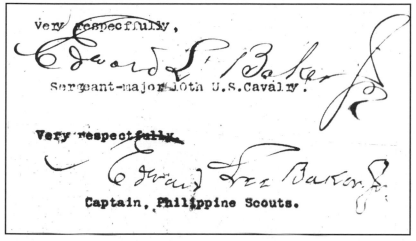

Edward Baker's signature, strong and clear when he applied for the French cavalry school in 1897, showed the effects of alcoholism when he resigned his commission in 1909. *Courtesy National Archives* (Microcopy M-929, roll 3)

Baker retired on January 12, 1910, with a total of just over twenty-eight years' service. Although he was only forty-four, he did not enjoy a lengthy retirement.[49] He died in August 1913 at the Army's Letterman General Hospital in San Francisco of peritonitis, the result of a partial intestinal blockage brought about by old adhesions. The Army shipped his remains to his widow in Los Angeles.[50] Like William McBryar, Baker had been an exceptional soldier in pursuit of a goal that he could not attain. But, unlike McBryar, Baker had followed his ambition back to the Philippines, where years of isolated frontier service brought his career to an unfortunate end. Despite long service, a Medal of Honor, and success as a volunteer officer, neither McBryar nor Baker was permitted to realize his dreams or potential.

~12~

The Recognition of
Black Valor

 ven in the period of the Indian wars, during which the Army was still resolving its ambiguity about the relative importance of the Medal of Honor and Certificate of Merit, the medal was the most obvious mark of bravery in battle. Soldiers pinned the medal to their uniforms, while the certificate remained framed in the recipient's quarters or tossed in a trunk or a desk drawer. The twenty-three buffalo soldiers who wore the gold star hanging from its silk ribbon constituted a select group—black men who had faced great danger, responded boldly, and won recognition for their valor from a society that did not readily acknowledge black achievement.

In the years just after the Spanish-American War, the medal gradually took precedence over the certificate. This development was already evident during the war with Spain. A number of soldiers of the Tenth Cavalry who were recommended for the medal by their commanders were given the certificate instead, thus implying the substitution of a lesser award. Chaplain Steward of the Twenty-fifth Infantry listed twenty-six black soldiers—eleven from the Tenth Cavalry, seven from the Ninth, and eight from the Twenty-fourth Infantry—who had received the certificate "for distinguished services in the Cuban campaign." Only five were awarded the Medal of Honor. The formal establishment of the medal's precedence over all other decorations was still a few years in the future, but the numbers indicate that an informal consensus on the ranking of the medal and the certificate had already been reached.[1]

With well-publicized efforts undertaken in the 1990s to scrutinize the lack of awards of the Medal of Honor to black soldiers in more recent wars, particularly in World War II, it is worth taking a brief look at the distribution of medals for the period of the Indian wars as well as the Cuban campaign.[2] For the years from 1866 to 1891, 416 soldiers were given the medal.[3] Black troopers received fewer than 4 percent of the awards but comprised 20 percent of the cavalry force and 12 percent of the infantry. They were definitely under-represented, especially when compared to units such as the Eighth Cavalry. Eighty-four men of the Eighth received the medal, yet the regiment was so undistinguished that it was not selected to join the large force that the Army mobilized for service in Cuba in 1898.[4]

What accounts for the underrepresentation of black soldiers? Certainly, their commanders had high expectations. Grierson, Hatch, and their successors assumed that their troopers would do their duty and were only rarely disappointed. They may not have been inclined to reward behavior that they felt entitled to expect. There were other reasons, too. One modern scholar, John Langellier, attributes the relatively few black holders of the medal to "bureaucratic red tape, prejudice, and other factors."[5] Indeed, the need to prepare recommendations and send them through the approval system did create problems. The pressure of operations prevented officers of all regiments, not only black units, from doing their administrative chores, including preparing and forwarding documentation for awards. Nevertheless, sooner or later they caught up with their paperwork. Five recommendations for buffalo soldier medals did not enter the approval process for nine years or longer, but they were eventually filed and approved.

One significant factor might have involved the tendency to station black soldiers in isolated places that were sometimes out of harm's way. Basically, these soldiers may have had less opportunity to gain recognition. A recent compilation of regimental participation in Indian campaigns for the period 1866 through 1891 ranked the Ninth Cavalry as seventh among the ten cavalry regiments with eight campaigns to its credit. Only the Fourth and Seventh, with six campaigns each, and the Tenth, with four, had fewer. In contrast, the First Cavalry had credit for twenty-one campaigns and the Second had nineteen.[6] By the same token, historian Thomas Phillips counted a total of 2,704 Indian engagements from 1866 through 1891. According to his data, soldiers of the four black regiments participated in 141 of these engagements, or just over 5 percent of the total. In this context the number of awards is not nearly as far out of line as it otherwise might be.[7]

Commanders also resorted to other methods to reward exemplary behavior. They saw to it that their soldiers were mentioned in official reports and in published orders, and they promoted them for valor as well. Corporal Asa Weaver of the Tenth Cavalry, who led a detachment of H Troop in a long-running fight against Victorio in August 1880, was promoted to sergeant on the spot for his "gallantry and qualities of leadership."[8] Benjamin Sayre of the Twenty-fourth Infantry, a sergeant when he went to Cuba in 1898, became sergeant major of his regiment for his bravery at San Juan Hill. Corporal John Mason of the Ninth Cavalry, who charged up San Juan Hill near the head of his regiment despite a severe wound, earned a mention in the annual report of the War Department. Others, such as Sergeant Thomas Griffin of the Tenth Cavalry, who helped cut the barbed wire in front of the Spanish positions while under heavy fire, never received the recognition that they deserved.[9] Nevertheless, many did, and no systematic effort to deny them recognition is apparent.

Whether they made up an equitable portion of soldiers who were recognized for their valor, the twenty-three black holders of the Medal of Honor shared a number of characteristics. Most were career soldiers: thirteen of the nineteen regulars and two of the four scouts served twenty-five years or more. Of the rest, only scout Adam Payne and deserter William Wilson served less than five years. Despite their long service and retirements before the age of fifty, which was early in life by civilian standards, few lived long enough to enjoy their retirement. They had worked hard under austere and perilous conditions, indulged in the usual amount of carousing along the way, and only survived a few years beyond retirement age; only George Wanton and Augustus Walley reached what could be considered a ripe old age. Many of these men, at least thirteen and perhaps as many as fifteen, were married. The group fit the expected profile of black soldiers at large. They were family men and inclined to stay in the Army.[10]

While the medal recipients met certain patterns, they also reflected the evolution of the buffalo soldier population, notably the emergence of a new generation of soldiers and noncommissioned officers in the 1880s and 1890s. Soldiers who matured later in the period showed a degree of worldliness and sophistication not apparent among their predecessors. Emanuel Stance's rough-and-tumble style became obsolete. Edward Baker had little in common with Stance or, for that matter, the first three sergeants major of his own regiment— Jacob B. Thomas, Frank Wilson, and George Goldsby—all of whom ended their careers by deserting.[11] William Thompkins, more of Baker's generation than Stance's, showed that awareness did not preclude activism. He was among the cavalrymen of the Ninth who retaliated against the white cowboys who insulted and threatened a fellow trooper at Suggs, Wyoming, in 1892.[12]

Overall, the twenty-three made up a group of heroes, not a group of saints. While Stance stands out for his duality as the bully and hero, there were also William Wilson, who deserted, as well as general problems with military discipline faced by several of the nineteen regulars. Eight had court martial convictions, and six were reduced to private at least once. At least two, McBryar and Wanton, also contracted a venereal disease.

Not surprisingly, most of the recipients came from the Ninth Cavalry. In the campaigns against the Apaches, the Ninth saw the most severe and protracted fighting experienced by any of the four black regiments. The nature of the combat against these fierce and tenacious native fighters, with small detachments engaged in long pursuits and short, violent skirmishes in which quick reaction sometimes meant the difference between life and death, put a premium on good judgment and unflinching courage. The struggles with Victorio and Nana tested the soldiers of the Ninth repeatedly and, when they met the challenge, brought them the most recognition. But the number of medals won by the regiment also says a great deal about their officers. They cared about the men who served under them and saw that they were rewarded.

The buffalo soldier heroes showed an enduring patriotism that withstood long years of second-class citizenship. The few who lived to see the onset of World War I volunteered their services to the Army despite their advanced age and previous rejections. None was quite as persistent as George W. Ford, the old cavalryman who had joined the Tenth when it was organized in 1866 and still volunteered for duty in 1917 at the age of seventy.[13] George Wanton, whose frequently interrupted career dated back to 1889, was still in the Army, the only one of the group remaining on active duty. Two others volunteered and were rebuffed because of their age—Augustus Walley, who was over sixty, and William McBryar, then in his late fifties.

None of the medal recipients achieved any postmilitary successes. Most were essentially used up by their service, and all were affected by the lack of opportunity in the pervasively racist climate of their time. But there may have been more to their general lack of accomplishment than exhaustion and discrimination. Murray Kempton recently observed that he could not "think of an enlisted man, tried in the line and certified a hero, who was ever afterward rewarded with large honors in peacetime." Kempton was thinking in particular of political success, but there may be something in the perspective gained by willingly putting one's life at great risk that makes other striving less important or meaningful.[14]

The careers of these men throw considerable light on the relations between blacks and Indians on the frontier. All but seven of the twenty-three received their medals for actions in wars against the Indian peoples. This fact clashes with the modern expectation that the mere state of nonwhiteness should constitute the basis for an alliance or common cause among people of color against a white oppressor. The soldiers were Anglophones who represented a sedentary agrarian-industrial English-speaking culture. Many were recently freed and new citizens in this framework, eager to validate their claims on citizenship by wearing the uniform of the United States Army. Very few looked across the cultural chasm that separated them from the seminomadic warrior-hunters with whom they did battle and perceived any similarity between their respective conditions. Culture created a gap that was virtually unbridgeable. This fundamental opposition may be frustrating and even seem incomprehensible to people seeking to impose a Rainbow Coalition frame of reference on the past, but it nevertheless cannot be discounted. It was basic to the worldview of virtually all who claimed American citizenship. As William Gwaltney, a descendant of buffalo soldiers who became superintendent at Fort Laramie National Monument, wrote, "Buffalo Soldiers fought for recognition as citizens in a racist country and . . . American Indian people fought to hold on to their traditions, their land, and their lives."[15]

Even today, the huge gap between the soldiers and the warrior tribes of the west sometimes continues to influence perceptions. In the summer of 1995 a busload of tourists to buffalo soldier historic sites visited the Pine Ridge reservation to view the scene of William Wilson's dash for help. At the base of the hill on which sits the Wounded Knee cemetery, a Sioux woman stopped her car and asked a black reporter what he was doing there. When he said that he was on a buffalo soldier tour, she replied: "Buffalo Soldiers and the white man killed my people. My ancestors are up there. And I don't appreciate you being here. Why don't you go visit Abraham Lincoln's grave?" The reporter said that he left Wounded Knee with "a dull, sick, guilty feeling at the pit of my stomach."[16]

Despite occasional twinges of discomfort about the role of buffalo soldiers in the subjugation of Indians, the troopers have increasingly become the focus of public commemora-

The buffalo soldier statue at the front gate of Fort Huachuca, Arizona. Photograph by Jeffry M. Platt

tions and monuments. Much of the attention has focused on the Medal of Honor recipients. These observances sometimes reflect ambivalence or unease about the fate of the Indians, but generally the outpouring of remembrances and memorialization focuses on the troopers rather than on their enemies. Since 1977, Fort Huachuca, Arizona, has been the site of a statue designed by Rose Murray. Fifteen years later, in 1992, a more widely known figure of a mounted trooper, designed by Eddie Dixon, was dedicated at Fort Leavenworth, Kansas, by General Colin Powell, then the chairman of the Joint Chiefs of Staff and a self-proclaimed descendant of the buffalo soldiers.[17] Dedicated the same year, a life-size bronze sculpture designed by Greg Whipple and commemorating the service of Corporal Clinton Greaves stands guard over the parade ground at Fort Bayard, near Silver City, New Mexico.[18] Another monumental statue, still unfinished in 1996, was planned for Fort D. A. Russell (now known as Francis E. Warren Air Force Base) near Cheyenne, Wyoming, and a room in a service club at the same base was named in honor of Edward L. Baker in the autumn of the same year.[19]

The Clinton Greaves monument at Fort Bayard, New Mexico. Photograph by Mark Erickson

Memorials focusing on Medal of Honor heroes in recent years have taken other forms as well. In 1984, Lorraine Smith of Somerset, Kentucky, led a successful effort to move Brent Woods's remains from a community cemetery where only a rock marked his grave to the Mill Springs National Cemetery in Pulaski County, where the Veterans Administration provided a proper Medal of Honor tombstone.[20] As noted earlier, William Wilson's native Hagerstown remembered his brave ride with a parade and re-

Lane next to St. Luke's Methodist Church, Reisterstown, Maryland, renamed in 1995 in honor of Augustus Walley. Photograph by author

named a small park for him.[21] Elsewhere in Maryland, a Medal of Honor marker was placed on Augustus Walley's grave at

Medal of Honor grave marker at St. Luke's Methodist Church, Reisterstown, Maryland, dedicated in 1995 to the memory of Augustus Walley. Photograph by author

St. Luke's Methodist Church in Reisterstown on Memorial Day 1995, and the small street alongside the church became Augustus Walley Way. One of the speakers, Brigadier General George Price of the Army, bemoaned the destruction of the western tribes but said that it was possible both to sympathize with the Indians' plight and celebrate the buffalo soldiers.[22]

Not everyone would agree. Certainly, the woman who directed the reporter at Wounded Knee to Lincoln's grave would not; nor would another Sioux, who objected to the depiction of an Indian warrior on the Ninth Cavalry's regimental crest: "You're going to offend some Indian folks, both young and old, when you talk about your proud history in battles with Indian people."[23] Because many peoples—Indians, black Americans, and others—prize their martial traditions, it is inevitable that the victories of one group remind another one of its defeats. Nevertheless, there seems to be room for celebrations of military accomplishments to coexist. For example, postage stamps since 1986 have shown three great Sioux warrior-chiefs and scourges of the United States Army—Red Cloud, Crazy Horse, and Sitting Bull—as well as Mort Kunstler's depiction of four mounted buffalo soldiers. The frontier past should be big enough to encompass the needs of all those who claim association with it.

The commemorative events continued into 1996. A Memorial Day ceremony at the U.S. Soldiers' and Airmen's Home in Washington, DC, honored three more of the Medal of Honor men—Thomas Boyne, Benjamin Brown, and John Denny—all of whom are interred in the home's national cemetery.[24] The saga of buffalo soldier recipients of the Medal of Honor is not over; the modern chapter is still being written.

Overall interest in black heroes and the question of adequate recognition of their valor remain high. At the African American Medal of Honor Day observance on the campus of Morgan State University in Baltimore on May 5, 1995, Wilson Smith's design for a memorial to all black Medal of Honor heroes was unveiled. Smith, a retired noncommissioned officer, first dreamed of completing this monument while he was a student at a segregated high school in Wilmington, Delaware. The featured speaker, retired Army Colonel William DeShields, remarked on the twofold significance of the memorial. According to DeShields, it symbolized the exceptional displays of battlefield bravery and gallantry by African Americans who fought the enemy at their front as well as racism from behind. It also reflected America's failure to tell the full story of black military contributions. "Let this monument be our inspiration and our moral strength," he went on, to continue the struggle for full participation in American society.[25] The monument, a dark marble square about seven feet high, has memorial plaques on all sides identifying some of the heroes. It also includes statuary on the top that feature the Civil War gallantry of William Carney as well as Milton Olive's heroism in the Vietnam War. The list of medals awarded has an asterisk after the World War II entry, pointedly noting that none of the 433 recipients was black.

As DeShields said, "The Department of Defense is currently reviewing its records to insure that African American participants were not overlooked." By the time that he spoke at Morgan State, the reassessment had already resulted in the posthumous award of a Medal of Honor in 1991 to the late Corporal Freddie Stowers, a squad leader in the black Ninety-third Division during World War I.[26] The review also included a study that recommended that the Army consider awarding Medals of Honor to ten black soldiers who had fought heroically in World War II. The Army agreed in seven of the ten cases. And one of the seven, seventy-six-year-old former Lieutenant Vernon Baker, was still alive to receive his medal.[27]

On January 13, 1997, President Bill Clinton awarded the Medal of Honor to seven black soldiers for valor during World War II. The U.S. Postal Service issued this commemorative envelope in conjunction with the White House ceremony at which the presentations were made. With its repetition of the buffalo soldier image, the envelope shows the continued importance of the buffalo soldier as a symbol of the black warrior. Photograph by Tony Skiscim

With black veterans of the Korean War successfully pressing the Army to reconsider the combat history of the much-maligned Twenty-fourth Infantry Regiment, the attempt to reevaluate black contributions and ensure adequate recognition for heroes of past wars continues.[28] The ongoing effort to honor those black soldiers who served with extraordinary courage, whether manifested in celebrations of acknowledged buffalo soldier heroes or in reevaluations of the deeds of men who may have been unfairly judged, shares a central recognition. The new research, the dramatic statuary at former frontier outposts, and the Memorial Day graveside services all attest to the long history of black valor in the service of the United States. The era of the buffalo soldier had started in acknowledgment of the importance of black troops to the Union victory. The soldiers of the new regiments and their successors in the twentieth century continue to contribute significantly to American military strength. Along the way, the buffalo soldier Medal of Honor heroes, Freddie Stowers and the black doughboys of General John Pershing's expeditionary force, G.I.s such as Vernon Baker in World War II, and the many gallant black soldiers of Korea and Vietnam affirmed as well the proud tradition of black valor.

Abbreviations Used in Notes

AAG	Assistant Adjutant General
AG	Adjutant General
AGO	Adjutant General's Office
CG	Commanding General
CO	Commanding Officer
GCMO	General Court Martial Order
GO	General Order
HQ	Headquarters
JAG	Judge Advocate General
LR	Letters Received
M	Microcopy
NA	National Archives
NCS	Noncommissioned Staff
OJAG	Office of the Judge Advocate General
PI	Philippine Islands
PRD	Principal Record Division
QMG	Quartermaster General
RG	Record Group
SO	Special Order
USA	United States Army
USV	United States Volunteers
VA	Veterans Administration
WD	War Department

Notes

Chapter 1, "Two Traditions: The Medal of Honor and Black Valor," pp. 1–8

1. For brief histories of all American military decorations, including the Certificate of Merit, see Evans E. Kerrigan, *American Medals and Decorations* (Noroton Heights, 1990).

2. U.S. Congress, Senate Committee on Veterans' Affairs, *Medal of Honor Recipients, 1863–1978*, 96th Cong., 1st sess., Senate Committee Print No. 3, February 14, 1979, 2–3.

3. Ibid., 4, 6; Kerrigan, *American Medals and Decorations*, 3–4, 10.

4. For information on the battle at New Market Heights, see John Brinsfield, "The Battle of New Market Heights," *Soldiers* 51 (February 1996): 50–51; Dudley T. Cornish, *The Sable Arm: Black Troops in the Union Army, 1861–1865* (Lawrence, 1987), 278–80; Joseph T. Glathaar, *Forged in Battle: The Civil War Alliance of Black Soldiers and White Officers* (New York, 1990), 150–51, 166; William Gwaltney, "New Market Heights," in *The Civil War Battlefield Guide*, ed. Frances Kennedy (Boston, 1990), 264–67; Hondon B. Hargrove, *Black Union Soldiers in the Civil War* (Jefferson, 1988), 187–89; and Richard J. Sommers, *Richmond Redeemed: The Siege at Petersburg* (Garden City, 1981), 13–49. Also see George Washington Williams, *A History of the Negro Troops in the War of the Rebellion, 1861–1865* (New York, 1968), 252–53; and Joseph T. Wilson, *The Black Phalanx: African American Soldiers in the War of Independence, the War of 1812, and the Civil War* (New York, 1994), 435.

5. Butler quoted in Cornish, *Sable Arm*, 280.

6. Senate Committee on Veterans' Affairs, *Medal of Honor Recipients*, 25; Hargrove, *Black Union Soldiers in the Civil War*, 216.

7. Senate Committee on Veterans' Affairs, *Medal of Honor Recipients*, 109.

8. Ibid., 88.

9. Ibid., 117, 129, 136–37, 246–47.

10. Ibid., 27; Hargrove, *Black Union Soldiers in the Civil War*, 216.

11. Senate Committee on Veterans' Affairs, *Medal of Honor Recipients*, 40, 119, 189–90, 197.

12. John McMurray, *Recollections of a Colored Troop*, comp. Randon W. Bartley (Brookville, 1994), 52.

13. Senate Committee on Veterans' Affairs, *Medal of Honor Recipients*, 51, 77, 109, 112.

14. Program, Dedication of the African-American Medal of Honor Monument, Morgan State University, Baltimore, Maryland, May 5, 1995.

15. Hargrove, *Black Union Soldiers*, 206–7, 212–13; Cornish, *Sable Arm*, 288. George Washington Williams erroneously stated in his *History of Negro Troops* (p. 328) that over 30,000 black soldiers were killed. This figure is still occasionally used.

16. *Congressional Globe*, 39th Cong., 1st sess. (March 14, 1866), 36: 1385.

17. Ibid. (June 21, 1866), 36: 3332.

18. "An Act to Increase and Fix the Military Establishment of the United States," 14 *United States Statutes at Large* (1866), 332.

19. The operational histories of these units on the frontier are covered in William H. Leckie, *The Buffalo Soldiers: A Narrative of the Negro Cavalry in the West* (Norman, 1967); and Arlen L. Fowler, *The Black Infantry in the West, 1869–1891* (Westport, 1971).

20. Edward M. Coffman, *The Old Army: A Portrait of the American Army in Peacetime, 1784–1898* (New York, 1968), 215, 218, 220; Frank N. Schubert, *On the Trail of the Buffalo Soldier: Biographies of African Americans in the U.S. Army, 1866–1917* (Wilmington, 1995), 509.

21. AG, USA, to CO, Department of Texas, February 2, 1875, AGO, LR, 1805–1889, NA, RG 94 (M-929, roll 2). Emphasis in original.

22. Terry quoted in U.S. Army, Public Information Division, *The Medal of Honor of the United States Army* (Washington, DC, 1948), 13–14; Washington *Times*, March 18, 1995.

23. Senate Committee on Veterans' Affairs, *Medal of Honor Recipients*, 10; Eugene V. McAndrews, "Sergeant Major Frederick Gerber: Engineer Legend," *The Military Engineer* 63 (July–August 1971): 240–41.

24. U.S. Army, Public Information Division, *Medal of Honor*, 6; Kerrigan, *American Medals and Decorations*, ix.

25. GO 2, USA, AGO, January 8, 1875 (M-929, roll 2).

26. Circular No. 2, AGO, General Correspondence File, 1890–1917, NA, RG 94 (M-929, roll 2).

27. AG, USA, to CG, USA, August 11, 1893, AGO, General Correspondence File, 1890–1917, NA, RG 94 (M-929, roll 2).

28. U.S. Army, Public Information Division, *Medal of Honor*, 15–16; Washington *Times*, March 18, 1995.

Chapter 2, "Emanuel Stance and the Emergence of the Black Professional Soldier," pp. 9–26

1. Schubert, *On the Trail of the Buffalo Soldier*, 400, 450; Harry E. Johnson, Sr., "The Formation of the Ninth Cavalry Regiment, July 1866

to March 1867" (Master of Military Art and Science thesis, U.S. Army Command and General Staff College, 1991), 59; Regimental Returns, 9th Cavalry, October 1866–February 1867, NA, RG 391 (M-744, roll 87).

2. Regimental Returns, 9th Cavalry, October 1866 (M-744, roll 87); Register of Enlistments in the United States Army, 1798–1914, Vol. 64, 1866, P-Z, p. 162, NA, RG 94 (M-233, roll 32). Just above Stance's name on the enlistment register was a soldier named Nathaniel Stanton from Charleston, South Carolina, who enlisted at Lake Providence on October 1, 1866. The regimental clerk conflated them in October 1866, noting that a soldier named "Nathaniel Stance" was on duty as the F Troop cook. Later returns showed that the real cook was Stanton. The confusion between Stance and Stanton did not last long, because Stanton deserted in March 1867, but it may still account for the occasional misidentification of Stance as having come from Charleston. See especially Leckie, *Buffalo Soldiers*, 10.

3. Regimental Returns, 9th Cavalry, October 1866 (M-744, roll 87); Moses Williams, Oath of Enlistment and Allegiance, October 10, 1871, NA, RG 94 (M-929, roll 2); Register of Enlistments, Vol. 62, 1866, A-G, p. 96, NA, RG 94 (M-233, roll 31); Schubert, *On the Trail of the Buffalo Soldier*, 50, 226–27, 473.

4. Johnson, "The Formation of the Ninth Cavalry Regiment," 47–48, 65; Colonel George F. Hamilton, "History of the Ninth Regiment U.S. Cavalry, 1866–1906" (unpublished manuscript, U.S. Military Academy Library); Leckie, *Buffalo Soldiers*, 6.

5. L. R. Hamersley, *Records of Living Officers of the United States Army* (Philadelphia, 1884), 177–80; William H. and Shirley A. Leckie, *Unlikely Warriors: General Benjamin H. Grierson and His Family* (Norman, 1984), 109; Fairfax D. Downey, *The Buffalo Soldiers in the Indian Wars* (New York, 1969), 23.

6. Glathaar, *Forged in Battle*, 17, 55, 94, 165, 234.

7. James G. Hollandsworth, Jr., *The Louisiana Native Guards: The Black Military Experience during the Civil War* (Baton Rouge, 1995), 106–7; Johnson, "Formation of the Ninth Cavalry Regiment," 61, 63; Regimental Returns, 9th Cavalry, October–December 1866; Robert S. Starobin, *Industrial Slavery in the Old South* (New York, 1970), 22; Richard C. Wade, *Slavery in the Cities: The South, 1820–1860* (New York, 1964), 36; "Preventing Cotton-Press Damage," *United States Department of Agriculture Leaflet No. 241*, 1944, 2–8.

8. Downey, *Buffalo Soldiers in the Indian Wars*, 29, 33; Johnson, "Formation of the Ninth Cavalry Regiment," 49–50, 63–66; Hamilton, "History of the Ninth Regiment U.S. Cavalry"; Byron Price, "Mutiny at San Pedro Springs," *By Valor & Arms: The Journal of American Military History* 1 (Spring 1975): 31–32.

9. Regimental Returns, 9th Cavalry, March 1867, NA, RG 391 (M-744, roll 87).

10. This narrative adheres to the conventional usage, referring to infantry units as companies and to cavalry units as troops, in discussing the period before the official change as well as afterward.

11. Don Rickey, Jr., *Forty Miles a Day on Beans and Hay: The Enlisted Soldier Fighting the Indian Wars* (Norman, 1963), 48–49, 75, 78; Robert M. Utley, *Frontier Regulars: The United States Army and the Indian, 1866–1890* (New York, 1973), 36.

12. Rickey, *Forty Miles a Day on Beans and Hay*, 77.

13. Price, "Mutiny at San Pedro Springs," 31–32; Hamilton, "History of the Ninth Regiment U.S. Cavalry." On the tendency toward heavy-handed and even vicious discipline that existed in the post-Civil War Army, see Rickey, *Forty Miles a Day on Beans and Hay*, 139–41, 181–82.

14. Price, "Mutiny at San Pedro Springs," 32–33.

15. Ibid.; Hamilton, "History of the Ninth Regiment U.S. Cavalry"; Charges and Specifications versus First Lieutenant E. M. Heyl, 9th Cavalry, Letters, Orders, and Reports Received from and Relating to Members of the 9th Cavalry ("Name File"), 1867–1898, NA, RG 391.

16. Price, "Mutiny at San Pedro Springs," 33–34; Downey, *Buffalo Soldiers in the Indian Wars*, 30; Coffman, *The Old Army*, 367.

17. Charges and Specifications versus First Lieutenant E. M. Heyl, "Name File," 1867–1898; Francis B. Heitman, *Historical Register and Dictionary of the United States Army*, 2 vols. (Washington, DC, 1903), 1:527.

18. Hamilton, "History of the Ninth Regiment U.S. Cavalry."

19. Utley, *Frontier Regulars*, 6.

20. Hamilton, "History of the Ninth Regiment U.S. Cavalry."

21. Regimental Returns, 9th Cavalry, May–September 1868 (M-744, roll 87); *Annual Report of the Secretary of War, 1870*, 1:41; Schubert, *On the Trail of the Buffalo Soldier*, 466.

22. GO 26, 5th Military District, March 17, 1869, and transcript of Court Martial, Fort Davis, January 6, 1869, OJAG, General Court Martial Case Files, NA, RG 153.

23. Regimental Returns, 9th Cavalry, September–November 1869 (M-744, roll 87); Leckie, *Buffalo Soldiers*, 89–90.

24. Hamilton, "History of the Ninth Regiment U.S. Cavalry"; Regimental Returns, 9th Cavalry, May 1870 (M-744, roll 87); Regimental Returns, 24th Infantry, Jan–June 1870, NA, RG 391 (M-665, roll 245).

25. Jerry M. Sullivan, *Fort McKavett: A Texas Frontier Post* (N.p., n.d.), 3, 6–7, 16, 28, 52.

26. Ibid., 44; Regimental Returns, 24th Infantry, January–June 1870 (M-665, roll 245); Regimental Returns, 9th Cavalry, July 1870 (M-744, roll 87).

27. SO 73, HQ, Fort McKavett, May 19, 1870, SO and GO, Fort McKavett, NA, RG 393 (M-929, roll 2); A. C. Greene, *The Last Captive* (Austin, 1972), 3.

28. Leckie, *Buffalo Soldiers*, 99.

29. The contemporaneous documentation—Stance's report, Carroll's endorsement, and the Medal of Honor citation—does not mention the rescue of either child. However, later materials assert that Stance did save them. The difference may be due to the delay involved in learning that Willie Lehmann managed to escape from the Apaches. See Orders 253, Fort Robinson, Nebraska, December 27, 1887, Post Orders, 1886–1898, NA, RG 393; *Army and Navy Journal* 25 (December 31, 1887): 442.

30. Sergeant Emanuel Stance to Lieutenant B. M. Custer, Post Adjutant, Fort McKavett, May 26, 1870, LR, AGO, 1805–1889, NA, RG 94 (M-929, roll 2); Greene, *Last Captive*, 10–11. Some writers credit Stance with freeing both boys, but the evidence only allows for the possibility that he could have been responsible for the escape of one. See Clinton Cox, *The Forgotten Heroes: The Story of the Buffalo Soldiers* (New York, 1993), 55.

31. Stance to Lieutenant Custer, May 26, 1870, LR, AGO, 1805–1889; Hamilton, "History of the Ninth Regiment U.S. Cavalry." Details of actions for which buffalo soldiers received Medals of Honor are scarce. In this case, Stance's account of the fighting is the only first-hand one. It has been embellished in recent years, most notably in Downey's *The Buffalo Soldiers in the Indian Wars*, 45–46, but actual details are limited to the Stance report, which I have followed.

32. Endorsement, Captain Henry Carroll, June 1, 1870, to Stance report to Lieutenant Custer, May 26, 1870; Stance to AG, USA, July 24, 1870; Memorandum, General William T. Sherman, June 28, 1870, all in LR, AGO, 1805–1889, NA, RG 94 (M-929, roll 2); Senate Committee on Veterans' Affairs, *Medal of Honor Recipients*, 315.

33. Lerone Bennett, Jr., *Before the Mayflower: A History of Black America* (New York, 1989), 211.

34. Frank N. Schubert, "The Violent World of Emanuel Stance, Fort Robinson, 1887," *Nebraska History* 55 (Summer 1974).

35. Frank N. Schubert, *Buffalo Soldiers, Braves, and the Brass: The Story of Fort Robinson, Nebraska* (Shippensburg, 1993), 84–85; Schubert, *On the Trail of the Buffalo Soldier*, 383; Proceedings of a General Court Martial, Fort Reno, Indian Territory, March 10, 1883, OJAG, Court Martial Case Files.

36. Schubert, *On the Trail of the Buffalo Soldier*, 121, 222, 301, 400. On the growing assertiveness of black soldiers in the late 1880s and 1890s, also see *Army and Navy Journal* 24 (December 25, 1886): 431; and Marvin E. Fletcher, "The Negro Soldier and the United States Army, 1891–1917" (Ph.D. diss., University of Wisconsin, 1968), 31.

37. Schubert, *Buffalo Soldiers, Braves, and the Brass*, 86–88.

38. *Army and Navy Journal* 25 (December 31, 1887): 442; ibid. 25 (January 14, 1888): 482; Inventory of Personal Effects of Emanuel Stance (copy in author's files).

39. Robert Miller, *Buffalo Soldiers: The Story of Emanuel Stance* (Morristown, 1995).

Chapter 3, "The Seminole Negro Scouts," pp. 27–40

1. Kevin Mulroy, *Freedom on the Border: The Seminole Maroons in Florida, the Indian Territory, Coahuila, and Texas* (Lubbock, 1993), 7.

2. Kenneth Wiggins Porter, *The Negro on the American Frontier* (New York, 1971), 475; Mulroy, *Freedom on the Border*, 110–11.

3. AG, USA, to CG, Department of Texas, June 25, 1870, and Captain Frank W. Perry, 24th Infantry, CO, Fort Duncan, Texas, to AAG, Department of Texas, May 15, 1870, Military Division of the Missouri, Special File, Seminole-Negro Indians, 1872–1876, NA, RG 393, Entry 2547.

4. Porter, *Negro on the American Frontier*, 472, 477–78; Major Zenas R. Bliss, 25th Infantry, CO, Fort Duncan, to AAG, Department of Texas, July 14, 1870, Military Division of the Missouri, Special File, Seminole-Negro Indians, 1872–1876, NA, RG 393, Entry 2547; Fort Worth *Star Telegram*, March 25, 1990.

5. Porter, *Negro on the American Frontier*, 472, 477–78; Major Zenas Bliss, 25th Infantry, CO, Fort Duncan, to AAG, Department of Texas, July 14, 1870; John Kibbetts, late sergeant of scouts and "Chief of Seminole Negro Indians," to CG, Department of Texas, December 10, 1872, Military Division of the Missouri, Special File, Seminole-Negro Indians, 1872–1876, NA, RG 393, Entry 2547; William Loren Katz, *Black Indians: A Hidden Heritage* (New York, 1986), 80.

6. Major Henry C. Merriam, 24th Infantry, CO, Fort Duncan, to AAG, Department of Texas, June 17, 1872, Colonel Ranald S. Mackenzie, CO, 4th Cavalry, Fort Clark, to AAG, Department of Texas, July 10, 1873, Military Division of the Missouri, Special File, Seminole-Negro Indians, 1872–1876, NA, RG 393, Entry 2547; Porter, *Negro on the American Frontier*, 472.

7. Thomas W. Dunlay, *Wolves for the Blue Soldiers: Indian Scouts and Auxiliaries with the United States Army, 1860–1890* (Lincoln, 1982), 48.

8. This summary is based on various documents in Military Division of the Missouri, Special File, Seminole-Negro Indians, 1872–1876, NA, RG 393, Entry 2547; Documents Relating to the Military and Naval Service of Blacks Awarded the Congressional Medal of Honor from the Civil War to the Spanish-American War, NA (M-929, roll 2); indexes to Veterans Administration pension files; the list in Donald A. Swanson, *Seminole, Lipan, Cherokee, Creek Indian Scouts: Enlistment Records, Fort Clark* (Bronte, n.d.); and the footnotes in Porter, *Negro on the American Frontier*, passim. A precise count of the actual number of men who served as scouts may be very difficult to assemble. In addition to the muster rolls in the Special File on Seminole-Negro Indians, only a handful of lists concerning the many detachments of various tribes is in the National Archives, listed in Entries 2053 through 2060 of Record Group 391. Only

one of those, a descriptive book of scouts who served from 1889 to 1893, concerns the Seminole Negroes. Rolls 70 and 71 of the Registers of Enlistments in the National Archives (Microcopy 233) also contain lists of Indian scouts enlisted between 1866 and 1914.

9. Katz, *Black Indians*, 80.

10. Porter, *Negro on the American Frontier*, 478–79; Hamersley, *Records of Living Officers*, 346, 479; Frost Woodhull, "The Seminole Indian Scouts on the Border," *Frontier Times* 15 (December 1937): 120; Dan L. Thrapp, *Al Sieber, Chief of Scouts* (Norman, 1964), 334.

11. Edward S. Wallace, "General John Lapham Bullis, Thunderbolt of the Texas Frontier, II," *Southwestern Historical Quarterly* 54 (July 1951): 78–80, 82–83.

12. Woodhull, "Seminole Indian Scouts," 120.

13. Porter, *Negro on the American Frontier*, 479, 483; Bullis, CO, Seminole Negro Scouts, San Antonio, to AAG, Department of Texas, through CO, Fort Clark, May 28, 1875, Military Division of the Missouri, Special File, Seminole-Negro Indians, 1872–1876, NA, RG 393, Entry 2547; Dunlay, *Wolves for the Blue Soldiers*, 105.

14. Porter, *Negro on the American Frontier*, 470–71, 483.

15. On the overall significance of Indian scouts for the frontier Army, see Dunlay, *Wolves for the Blue Soldiers*; and Thrapp, *Al Sieber*.

16. Preston E. Amos, *Above and Beyond in the West: Black Medal of Honor Winners, 1870–1890* (Washington, DC, 1974), 4; Fort Worth *Star Telegram*, March 25, 1990. Payne's name is sometimes written "Paine," based on an incorrect spelling introduced by Colonel Ranald Mackenzie in an 1875 report. See Swanson, *Seminole, Lipan, Cherokee, Creek Indian Scouts,* 32.

17. Charles M. Robinson III, *Bad Hand: A Biography of General Ranald S. Mackenzie* (Austin, 1993), 159–68.

18. William H. Leckie, *The Military Conquest of the Southern Plains* (Norman, 1963), 220; Frank N. Schubert, *Vanguard of Expansion: Army Engineers in the Trans-Mississippi West, 1819–1879* (Washington, DC, 1980), 105; Amos, *Above and Beyond in the West*, 3–4; Robinson, *Bad Hand*, 167–68; Porter, *Negro on the American Frontier*, 479; Fort Worth *Star Telegram*, March 25, 1990.

19. Amos, *Above and Beyond in the West*, 3–4; Leckie, *Military Conquest of the Southern Plains*, 220–23; Robinson, *Bad Hand*, 169, 171.

20. Colonel Ranald S. Mackenzie, CO, 4th Cavalry, to AG, USA, March 28, 1875, Military Division of the Missouri, Special File, Seminole-Negro Indians, 1872–1876; Robinson, *Bad Hand*, 185–86.

21. Mackenzie to AG, USA, August 31, 1875, AGO, LR, 1805–1889, NA, RG 94 (M-929, roll 2).

22. Quoted in Amos, *Above and Beyond in the West*, 3.

23. Report, First Lieutenant John L. Bullis, 24th Infantry, Fort Clark, April 27, 1875, published in GO 10, HQ, Department of Texas, May 12, 1875, AGO, LR, 1805–1889, NA, RG 94 (M-929, roll 2).

24. Amos, *Above and Beyond in the West,* 7; John Allen Johnson, "The Medal of Honor and Sergeant John Ward and Private Pompey Factor," *Arkansas Historical Quarterly* 29 (1970): 372; Swanson, *Seminole, Lipan, Cherokee, Creek Indian Scouts,* 46.

25. Report, First Lieutenant John L. Bullis, 24th Infantry, Fort Clark, April 27, 1875, published in GO 10, HQ, Department of Texas, May 12, 1875. Unless otherwise noted, this account of the reconnaissance to the Pecos and the fight that ensued is based on this report.

26. Woodhull, "Seminole Indian Scouts," 122.

27. Memorandum, Secretary of War William W. Belknap, May 22, 1875; Receipt, Private Pompey Factor, March 15, 1876, AGO, LR, 1805–1889, NA, RG 94 (M-929, roll 2); U.S. Army, Headquarters, Military Division of the Missouri, *Record of Engagements with Hostile Indians within the Military Division of the Missouri from 1868 to 1882, Lieutenant General P. H. Sheridan, Commanding* (Washington, DC, 1882), 46.

28. Petition, Citizens of Kinney County, Texas, April 24, 1876; Lieutenant Colonel William Shafter, CO, Fort Duncan, to AAG, Department of Texas, May 10, 1875; Endorsement, Colonel Mackenzie, CO, Fort Sill, Indian Territory, April 20, 1876, to letter, First Sergeant Elijah Daniels, March 7, 1876; Colonel John I. Gregg, CO, 8th Cavalry, Fort Clark, to AAG, Department of Texas, May 23, 1876, all in Military Division of the Missouri, Special File, Seminole-Negro Indians, 1872–1876.

29. Petition, Citizens of Kinney County, Texas, April 24, 1876; Lieutenant Colonel William Shafter, CO, Fort Duncan, to AAG, Department of Texas, May 10, 1875; Colonel John I. Gregg, CO, 8th Cavalry, Fort Clark, to AAG, Department of Texas, May 23, 1876, all in Military Division of the Missouri, Special File, Seminole-Negro Indians, 1872–1876.

30. Colonel Hatch to AAG, Department of Texas, August 9, 1875, Military Division of the Missouri, Special File, Seminole-Negro Indians, 1872–1876.

31. Endorsement, Brigadier General Edward O. C. Ord, CG, Department of Texas, May 29, 1876, to letter, Colonel John I. Gregg, CO, 8th Cavalry, Fort Clark, to AAG, Department of Texas, May 25, 1876, Military Division of the Missouri, Special File, Seminole-Negro Indians, 1872–1876.

32. Ibid.; Endorsement, Lieutenant General Philip H. Sheridan, CG, Military Division of the Missouri, to letter, Colonel John I. Gregg, CO, 8th Cavalry, Fort Clark, to AAG, Department of Texas, May 25, 1876; Francis A. Walker, Commissioner of Indian Affairs, to Secretary of the Interior, December 16, 1872; Colonel Edward L. Hatch to AAG, Department of Texas, August 9, 1875; Colonel Mackenzie, CO, 4th Cavalry, Fort Sill, to AG, USA, March 28, 1875, all in Military Division of the Missouri, Special File, Seminole-Negro Indians, 1872–1876.

33. Lieutenant Bullis, Fort Clark, to AAG, Department of Texas, June 14, 1880, and Endorsements, Colonel David S. Stanley, 22d Infantry, CO, Fort Clark, June 15, 1880, and Brigadier General Ord, CO, Department of Texas, June 22, 1880; E. J. Brooks, Acting Commissioner of Indian Affairs, to Secretary of the Interior, July 10, 1880, all in AGO, LR, 1805–1889, NA, RG 94 (M-929, roll 2); Porter, *Negro on the American Frontier*, 486.

34. Amos, *Above and Beyond in the West*, 7; SO 113, HQ, Department of Texas, May 31, 1879, AGO, Orders and Circulars, 1797–1910, NA, RG 94 (M-929, roll 2).

35. Johnson, "Medal of Honor and Sergeant John Ward and Private Pompey Factor," 372; Amos, *Above and Beyond in the West*, 7, 41.

36. Statement of Service, Isaac Payne, January 14, 1896, AGO, General Correspondence File, 1890–1917, NA, RG 94 (M-929, roll 2); Amos, *Above and Beyond in the West*, 7.

37. SO 104, Department of Texas, August 18, 1884, AGO, General Correspondence File, 1890–1917, NA, RG 94 (M-929, roll 2); Porter, *Negro on the American Frontier*, 471, 490–91.

38. Porter, *Negro on the American Frontier*, 490–91; Wallace, "General John Lapham Bullis, Thunderbolt of the Texas Frontier, II," 85.

39. Quoted in Scott Thybony, "Against All Odds, Black Seminoles Won Their Freedom," *Smithsonian* 22 (August 1991): 90.

Chapter 4, "The Apache Wars, 1877–1879," pp. 41–59

1. Hamilton, "History of the Ninth Regiment U.S. Cavalry."

2. Ibid.

3. Regimental Returns, 9th Cavalry, June 1876, NA, RG 391 (M-744, roll 88); Leckie, *Buffalo Soldiers*, 176.

4. Hamilton, "History of the Ninth Regiment U.S. Cavalry"; Leckie, *Buffalo Soldiers*, 177.

5. Leckie, *Buffalo Soldiers*, 176.

6. Quoted in Eve Ball, *In the Days of Victorio: Recollections of a Warm Springs Apache* (Tucson, 1970), 50.

7. Hamilton, "History of the Ninth Regiment U.S. Cavalry"; Leckie, *Buffalo Soldiers*, 176.

8. Hamilton, "History of the Ninth Regiment U.S. Cavalry."

9. Schubert, *On the Trail of the Buffalo Soldier*, 72; William Henry Bush to Commissioner of Pensions, May 3, 1915, VA Pension File C 2577213, William Henry Bush.

10. Regimental Returns, 9th Cavalry, January 1877, NA, RG 391 (M-744, roll 88); Leckie, *Buffalo Soldiers*, 178.

11. GO 5, HQ, Fort Bayard, New Mexico, February 5, 1877, LR, Enlisted Branch, AGO, NA, RG 94 (M-929, roll 2); Downey, *Buffalo Soldiers in the Indian Wars*, 68–69.

12. Senate Committee on Veterans' Affairs, *Medal of Honor Recipients*, 286; Memorandum, Major Samuel N. Benjamin, AAG, February 3, 1879, LR, Enlisted Branch, AGO, NA, RG 94 (M-929, roll 2).

13. Hamilton, "History of the Ninth Regiment U.S. Cavalry."

14. GO 5, HQ, Fort Bayard, New Mexico, February 5, 1877, and Memorandum, Major Samuel N. Benjamin, AAG, February 3, 1879, LR, Enlisted Branch, AGO, NA, RG 94 (M-929, roll 2).

15. Memorandum, Major Samuel N. Benjamin, AAG, February 3, 1879, LR, Enlisted Branch, AGO, NA, RG 94 (M-929, roll 2); Senate Committee on Veterans' Affairs, *Medal of Honor Recipients*, 286.

16. Hamilton, "History of the Ninth Regiment U.S. Cavalry."

17. Amos, *Above and Beyond in the West*, 8; Bureau of Pensions, Request for Medical History, February 1906, and General Affidavit, Peter Watson, June 18, 1908, VA File C 922002, Clinton Greaves; Captain George A. Purrington, 9th Cavalry, CO, Fort Bayard, New Mexico, to AG, USA, March 22, 1881, LR, Enlisted Branch, AGO, NA, RG 94 (M-929, roll 2).

18. Lieutenant Colonel William H. Jordan, CO, Depot, General Recruiting Service, USA, Columbus Barracks, Ohio, November 18, 1889, to AG, USA, LR, AGO, 1805–1889, NA, RG 94 (M-929, roll 2).

19. General Affidavit, Peter Watson, June 18, 1908, VA File C 922002, Clinton Greaves.

20. General Affidavit, John F. O'Connor, November 1, 1906, VA File C 922002, Clinton Greaves.

21. General Affidavit, Peter Watson, June 18, 1908; General Affidavit, Bertha Greaves, June 18, 1908; General Affidavit, John W. Adams, June 18, 1908; Physician's Affidavit, H. L. Agler, M.D., June 18, 1908; Declaration for Original Pension, Bertha Greaves, August 28, 1906; Declaration for Pension, Bertha Greaves, May 15, 1917; Declaration for Pension, Bertha Greaves, December 3, 1927, all in VA File C 922002, Clinton Greaves.

22. Dan L. Thrapp, *The Conquest of Apacheria* (Norman, 1967), vii–viii, x–xi, 66.

23. Ibid., x, xv, 5, 21–23, 58, 166, 171–77; C. L. Sonnichsen, *The Mescalero Apaches* (Norman, 1973), 177–78; Leckie, *Buffalo Soldiers*, 180; Porter, *Negro on the American Frontier*, 470.

24. Dan L. Thrapp, *Victorio and the Mimbres Apaches* (Norman, 1974), 215–16; Regimental Returns, 9th Cavalry, May 1879, NA, RG 391 (M-744, roll 88); Hamilton, "History of the Ninth Regiment U.S. Cavalry."

25. Amos, *Above and Beyond in the West*, 9; Captain Charles D. Beyer, Report of Scout, June 16, 1879, District of New Mexico, Letters and Reports Received, 1867–1890, NA, RG 393 (M-929, roll 2). Beyer's report contained an extensive, detailed day-by-day account of his travels. His exertions were not everywhere appreciated. In an endorsement of June 25, 1879, First Lieutenant Clarence A. Stedman of the Ninth Cav-

alry, then serving as acting District of New Mexico engineer, complained that "the notes are of no value to this office, Genl Orders 4, Hdqrs, Dist of New Mexico series of 1878 not having been complied with, no compass or odometer having been used, although both these instruments are available at Fort Bayard."

26. Thomas Boyne, Application for Certificate in Lieu of Discharge, November 21, 1891, and Statement of Service, December 4, 1891, filed with Application for Certificate in Lieu of Discharge, November 21, 1891, Record and Pension Office General Correspondence File, 1889–1904, NA, RG 94 (M-929, roll 2); William A. Gladstone, *United States Colored Troops, 1863–1867* (Gettysburg, 1990), 113, 115.

27. Captain Charles D. Beyer, Report of Scout, June 16, 1879, District of New Mexico, Letters and Reports Received, 1867–1890, NA, RG 393 (M-929, roll 2). The account of the fight of May 29 is based on Beyer's report.

28. Regimental Returns, 9th Cavalry, September 1879, NA, RG 391 (M-744, roll 88); Thrapp, *Conquest of Apacheria*, 182, 218; Amos, *Above and Beyond in the West*, 11; Leckie, *Buffalo Soldiers*, 211.

29. Quoted in Leckie, *Buffalo Soldiers*, 213–14.

30. Thrapp, *Conquest of Apacheria*, 186.

31. Ibid., 183; Thrapp, *Victorio and the Mimbres Apaches*, 240.

32. Descriptive List and Pay Account of Corporal John Denny, Retired, AGO, General Correspondence File, 1890–1917, NA, RG 94 (M-929, roll 2); Senate Committee on Veterans' Affairs, *Medal of Honor Recipients*, 280.

33. Regimental Returns, 9th Cavalry, September 1879, NA, RG 391 (M-744, roll 88); Hamilton, "History of the Ninth Regiment U.S. Cavalry"; Thrapp, *Conquest of Apacheria*, 183–84.

34. Regimental Returns, 9th Cavalry, September 1879, NA, RG 391 (M-744, roll 88); Hamilton, "History of the Ninth Regiment U.S. Cavalry"; Leckie, *Buffalo Soldiers*, 211; Thrapp, *Victorio and the Mimbres Apaches*, 240; Amos, *Above and Beyond in the West*, 13; Captain Matthias W. Day, 9th Cavalry, Mansfield, Ohio, to Captain Charles W. Taylor, C/9th Cavalry, August 22, 1894, AGO, General Correspondence File, 1890–1917, NA, RG 94 (M-929, roll 2).

35. Regimental Returns, 9th Cavalry, September–October 1879, NA, RG 391 (M-744, roll 88); Captain Matthias W. Day, 9th Cavalry, Mansfield, Ohio, to Captain Charles W. Taylor, C/9th Cavalry, August 22, 1894, and Affidavits, Corporal George Lyman and Private James Jackson, A/9th Cavalry, Fort Robinson, Nebraska, September 7, 1894, AGO, General Correspondence File, 1890–1917, NA, RG 94 (M-929, roll 2).

36. Regimental Returns, 9th Cavalry, September 1879, NA, RG 391 (M-744, roll 88); Hamilton, "History of the Ninth Regiment U.S. Cavalry"; Leckie, *Buffalo Soldiers*, 211; Thrapp, *Victorio and the Mimbres Apaches*, 240; Amos, *Above and Beyond in the West*, 13; Captain Matthias W. Day, 9th Cavalry, Mansfield, Ohio, to Captain Charles W.

Taylor, C/9th Cavalry, August 22, 1894, AGO, General Correspondence File, 1890–1917, NA, RG 94 (M-929, roll 2).

37. Thrapp, *Victorio and the Mimbres Apaches*, 240; Senate Committee on Veterans' Affairs, *Medal of Honor Recipients*, 279.

38. Captain Charles W. Taylor, C/9th Cavalry, to AG, USA, September 28, 1894, and Affidavit, Private James Jackson, A/9th Cavalry, Fort Robinson, Nebraska, September 7, 1894, AGO, General Correspondence File, 1890–1917, NA, RG 94 (M-929, roll 2); Schubert, *On the Trail of the Buffalo Soldier*, 221; Memorandum, Acting Secretary of War Joseph B. Doe, November 27, 1894, AGO, General Correspondence File, 1890–1917, NA, RG 94 (M-929, roll 2).

39. Schubert, *On the Trail of the Buffalo Soldier*, 119; GCMO 39, Department of the Platte, Omaha, May 19, 1891, OJAG, Court Martial Case Files, 1809–1894, NA, RG 153 (M-929, roll 2).

40. Schubert, *On the Trail of the Buffalo Soldier*, 119; Descriptive List and Pay Account of Corporal John Denny, Retired, and Chief Disbursing Officer, Paymaster General's Office, WD, to AG, USA, November 30, 1901, AGO, General Correspondence File, 1890–1917, NA, RG 94 (M-929, roll 2).

41. Leckie, *Buffalo Soldiers*, 211.

42. Certificate, First Lieutenant Henry H. Wright, 9th Cavalry, [date illegible but 1881], VA Pension File SC 441287, Thomas Boyne.

43. Amos, *Above and Beyond in the West*, 10–11; Leckie, *Buffalo Soldiers*, 212; Hamilton, "History of the Ninth Regiment U.S. Cavalry."

44. Regimental Returns, 9th Cavalry, September 1879, NA, RG 391 (M-744, roll 88); Thrapp, *Victorio and the Mimbres Apaches*, 250; Leckie, *Buffalo Soldiers*, 212–13; Dunlay, *Wolves for the Blue Soldiers*, 76.

45. Corporal Thomas Boyne to Lieutenant Henry Wright, Fort Cummings, New Mexico, January 16, 1881, LR, Enlisted Branch, AGO, NA, RG 94 (M-929, roll 2); Grote Hutcheson, "The Ninth Regiment of Cavalry," in *The Black Military Experience in the American West*, ed. John M. Carroll (New York, 1969), 73.

46. Certificate, First Lieutenant Henry H. Wright, 9th Cavalry, [date illegible but 1881], with Endorsement, Major Albert B. Morrow, March 5, 1881, VA Pension File SC 441287, Thomas Boyne.

47. Major Henry C. Corbin, AAG, to Chief Clerk, WD, December 13, 1881, and AG to Chief Clerk, WD, January 5, 1882, LR, Enlisted Branch, AGO, NA, RG 94 (M-929, roll 2); Senate Committee on Veterans' Affairs, *Medal of Honor Recipients*, 272–73.

48. Hamilton, "History of the Ninth Regiment U.S. Cavalry"; Leckie, *Buffalo Soldiers*, 250–51; General Affidavit, George Brown, May 1893, VA Pension File SC 441287, Thomas Boyne.

49. Certificate of Disability for Discharge, Fort Missoula, Montana, January 2, 1889; Certificate of Pension, December 29, 1893, VA Pension File SC 441287, Thomas Boyne.

50. General Affidavit, George Brown, May 1893, VA Pension File SC 441287, Thomas Boyne; Secretary of War, *Annual Report, 1889*, 1013; Secretary of War, *Annual Report, 1896*, 640.

Chapter 5, "Henry Johnson and the Ute War," pp. 61–71

1. Hamilton, "History of the Ninth Regiment U.S. Cavalry"; Leckie, *Buffalo Soldiers*, 179, 206–7; Amos, *Above and Beyond in the West*, 14.

2. Regimental Returns, 9th Cavalry, 1879, NA, RG 391 (M-744, roll 88).

3. Leckie, *Buffalo Soldiers*, 207; Downey, *Buffalo Soldiers in the Indian Wars*, 73.

4. Robert Emmitt, *The Last War Trail: The Utes and the Settlement of Colorado* (Norman, 1954), 195, 199–200, 217; Downey, *Buffalo Soldiers in the Indian Wars*, 74; Leckie, *Buffalo Soldiers*, 208; Amos, *Above and Beyond in the West*, 14–15; Russel D. Santala, *The Ute Campaign: A Study in the Use of the Military Instrument* (Fort Leavenworth, 1994), 57.

5. Leckie, *Buffalo Soldiers*, 208; Emmitt, *Last War Trail*, 204; Santala, *Ute Campaign*, 61.

6. Emmitt, *Last War Trail*, 217–18.

7. Ibid., 205; Santala, *Ute Campaign*, 61.

8. Hamilton, "History of the Ninth Regiment U.S. Cavalry"; Military Division of the Missouri, *Record of Engagements with Hostile Indians*, 90; Amos, *Above and Beyond in the West*, 16.

9. Statements of Service for Privates Greaves, Epps, Mackadoo, and Adams, LR, Enlisted Branch, AGO, NA, RG 94 (M-929, roll 2); Schubert, *On the Trail of the Buffalo Soldier*, 35, 209, 217; Hamilton, "History of the Ninth Regiment U.S. Cavalry."

10. Schubert, *On the Trail of the Buffalo Soldier*, 217; Descriptive List and Pay Account, Henry Johnson, and Summary of Service, Henry Johnson, June 22, 1898, Record and Pension Office, General Correspondence File, 1889–1904, NA, RG 94 (M-929, roll 2). On the Republican River fight, see Leckie, *Buffalo Soldiers*, 34–36.

11. Hamilton, "History of the Ninth Regiment U.S. Cavalry."

12. Quoted in Amos, *Above and Beyond in the West*, 16.

13. Military Division of the Missouri, *Record of Engagements with Hostile Indians*, 90.

14. Emmitt, *Last War Trail*, 93, 219–20.

15. Senate Committee on Veterans' Affairs, *Medal of Honor Recipients*, 280.

16. Dodge's telegram to Department of the Missouri headquarters, drafted on the morning of October 2 and actually sent on October 8, is quoted in Amos, *Above and Beyond in the West*, 16.

17. Santala, *Ute Campaign*, 61–62; Amos, *Above and Beyond in the West*, 17.

18. Affidavit, Henry Johnson, August 1890, and AG, USA, to CG, USA, August 26, 1890, General Correspondence File, AGO, 1890–1917, NA, RG 94 (M-929, roll 2).

19. Leckie, *Buffalo Soldiers*, 208; Dodge quoted in Amos, *Above and Beyond in the West*, 17.

20. Affidavit, Johnson, August 1890, General Correspondence File, AGO, 1890–1917, NA, RG 94 (M-929, roll 2). Modern accounts accept this document's version of what occurred. See, for example, Leckie, *Buffalo Soldiers*, 208; and Downey, *Buffalo Soldiers in the Indian Wars*, 77–78.

21. Santala, *Ute Campaign*, 63; Military Division of the Missouri, *Record of Engagements with Hostile Indians*, 91; Leckie, *Buffalo Soldiers*, 209; Amos, *Above and Beyond in the West*, 17.

22. Hamilton, "History of the Ninth Regiment U.S. Cavalry."

23. Statement of Service, Henry Johnson, File 5993 PRD 1890, NA, RG 94 (M-929, roll 2); Regimental Returns, 9th Cavalry, 1881, NA, RG 391 (M-744, roll 89).

24. Statement of Service, Henry Johnson, and Depositions, Sergeant Madison Ingoman and Trumpeter Lewis Fort, Fort McKinney, Wyoming, August 14, 1890, File 5993 PRD 1890, NA, RG 94 (M-929, roll 2); Johnson to Major Francis S. Dodge, Paymaster, USA, New York City, March 23, 1890, General Correspondence File, AGO, 1890–1917, NA, RG 94 (M-929, roll 2); *Army and Navy Journal* 27 (December 28, 1889): 352.

25. (Crawford) *Northwest Nebraska News*, August 9, 1934.

26. Emmitt, *Last War Trail*, 105.

27. Ibid., 221.

28. Memorandum, Acting Secretary of War Grant, September 18, 1890, General Correspondence File, 1890–1917, AGO, NA, RG 94 (M-929, roll 2); Senate Committee on Veterans' Affairs, *Medal of Honor Recipients*, 293.

29. See Chapter 9, this volume, for detailed coverage of the events surrounding the Pine Ridge campaign and the assignment to Fort Myer.

30. Captain Martin B. Hughes, CO, K/9th Cavalry, Fort Myer, Virginia, to Adjutant, 9th Cavalry, Fort Robinson, Nebraska, July 26, 1893, and AG, USA, to CG, USA, August 11, 1893, General Correspondence File, 1890–1917, AGO, NA, RG 94 (M-929, roll 2); AAG, USA, endorsement, August 17, 1893, to Deposition, Private Henry Johnson, Fort Robinson, August 1890, and Statement of Service, Henry Johnson, File 5993 PRD 1890, NA, RG 94 (M-929, roll 2).

31. Private Henry Johnson, Crawford, Nebraska, to AG, USA, through military channels, June 1, 1898, Record and Pension Office, General Correspondence File, 1889–1904, NA, RG 94 (M-929, roll 2); SO 180, WD, August 2, 1898.

32. W. H. Stoutanburgh, Intendant, Washington Asylum, to AG, USA, January 31, 1904, and Chief Disbursing Officer, Paymaster General's Office, to AG, USA, February 11, 1904, Record and Pension Office, General Correspondence File, 1889–1904, NA, RG 94 (M-929, roll 2).

33. Descriptive List and Pay Account, Henry Johnson, Record and Pension Office, General Correspondence File, 1889–1904, NA, RG 94 (M-929, roll 2).

34. Telegram, AAG, USA, to CO, Fort Myer, Virginia, February 10, 1904, Record and Pension Office, General Correspondence File, 1889–1904, NA, RG 94 (M-929, roll 2).

Chapter 6, "The Apache Wars Continue, 1880–81," pp. 73–89

1. Thrapp, *Victorio and the Mimbres Apaches*, 268; Leckie, *Buffalo Soldiers*, 215.

2. Leckie, *Buffalo Soldiers*, 217–18.

3. W. F. Beyer and O. F. Keydel, *Deeds of Valor: How America's Heroes Won the Medal of Honor*, 2 vols. (Detroit, 1903), 2:275.

4. Schubert, *On the Trail of the Buffalo Soldier*, 249.

5. Beyer and Keydel, *Deeds of Valor*, 2:273–76. According to the authors, their account draws directly on Jordan's own recollection of the affair at Tularosa.

6. Ibid.

7. Ibid.; Leckie, *Buffalo Soldiers*, 221.

8. Beyer and Keydel, *Deeds of Valor*, 2:273–76.

9. Ibid.

10. Ibid., 2:276; Leckie, *Buffalo Soldiers*, 221; Downey, *Buffalo Soldiers in the Indian Wars*, 70; Descriptive List and Pay Account, First Sergeant George Jordan, AGO, General Correspondence File, 1890–1917, NA, RG 94 (M-929, roll 2).

11. Senate Committee on Veterans' Affairs, *Medal of Honor Recipients*, 294.

12. Regimental Returns, 9th Cavalry, May 1880, NA, RG 391 (M-744, roll 88).

13. Leckie, *Buffalo Soldiers*, 221–22; Thrapp, *Conquest of Apacheria*, 202; Dunlay, *Wolves for the Blue Soldiers*, 101.

14. Colonel Edward Hatch, Santa Fe, New Mexico, to AG, USA, August 17, 1880, filed with Regimental Returns, 9th Cavalry, June 1880, NA, RG 391 (M-744, roll 88).

15. Sonnichsen, *Mescalero Apaches*, 207; Leckie, *Buffalo Soldiers*, 224–28; Thrapp, *Conquest of Apacheria*, 209, 314.

16. Leckie, *Buffalo Soldiers*, 230; Edward L. N. Glass, *The History of the Tenth Cavalry, 1866–1921* (Fort Collins, 1972), 95; Schubert, *On the Trail of the Buffalo Soldier*, 514. The five men killed were Corporal

William Backers of K Troop, Privates Carter Burns and George Mills of B Troop, and Privates J. K. Griffin and James Stanley of K Troop.

17. Thrapp, *Conquest of Apacheria*, 212; Sonnichsen, *Mescalero Apaches*, 210.

18. Thomas E. Dowling, "Intelligence in the Final Indian Wars, 1866–1887" (Master of Science of Strategic Intelligence thesis, Joint Military Intelligence College, 1996), 190; Regimental Returns, 9th Cavalry, August 1881, NA, RG 391 (M-744, roll 88); Thrapp, *Conquest of Apacheria*, 212–14.

19. Regimental Returns, 9th Cavalry, August 1881, NA, RG 391 (M-744, roll 88); Thrapp, *Conquest of Apacheria*, 212–14; Beyer and Keydel, *Deeds of Valor*, 2:276–77; Amos, *Above and Beyond in the West*, 20; Military Division of the Missouri, *Record of Engagements against Hostile Indians*, 100; Hamilton, "History of the Ninth Regiment U.S. Cavalry."

20. Descriptive List and Pay Account, First Sergeant George Jordan, AGO, General Correspondence File, 1890–1917, NA, RG 94 (M-929, roll 2); Senate Committee on Veterans' Affairs, *Medal of Honor Recipients*, 313. As a sergeant, Jordan should not have been awarded a certificate, but his pay records show the additional $2 per month that went with such recognition.

21. Leckie, *Buffalo Soldiers*, 232–33; Beyer and Keydel, *Deeds of Valor*, 2:277–78; Regimental Returns, 9th Cavalry, October 1866; Descriptive List of Ordnance Sergeant Moses Williams, Fort Buford, North Dakota, October 9, 1895, AGO, General Correspondence File, 1890–1917, NA, RG 94 (M-929, roll 2); George R. Burnett, formerly Second Lieutenant, 9th Cavalry, Consulate of the United States, Kehl [*sic*], Germany, to Sergeant Williams, June 20, 1896, AGO Document File 41940, NA, RG 94.

22. Burnett to Williams, June 20, 1896, AGO Document File 41940, NA, RG 94.

23. Ibid.

24. Ibid.; Leckie, *Buffalo Soldiers*, 232–33; Beyer and Keydel, *Deeds of Valor*, 2:277–78.

25. Leckie, *Buffalo Soldiers*, 232–33; Beyer and Keydel, *Deeds of Valor*, 2:277–78.

26. Burnett to Williams, June 20, 1896, AGO Document File 41940, NA, RG 94.

27. Ibid.; Leckie, *Buffalo Soldiers*, 232–33; Beyer and Keydel, *Deeds of Valor*, 2:277–79.

28. Burnett to Williams, June 20, 1896, AGO Document File 41940; Leckie, *Buffalo Soldiers*, 232–33; Beyer and Keydel, *Deeds of Valor*, 2:277–79.

29. Burnett, Altoona, Pennsylvania, to AG, USA, August 21, 1890, Document File 12608 PRD 1890, Augustus Walley; Burnett to Williams, June 20, 1896, AGO Document File 41940, NA, RG 94.

30. Ordnance Sergeant Moses Williams, Fort Stevens, Oregon, to President of the United States, through HQ, Department of the Columbia, July 29, 1896, AGO Document File 41940, NA, RG 94; Senate Committee on Veterans' Affairs, *Medal of Honor Recipients*, 275, 322.

31. Regimental Returns, 9th Cavalry, August 1881, NA, RG 391 (M-744, roll 88).

32. Schubert, *On the Trail of the Buffalo Soldier*, 20; Hamilton, "History of the Ninth Regiment U.S. Cavalry."

33. Hamilton, "History of the Ninth Regiment U.S. Cavalry"; Affidavit, Saddler Henry Trout, E/9th Cavalry [signed with Trout's mark], Fort Robinson, Nebraska, June 24, 1894, AGO, General Correspondence File, 1890–1917, NA, RG 94 (M-929, roll 2); Schubert, *On the Trail of the Buffalo Soldier*, 431; Leckie, *Buffalo Soldiers*, 233.

34. Endorsement, Captain Charles Taylor, CO, C/9th Cavalry, Fort McKinney, Wyoming, June 5, 1894, to Captain Byron Dawson, U.S. Army, Retired, Indianapolis, Indiana, to AG, USA, April 6, 1894, and Statement of Service of Sergeant Brent Woods, AGO, General Correspondence File, 1890–1917, NA, RG 94 (M-929, roll 2).

35. Hamilton, "History of the Ninth Regiment U.S. Cavalry"; Endorsement, Taylor, June 5, 1894, to Dawson to AG, USA, April 6, 1894, AGO, General Correspondence File, 1890–1917, NA, RG 94 (M-929, roll 2).

36. Endorsement, Taylor, June 5, 1894, to Dawson to AG, USA, April 6, 1894, AGO, General Correspondence File, 1890–1917, NA, RG 94 (M-929, roll 2).

37. Affidavit, Private John Denny, C/9th Cavalry, Fort McKinney, Wyoming, June 4, 1894, AGO, General Correspondence File, 1890–1917, NA, RG 94 (M-929, roll 2).

38. Captain Charles Taylor, CO, C/9th Cavalry, Fort McKinney, Wyoming, to Adjutant, 9th Cavalry, and Affidavit, Private Denny, C/9th Cavalry, Fort McKinney, Wyoming, June 4, 1894, AGO, General Correspondence File, 1890–1917, NA, RG 94 (M-929, roll 2).

39. Dawson to AG, USA, April 6, 1894, and Endorsements, AGO, General Correspondence File, 1890–1917, NA, RG 94 (M-929, roll 2); Senate Committee on Veterans' Affairs, *Medal of Honor Recipients*, 324.

40. Thrapp, *Conquest of Apacheria*, 215–16; Leckie, *Buffalo Soldiers*, 234, 242.

41. First Sergeant Augustus Walley, Fort Washakie, Wyoming, February 2, 1907, to Military Secretary, USA, AGO, General Correspondence File, 1890–1917, NA, RG 94 (M-929, roll 2); Baltimore *Sun*, April 13, 1938; Captain Charles G. Ayres, CO, E/10th Cavalry, to AAG, Young's Brigade, June 27, 1898; Report, CO, Cavalry Division, USA, Fort San Juan, Cuba, July 17, 1898; Ayres, Holguín, Cuba, to AG, USA, October 23, 1899, all three in AGO, General Correspondence File, 1890–1917,

NA, RG 94 (M-929, roll 2); Preston Amos, " 'Augustus Walley Day' Observed in Maryland County," *The Annals, Official Publication of the Medal of Honor Historical Society* 17, no. 1 (September 1995): 11.

42. Senate Committee on Veterans' Affairs, *Medal of Honor Recipients*, 313; Amos, *Above and Beyond in the West*, 22, 44; Schubert, *On the Trail of the Buffalo Soldier*, 353.

43. Ordnance Sergeant Moses Williams, Vancouver Barracks, Washington, to AAG, Department of the Columbia, November 9, 1896, and Endorsements; Major A. C. Markley, 24th Infantry, CO, Vancouver Barracks, Washington, to AG, USA, November 16, 1899, all in AGO, General Correspondence File, 1890–1917, NA, RG 94 (M-929, roll 2).

44. Brent Woods to AG, USA, January 27, 1903; Descriptive List and Pay Account of Brent Woods, Retired Sergeant of Cavalry, Somerset, Kentucky; Mayor T. R. Griffin, Somerset, Kentucky, to Military Secretary, WD, August 8, 1906, all in AGO, General Correspondence File, 1890–1917, NA, RG 94 (M-929, roll 2).

45. Schubert, *On the Trail of the Buffalo Soldier*, 249; Schubert, *Buffalo Soldiers, Braves, and the Brass*, 150–57.

46. Crawford *Tribune*, October 28, 1904; Schubert, *On the Trail of the Buffalo Soldier*, 249.

47. Schubert, *On the Trail of the Buffalo Soldier*, 249.

Chapter 7, "The Wham Paymaster Robbery," pp. 91–100

1. Downey, *Buffalo Soldiers in the Indian Wars*, 80–81.

2. On the economic impact of the Army on one western community, see Schubert, *Buffalo Soldiers, Braves, and the Brass*, chapter 13. For the military impact on the southwest, see Darlis A. Miller, *Soldiers and Settlers: Military Supply in the Southwest, 1861–1885* (Albuquerque, 1989).

3. Regimental Returns, 10th Cavalry, May 1889, NA, RG 391 (M-744, roll 98); Regimental Returns, 24th Infantry, May 1889, NA, RG 391 (M-665, roll 247).

4. Schubert, *On the Trail of the Buffalo Soldier*, 57, 150–51; Private Isaiah Mays, D/24th Infantry, Fort Bayard, New Mexico, to AG, USA, August 2, 1893, and Statements of Service, February 13, 1890, AGO, General Correspondence File, 1890–1917, NA, RG 94 (M-929, roll 2).

5. This account of the robbery is based on Wham's report: Major Joseph W. Wham, Tucson, Arizona, to Secretary of War, September 1, 1889, AGO, General Correspondence File, 1890–1917, NA, RG 94 (M-929, roll 2).

6. Downey, *Buffalo Soldiers in the Indian Wars*, 82.

7. Regimental Returns, 24th Infantry, May 1889, NA, RG 391 (M-665, roll 247).

8. Quoted in Amos, *Above and Beyond in the West*, 32.

9. Major Joseph W. Wham, Tucson, Arizona, to Secretary of War, September 1, 1889, AGO, General Correspondence File, 1890–1917, NA, RG 94 (M-929, roll 2).

10. Colonel Zenas R. Bliss to AG, USA, November 9, 1889; Lieutenant Colonel George G. Huntt, Fort Apache, to AG, USA, February 14, 1890; Brevet Major General Benjamin H. Grierson, Colonel, 10th Cavalry, and CO, Department of Arizona, to AAG, Division of the Pacific, November 14, 1889; Orders 56, HQ, 24th Infantry, Fort Bayard, New Mexico, November 1, 1889, all in AGO, General Correspondence File, 1890–1917, NA, RG 94 (M-929, roll 2).

11. Endorsement, Lieutenant Colonel Robert H. Hall, Acting Inspector General, Department of Arizona, November 14, 1889, and Memorandum, Brigadier General John C. Kelton, AG, January 28, 1890, AGO, General Correspondence File, 1890–1917, NA, RG 94 (M-929, roll 2).

12. Memorandum, AGO, to CO, 24th Infantry, February 27, 1890, AGO, General Correspondence File, 1890–1917, NA, RG 94 (M-929, roll 2).

13. "National Capital Notes," Chicago *Inter-Ocean*, February 24, 1890; Memorandum, AGO, February 27, 1890, AGO, General Correspondence File, 1890–1917, NA, RG 94 (M-929, roll 2).

14. Statements of Service, AGO, February 13, 1890, AGO, General Correspondence File, 1890–1917, NA, RG 94 (M-929, roll 2).

15. AAG, USA, to CO, Fort Grant, Arizona, March 10, 1892, and Mays Endorsement, March 26, 1892; Memorandum, AAG, USA, to CO, Fort Thomas, Arizona, April 28, 1892; Application for Discharge and Endorsements, Mays, 1892, all in AGO, General Correspondence File, NA, RG 94 (M-929, roll 2).

16. GCMO 16, HQ, Department of Arizona, April 19, 1892, Court Martial Case Files, OJAG, USA, NA, RG 153 (M-929, roll 2); Regimental Returns, 24th Infantry, April–June 1892, NA, RG 391 (M-665, roll 248).

17. Private Isaiah Mays, D Company, 24th Infantry, Fort Bayard, New Mexico, to AG, USA, August 2, 1893, and Endorsement, AAG, USA, August 25, 1893; SO 197, HQ, USA, August 28, 1893; Mays, Clifton, Arizona, to AG, USA, August 29, 1896; Mays, Guthrie, Arizona, to Ralph Cameron, Member of Congress, May 1910, all in AGO, General Correspondence File, 1890–1917, NA, RG 94 (M-929, roll 2); Amos, *Above and Beyond in the West*, 33.

18. Schubert, *On the Trail of the Buffalo Soldier*, 57, 512.

19. Ibid., 57; Amos, *Above and Beyond in the West*, 33; James DeSalvo, "The Home's Heroes Span 5 Wars," *United States Soldiers' and Airmen's Home* 11 (December 18, 1992): 14–15.

Chapter 8, "William McBryar and the End of the Indian Wars in the South," pp. 101–15

1. Efficiency Report, William McBryar, Second Lieutenant, 49th Infantry, 1900, AGO, General Correspondence File, 1890–1917, NA, RG 94 (M-929, roll 2); Affidavit, McBryar, September 22, 1933, VA Pension File XC 2419213, William McBryar.

2. Statement of Regular Army Service, McBryar, VA File XC 2419213, William McBryar; Regimental Returns, 10th Cavalry, March–June 1887, NA, RG 391 (M-744, roll 97); AGO, Statement of Service of William McBryar, February 21, 1899, accompanying letter from Rose Black, July 20, 1899, to "His Excellency the President of the United States," AGO, General Correspondence File, 1890–1917, NA, RG 94 (M-929, roll 2); Descriptive Book, K Company, 49th Infantry, NA, RG 94.

3. Glass, *History of the Tenth Cavalry*, 28.

4. Quoted in Herbert M. Hart, *Old Forts of the Far West* (New York, 1965), 167.

5. Edward L. Baker, Jr., *Roster of Non-Commissioned Officers of the Tenth Cavalry with Some Regimental Reminiscences, Appendixes, etc., connected with the Early History of the Regiment* (1897; reprint ed., Mattituck, 1983), 44

6. Baker, *Roster of Non-Commissioned Officers*, 44; Senate Committee on Veterans' Affairs, *Medal of Honor Recipients*, 277; Schubert, *On the Trail of the Buffalo Soldier*, 372; Powhatan Clarke, "A Hot Trail," *Cosmopolitan* 22 (October 1894): 706, 710; Leckie, *Buffalo Soldiers*, 243–44.

7. Baker, *Roster of Non-Commissioned Officers*, 44, 49–50; Amos, *Above and Beyond in the West*, 34; Regimental Returns, 10th Cavalry, March 1890, NA, RG 391 (M-929, roll 98); Clarke, "A Hot Trail," 707, 710; James W. Watson, "Scouting in Arizona," *Journal of the U.S. Cavalry Association* 10 (June 1897): 128. On scouting techniques, see Dunlay, *Wolves for the Blue Soldiers*, 77–79.

8. Watson, "Scouting in Arizona," 130–31; Clarke, "A Hot Trail," 713.

9. Watson, "Scouting in Arizona," 130–32; Baker, *Roster of Non-Commissioned Officers*, 44, 49–50; Amos, *Above and Beyond in the West*, 34; Regimental Returns, 10th Cavalry, March 1890, NA, RG 391 (M-929, roll 98).

10. Watson, "Scouting in Arizona," 131–34; Baker, *Roster of Non-Commissioned Officers*, 44, 49–50; Regimental Returns, 10th Cavalry, March 1890, NA, RG 391 (M-929, roll 98); Clarke, "A Hot Trail," 715–17.

11. Baker, *Roster of Non-Commissioned Officers*, 44, 49–50; Regimental Returns, 10th Cavalry, March 1890, NA, RG 391 (M-929, roll 98).

12. Senate Committee on Veterans' Affairs, *Medal of Honor Recipients*, 300. The contemporary literature of the Salt River fight is very frustrating. Neither the two firsthand accounts by Lieutenants Watson and Clarke nor Frederic Remington's "Two Gallant Young Cavalrymen," published in *Harper's Magazine* shortly after the fight and reprinted in *The Collected Writings of Frederic Remington*, ed. Peggy and Harold Samuels (Garden City, NY, 1979), 47–49, mention McBryar by name. All three profess admiration and respect for the buffalo soldiers, but only Rowdy and Daniels receive ample attention in their essays.

13. Glass, *History of the Tenth Cavalry*, 28.

14. John H. Nankivell, *The History of the Twenty-Fifth Regiment United States Infantry, 1869–1926* (Fort Collins, 1972), 58–64.

15. Descriptive Book, K Company, 49th Infantry, NA, RG 94; AGO, Statement of Service of William McBryar, February 21, 1899, accompanying letter from Rose Black, July 20, 1899, to "His Excellency the President of the United States," AGO, General Correspondence File, 1890–1917, NA, RG 94 (M-929, roll 2); WD, Statement of Regular Army Service of William McBryar, VA Pension File XC 2419213, William McBryar.

16. Captain Eaton A. Edwards, 25th Infantry, Tampa, Florida, to AG, State of North Carolina, May 30, 1898, AGO, General Correspondence File, 1890–1917, NA, RG 94 (M-929, roll 2); U.S. Army, AGO, *Correspondence Relating to the War with Spain, including the Insurrection in the Philippine Islands and the China Relief Expedition, April 15, 1898, to July 30, 1902*, 2 vols. (Washington, DC, 1993), 1:609; Nankivell, *History of the Twenty-Fifth Infantry*, 69; Heitman, *Historical Register and Dictionary of the United States Army*, 1:398; Graham A. Cosmas, *An Army for Empire: The United States Army in the Spanish-American War* (Columbia, 1971), 136.

17. Theophilus G. Steward, *The Colored Regulars in the United States Army* (Philadelphia, 1904), 152; Herschel V. Cashin et al., *Under Fire with the Tenth Cavalry* (London, 1899), 144–45.

18. Lieutenant Vernon A. Caldwell to Quartermaster Sergeant William McBryar, [undated but 1898], AGO, General Correspondence File, 1890–1917, NA, RG 94 (M-929, roll 2); Steward, *Colored Regulars*, 160; Cashin et al., *Under Fire with the Tenth Cavalry*, 144–45.

19. Cashin et al., *Under Fire with the Tenth Cavalry*, 144–45.

20. Ibid.; Schubert, *On the Trail of the Buffalo Soldier*, 73; Nankivell, *History of the Twenty-Fifth Infantry*, 78, 82.

21. Steward, *Colored Regulars*, 160; GO 19, 25th Infantry, near Santiago, Cuba, August 11, 1898, quoted in Steward, *Colored Regulars*, 177.

22. Lieutenant Vernon A. Caldwell to Quartermaster Sergeant William McBryar, [undated but 1898], AGO, General Correspondence File, 1890–1917, NA, RG 94 (M-929, roll 2).

23. Telegram, Lieutenant Colonel Andrew S. Daggett to AG, USA, July 25, 1898, and AAG, USA, to CO, 8th USV, Fort Thomas, Kentucky, July 30, 1898, AGO, Record and Pension Office, General Correspondence File, 1889–1904, NA, RG 94 (M-929, roll 2); Schubert, *On the Trail of the Buffalo Soldier*, 286, 385, 513; Cosmas, *An Army for Empire*, 136.

24. Telegram, William McBryar, Fort Thomas, Kentucky, to AG, USA, September 13, 1898, AGO, General Correspondence File, 1890–1917, NA, RG 94 (M-929, roll 2); Rayford W. Logan, *The Betrayal of the Negro, from Rutherford B. Hayes to Woodrow Wilson* (New York, 1965), 335. For the popular acclaim that came to McBryar and others like him, see, for example, Hiram Thweatt, *What the Newspapers Say of the Negro Soldier in the Spanish-American War* (Thomasville, n.d.), 9–10; Edward A. Johnson, *History of Negro Soldiers in the Spanish-American War* (Raleigh, 1899), 32; and the Richmond *Planet*, August 13, 1898.

25. Lieutenant Vernon A. Caldwell to Quartermaster Sergeant William McBryar, [undated but 1898], AGO, General Correspondence File, 1890–1917, NA, RG 94 (M-929, roll 2); Descriptive Book, K Company, 49th Infantry, NA, RG 94; WD, Statement of Volunteer Service of William McBryar, VA Pension File XC 2419213, William McBryar.

26. Telegram, General Elwell S. Otis to the Secretary of War, September 25, 1899, and Chaplain Theophilus G. Steward, Wilberforce, Ohio, August 25, 1899, to AG, USA, AGO, General Correspondence File, 1890–1917, NA, RG 94 (M-929, roll 2); Steward, *Colored Regulars*, 292; Rose Black, July 20, 1899, to "His Excellency the President of the United States," AGO, General Correspondence File, 1890–1917, NA, RG 94 (M-929, roll 2).

27. Memorandum, Chief of Ordnance to Secretary of War, August 29, 1899; Telegram, AG, USA, to General Otis, Manila, September 29, 1899; AAG, USA, to CG, Division of the Philippines, November 10, 1899, all in AGO, General Correspondence File, 1890–1917, NA, RG 94 (M-929, roll 2); *Army and Navy Journal* 37 (December 9, 1899): 345b; Descriptive Book, M Company, 49th Infantry, NA, RG 94.

28. "Succinct Account of Service," Efficiency Report of Second Lieutenant William McBryar, 49th Infantry, 1900, AGO, General Correspondence File, 1890–1917, NA, RG 94 (M-929, roll 2); Nankivell, *History of the Twenty-Fifth Infantry*, 90.

29. Descriptive Book, K Company, 49th Infantry, NA, RG 94; *Army and Navy Journal* 38 (November 24, 1900): 307; "Succinct Account of Service," Efficiency Report of Second Lieutenant William McBryar, 49th Infantry, 1900, AGO, General Correspondence File, 1890–1917, NA, RG 94 (M-929, roll 2); Statement of Volunteer Service of William McBryar, WD, VA Pension File XC 2419213, William McBryar.

30. Lieutenant Colonel Charles H. Noble, 16th Infantry, Recruiting Station, Indianapolis, Indiana, May 6, 1901, to Members of Examining Board, San Francisco, May 6, 1901, AGO, General Correspondence File, 1890–1917, NA, RG 94 (M-929, roll 2).

31. William McBryar to AG, USA, August 24, 1901, and Endorsement, Chief of Ordnance, September 24, 1901, AGO, General Correspondence File, 1890–1917, NA, RG 94 (M-929, roll 2).

32. 60 *Stat.* 757; Memorandum, Miscellaneous Division, AGO, July 8, 1901; William McBryar, late First Lieutenant, 49th Infantry, Lincolnton, North Carolina, to AG, USA, July 28, August 16, and August 24, 1901; AAG, USA, to McBryar, August 22, 1901, all in AGO, General Correspondence File, 1890–1917, NA, RG 94 (M-929, roll 2).

33. AAG, USA, to William McBryar, late First Lieutenant, 49th Infantry, Lincolnton, North Carolina, September 5, 1901, AGO, General Correspondence File, 1890–1917, NA, RG 94 (M-929, roll 2).

34. William McBryar, Lincolnton, North Carolina, to Military Secretary, WD, February 3, 1905; AAG, USA, to Recruiting Officer, Charlotte, North Carolina, February 6, 1905; CO, 2d Squadron, 9th Cavalry, to Military Secretary, WD, March 23, 1905, all in AGO, General Correspondence File, 1890–1917, NA, RG 94 (M-929, roll 2).

35. Military Secretary, WD, to Corporal William McBryar, June 15, 1905, and Corporal William McBryar, G Troop, 9th Cavalry, Arlington, Virginia, to Military Secretary, WD, February 26, 1906, AGO, General Correspondence File, 1890–1917, NA, RG 94 (M-929, roll 2).

36. William McBryar, Declarations for Pension, June 8, 1911, and March 29, 1923, VA Pension File XC 2419213, William McBryar; Major H. B. Shattuck, 4th Infantry, Letter of Recommendation, April 15, 1909, and Application for Commission, William McBryar, February 24, 1916, AGO, General Correspondence File, 1890–1917, NA, RG 94 (M-929, roll 2).

37. William McBryar, McNeil Island, Washington, June 10, 1914, to AG, USA; Application for Commission, William McBryar, February 24, 1916; AG, USA, to William McBryar, Route 4, Box 190, Greensboro, North Carolina, March 31, 1916, all in AGO, General Correspondence File, 1890–1917, NA, RG 94 (M-929, roll 2).

38. William McBryar to Veterans Administration, May 20, 1933; Application for Burial Flag, March 10, 1941; Application for Burial Allowance, March 17, 1941, all in VA Pension File XC 2419213, William McBryar.

Chapter 9, "William Wilson and the End of the Indian Wars in the North," pp. 117–32

1. Robert M. Utley, *The Last Days of the Sioux Nation* (New Haven, 1963), 22, 30–31, 33.

2. Ibid., 39.

3. Ibid., 61–62; Robert A. Wooster, *The Military and the United States Indian Policy, 1865–1903* (New Haven, 1988), 193.

4. Quoted in Utley, *Last Days of the Sioux Nation*, 59.

5. Ibid., 60, 69–73; Robert Lee, *Fort Meade and the Black Hills* (Lincoln, 1991), 100.

6. Regimental Returns, 9th Cavalry, November 1890, NA, RG 391 (M-744, roll 90). For a clear statement of the changes wrought by the railroad and telegraph at the time of the Pine Ridge campaign, see R. Eli Paul', "Your Country Is Surrounded," in Richard E. Jensen et al., *Eyewitness at Wounded Knee* (Lincoln, 1991), 23–36.

7. Alexander Perry, "The Ninth U.S. Cavalry in the Sioux Expedition of 1890," in *The Black Military Experience in the American West*, ed. John M. Carroll (New York, 1969), 251–52; Report of Brigadier General Wesley Merritt, CG, Department of the Missouri, in *Annual Report of the Secretary of War, 1891*, 169; Perry D. Jamieson, *Crossing the Deadly Ground: United States Army Tactics, 1865–1899* (Tuscaloosa, 1994), 37.

8. Report of Brigadier General Thomas H. Ruger, CG, Department of Dakota, in *Annual Report of the Secretary of War, 1891*, 179; Utley, *Last Days of the Sioux Nation*, 117–18; Utley, *Frontier Regulars*, 409.

9. George B. Sanford, *Fighting Rebels and Redskins: Experiences in Army Life of Colonel George B. Sanford, 1861–1892*, ed. E. R. Hagemann (Norman, 1969), 91–92; Report of Major General Nelson A. Miles, CG, Military Division of the Missouri, in *Annual Report of the Secretary of War, 1891*, 148.

10. Virginia W. Johnson, *The Unregimented General: A Biography of Nelson A. Miles* (Boston, 1962), 283; Jamieson, *Crossing the Deadly Ground*, 123.

11. Johnson, *Unregimented General*, 283; Perry, "The Ninth U.S. Cavalry in the Sioux Expedition of 1890," 252; Sanford, *Fighting Rebels and Redskins*, 91; Jamieson, *Crossing the Deadly Ground*, 123; William F. Kelley, *Pine Ridge, 1890: An Eye Witness Account of the Events Surrounding the Fighting at Wounded Knee* (San Francisco, 1971), 149.

12. Utley, *Last Days of the Sioux Nation*, 4; Report of General Miles, *Annual Report of the Secretary of War, 1891*, 150; Kelley, *Pine Ridge, 1890*, 148–50.

13. Utley, *Last Days of the Sioux Nation*, 235–36; Perry, "The Ninth U.S. Cavalry in the Sioux Expedition of 1890," 253; Regimental Returns, 9th Cavalry, December 1890, NA, RG 391 (M-744, roll 90).

14. Endorsement, Captain John S. Loud, August 21, 1891, to William O. Wilson, Fort Robinson, to AG, USA, August 14, 1891, AGO, General Correspondence File, 1890–1917, NA, RG 94 (M-929, roll 2); Regimental Returns, 9th Cavalry, December 1890, NA, RG 391 (M-744, roll 90); Perry, "The Ninth U.S. Cavalry in the Sioux Expedition of 1890," 254.

15. Endorsement, Captain John S. Loud, August 21, 1891, to William O. Wilson, Fort Robinson, to AG, USA, August 14, 1891, AGO, General Correspondence File, 1890–1917, NA, RG 94 (M-929, roll 2); Testimony of Lieutenant Philip P. Powell, Proceedings of Wilson General

Court Martial, May 1891, OJAG, Court Martial Case Files, 1809–1894, NA, RG 153 (M-929, roll 2).

16. Proceedings of Wilson General Court Martial, May 1891, OJAG, Court Martial Case Files, 1809–1894, NA, RG 153 (M-929, roll 2).

17. Testimony of Lieutenant Philip P. Powell in ibid.

18. Ibid.; Fred Erisman and Patricia L. Erisman, "Letters from the Field: John Sylvanus Loud and the Pine Ridge Campaign of 1890–1891," *South Dakota History* 26 (Spring 1996): 33.

19. Perry, "The Ninth U.S. Cavalry in the Sioux Expedition of 1890," 253–54.

20. Ibid., 254; Johnson, *Unregimented General*, 287.

21. Johnson, *Unregimented General*, 288; Report of General Miles, in *Annual Report of the Secretary of War, 1891*, 151; John G. Neihardt, *Black Elk Speaks, Being the Life of a Holy Man of the Oglala Sioux* (Lincoln, 1961), 273; Brian C. Pohanka, ed., *Nelson A. Miles, A Documentary Biography of His Military Career, 1861–1903* (Glendale, 1985), 188–89.

22. Regimental Returns, 9th Cavalry, December 1890, NA, RG 391 (M-744, roll 90); Perry, "The Ninth U.S. Cavalry in the Sioux Expedition of 1890," 254; Hamilton, "History of the Ninth Regiment U.S. Cavalry"; Johnson, *Unregimented General*, 288.

23. Report of General Miles, in *Annual Report of the Secretary of War, 1891*, 151–52; Utley, *Last Days of the Sioux Nation*, 1; Kelley, *Pine Ridge, 1890*, 192, 204; Sanford, *Fighting Rebels and Redskins*, 93; Pohanka, ed., *Miles, A Documentary Biography*, 198–99. Private Creek is quoted in Rickey, *Forty Miles a Day on Beans and Hay*, 10.

24. Orders No. 1, Headquarters, Battalion, 9th Cavalry, Pine Ridge Agency, January 1, 1891, AGO, General Correspondence File, 1890–1917, NA, RG 94 (M-929, roll 2); *Army and Navy Journal* 28 (January 17, 1891): 355.

25. Hutcheson, "The Ninth Regiment of Cavalry," 74.

26. William Wilson to CO, Fort Robinson, March 21, 1891, and Proceedings of Wilson General Court Martial, May 1891, OJAG, Court Martial Case Files, 1809–1894, NA, RG 153 (M-929, roll 2).

27. William Wilson to CO, Fort Robinson, March 21, 1891, and to the President of the United States, May 30, 1891, OJAG, Court Martial Case Files, 1809–1894, NA, RG 153 (M-929, roll 2).

28. Regimental Returns, 9th Cavalry, March 1891, NA, RG 391 (M-744, roll 90); Schubert, *Buffalo Soldiers, Braves, and the Brass*, 31.

29. This poem appeared in *Army and Navy Journal* 28 (March 7, 1891): 483. It is sometimes quoted without the last two lines, implying that Prather concluded with unmitigated bitterness. For example, see Jack D. Foner, *The United States Soldier between Two Wars: Army Life and Reforms, 1865–1898* (New York, 1970), 135. Jensen et al., *Eyewitness at Wounded Knee*, 176, quotes Prather in full.

30. For example, Prather wrote that "the Red Skins heard the 9th was near and fled in great dismay." Quoted in Fairfax D. Downey, *Indian-Fighting Army* (New York, 1943), 304–5.

31. Sidney (Nebraska) *Telegraph*, July 25, 1885; *Winners of the West* 1 (September 1924): 1; ibid. 1 (October 1924): 19; ibid. 3 (December 1926): 2; ibid. 4 (December 1927): 3; *Army and Navy Journal* 31 (February 10, 1894): 407.

32. Porter, *Negro on the American Frontier*, 408–9.

33. GCMO 51, Department of the Platte, Omaha, June 26, 1891, OJAG, Court Martial Case Files, 1809–1894, NA, RG 153 (M-929, roll 2).

34. William Wilson to AG, USA, August 14, 1891, and Endorsements; AAG, USA, to CO, Fort Robinson, September 17, 1891, and Endorsements, both in AGO, General Correspondence File, 1890–1917, NA, RG 94 (M-929, roll 2); Amos, *Above and Beyond in the West*, 36; Erisman and Erisman, "Letters from the Field," 33.

35. Amos, *Above and Beyond in the West*, 36; Proceedings of Board of Survey, Fort Duchesne, Utah, September 19, 1893; Captain E. D. Dimmick, CO, H Troop, 9th Cavalry, to AG, USA, November 2, 1893, both in AGO, General Correspondence File, 1890–1917, NA, RG 94 (M-929, roll 2); Preston E. Amos, "Buffalo Soldier Found," *The Annals, Official Publication of the Medal of Honor Historical Society* 16, no. 3 (March 1995): 57.

36. Amos, "Buffalo Soldier Found," 58; Hagerstown *Daily Mail*, May 22, 1988. On a visit to the cemetery in the winter of 1995–96, I found no headstone with Wilson's name on it.

37. Report of General Miles, in *Annual Report of the Secretary of War, 1891*, 154; Sanford, *Fighting Rebels and Redskins*, 93; Utley, *Last Days of the Sioux Nation*, viii, 5; Lee, *Fort Meade*, 127.

38. Foner, *United States Soldier between Two Wars*, 143–44; *Illustrated Review, Ninth Cavalry, U.S.A., Fort D. A. Russell, Wyoming, 1910* (Denver, 1910), 65.

Chapter 10, "Four Cavalrymen in Cuba," pp. 133–44

1. For a summary of the events surrounding the deployment of the *Maine*, the explosion, and the public outcry that followed, see Stanley Karnow, *In Our Image: America's Empire in the Philippines* (New York, 1989), 94–99.

2. Schubert, *On the Trail of the Buffalo Soldier*, 26, 149.

3. "Diary of E. L. Baker, Sergeant-Major Tenth U.S. Cavalry," in Steward, *Colored Regulars*, 255–56; Willard B. Gatewood, Jr., *"Smoked Yankees" and the Struggle for Empire: Letters from Negro Soldiers, 1898–1902* (Urbana, 1971), 31.

4. Gatewood, *"Smoked Yankees" and the Struggle for Empire*, 31–32.

5. Hal Hubener, "Lakeland Jubilee: The African-American Experience, 1882–1954" (unpublished manuscript, n.d.), 4; Glass, *History of the Tenth Cavalry*, 31; Schubert, *On the Trail of the Buffalo Soldier*, 509.

6. Gatewood, *"Smoked Yankees" and the Struggle for Empire*, 32; Willard B. Gatewood, Jr., "Negro Troops in Florida, 1898," *Florida Historical Quarterly* 49 (July 1970): 1–15.

7. Glass, *History of the Tenth Cavalry*, 31.

8. Walter Millis, *The Martial Spirit: A Study of Our War with Spain* (New York, 1965), 147; AGO, *Correspondence Relating to the War with Spain*, 1:51–52; Report of Major General Nelson A. Miles, *Annual Report of the Secretary of War, 1898*, vol. 1, pt. 2:10–11; Report of Lieutenant Carter P. Johnson, *Annual Report of the Secretary of War, 1898*, vol. 1, pt. 2:325; Chaplain C. C. Bateman, "Biographical Sketch of Edward L. Baker, Jr., Sergeant-Major 10th United States Cavalry," AGO, General Correspondence File, 1890–1917, NA, RG 94 (M-929, roll 3).

9. Schubert, *On the Trail of the Buffalo Soldier*, 392; Captain Carter P. Johnson to Adjutant, Fort Robinson, Nebraska, October 4, 1904, AGO, General Correspondence File, 1890–1917, NA, RG 94 (M-929, roll 3); GCMO 17, HQ, Department of the Platte, October 1, 1892, OJAG, Court Martial Case Files, 1809–1894, NA, RG 153 (M-929, roll 3). On the incident at Suggs, Wyoming, see Schubert, "The Suggs Affray: The Black Cavalry in the Johnson County War," *Western Historical Quarterly* 4 (January 1973): 57–68.

10. Steward, *Colored Regulars*, 203–4; Fourth Endorsement, Johnson, Fort Sam Houston, Texas, April 6, 1899, to Johnson to CO, 10th Cavalry, February 18, 1899, and Affidavits, Trumpeter Frank C. Henry and Private William K. Porter, H/10th Cavalry, Bexar County, Texas, April 11, 1899, AGO, General Correspondence File, 1890–1917, NA, RG 94 (M-929, roll 3); Report of Lieutenant Johnson, *Annual Report of the Secretary of War, 1898*, vol. 1, pt. 2:325.

11. Fourth Endorsement, Johnson, Fort Sam Houston, Texas, April 6, 1899, to Johnson to CO, 10th Cavalry, February 18, 1899, AGO, General Correspondence File, 1890–1917, NA, RG 94 (M-929, roll 3).

12. Johnson to CO, 10th Cavalry, February 18, 1899, and Fourth Endorsement, April 6, 1899, ibid.

13. Senate Committee on Veterans' Affairs, *Medal of Honor Recipients*, 350; Memorandum, AGO, December 28, 1897, and AAG to CO, Washington Barracks, December 28, 1897, AGO, General Correspondence File, 1890–1917, NA, RG 94 (M-929, roll 3); Declaration for an Original Invalid Pension, Fitz Lee, 920 North 3rd Street, Leavenworth, Kansas, September 11, 1899, and AG, USA, Statement of Service of Fitz Lee, September 28, 1899, VA Pension File SO 1231751, Fitz Lee.

14. Senate Committee on Veterans' Affairs, *Medal of Honor Recipients*, 365; Proceedings of Board of Officers, Fort Leavenworth, Kansas, July 25, 1892, and Private Wanton, Fort Leavenworth, to AAG, Department of the Missouri, July 18, 1892, with Endorsements, AGO, General Correspondence File, 1890–1917, NA, RG 94 (M-929, roll 3).

15. Fourth Endorsement, Johnson, Fort Sam Houston, Texas, April 6, 1899, to Johnson to CO, 10th Cavalry, February 18, 1899, AGO, General Correspondence File, 1890–1917, NA, RG 94 (M-929, roll 3).

16. Ibid.; Schubert, *On the Trail of the Buffalo Soldier*, 424; Paterson, New Jersey, *Morning Call*, no date [between June 10 and 17, 1899], AGO, General Correspondence File, 1890–1917, NA, RG 94 (M-929, roll 3).

17. Report of Lieutenant Johnson, *Annual Report of the Secretary of War, 1898*, vol. 1, pt. 2:325–26; Cosmas, *An Army for Empire*, 242.

18. Johnson to CO, 10th Cavalry, February 18, 1899, and Fourth Endorsement, April 6, 1899, AGO, General Correspondence File, 1890–1917, NA, RG 94 (M-929, roll 3).

19. Senate Committee on Veterans' Affairs, *Medal of Honor Recipients*, 359, 365.

20. Captain Samuel L. Woodward, 10th Cavalry, Fort Bliss, Texas, to AG, USA, June 18, 1899, and AAG to Fitz Lee, June 23, 1899, AGO, General Correspondence File, 1890–1917, NA, RG 94 (M-929, roll 3); Declaration for an Original Invalid Pension, Fitz Lee, 127 Cheyenne Street, Leavenworth, Kansas, July 10, 1899, and Claimant's Affidavit, Fitz Lee, Leavenworth, Kansas, September 11, 1899, VA Pension File SO 1231751, Fitz Lee.

21. Schubert, *On the Trail of the Buffalo Soldier*, 415; General Affidavit, Charles Taylor and Charles F. Giles, Leavenworth, Kansas, September 11, 1899, and J. L. Davenport, Acting Commissioner, Bureau of Pensions, to Lee, September 22, 1899, VA Pension File SO 1231751, Fitz Lee; Henry Schindler, National Commander, Regular Army and Navy Union, Leavenworth, Kansas, to AG, USA, October 5, 1899, AGO, General Correspondence File, 1890–1917, NA, RG 94 (M-929, roll 3). On the cohesive, mutually supportive community of former buffalo soldiers at Crawford, near Fort Robinson, Nebraska, see Schubert, *Buffalo Soldiers, Braves, and the Brass*, chapter 12.

22. Memorandum, Dr. George N. Perry, October 19, 1898; SO 279, AGO, November 26, 1898; Bell to AG, USA, January 23, 1902; Bell to Secretary of War, March 3, 1906; Affidavit, First Sergeant Lewis M. Smith, USA, Retired, May 18, 1906; Affidavit, G. H. Robinson, formerly of H/10th Cavalry, March 14, 1906; Military Secretary, WD, to Dennis Bell, 1436 T Street, N.W., Washington, D.C., June 6, 1906, all in AGO, General Correspondence File, 1890–1917, NA, RG 94 (M-929, roll 3).

23. AAG to Thompkins, June 23, 1899; Affidavit, First Sergeant Carter Smith, A/10th Cavalry, Manzanillo, Cuba, August 4, 1900; SO 260, WD, November 4, 1914; Descriptive List and Pay Account, Thompkins; AG,

USA, to First Sergeant Thompkins, USA, Retired, April 26, 1915, all in AGO, General Correspondence File, 1890–1917, NA, RG 94 (M-929, roll 3).

24. Paterson, New Jersey, *Morning Call*, no date [between June 10 and 17, 1899], and Memorandum, AGO, July 12, 1901, AGO, General Correspondence File, 1890–1917, NA, RG 94 (M-929, roll 3).

25. Wanton to CO, I/10th Cavalry, July 29, 1909; First Lieutenant Les P. Quinn, Recruiting Office, Newark, New Jersey, to AG, USA, August 5, 1909; Affidavit, Wanton, Fort Ethan Allen, November 5, 1910; Wanton, Naco, Arizona, to CO, 10th Cavalry, August 6, 1915, and Endorsements, all in AGO, General Correspondence File, 1890–1917, NA, RG 94 (M-929, roll 3); "George Henry Wanton," *Negro History Bulletin* 4, no. 1 (January 1941): 87.

26. "George Henry Wanton," 87.

Chapter 11, "Edward Baker and the Limits of Upward Mobility," pp. 145–61

1. Heitman, *Historical Register and Dictionary of the United States Army*, 2:291; Cosmas, *An Army for Empire*, 209; Schubert, *On the Trail of the Buffalo Soldier*, 509.

2. "Diary of E. L. Baker," in Steward, *Colored Regulars*, 258; Glass, *History of the Tenth Cavalry*, 32. The Baker diary covers pages 255 through 279 of Steward's book. Steward is silent on the provenance of the diary; and, after nearly thirty years of intermittent research on buffalo soldiers, I have never seen the manuscript. Nevertheless, I am confident that the diary is authentic.

3. Schubert, *On the Trail of the Buffalo Soldier*, 23–24; Chaplain C. C. Bateman, "Biographical Sketch of Edward L. Baker, Jr., Sergeant-Major 10th United States Cavalry," and Efficiency Report, Edward L. Baker, Jr., Captain, 49th Infantry, USV, Claveria, PI, June 30, 1900, AGO, General Correspondence File, 1890–1917, NA, RG 94 (M-929, roll 3).

4. Schubert, *On the Trail of the Buffalo Soldier*, 23–24; Private Baker, B/10th Cavalry, Fort Apache, Arizona, to Honorable J. M. Carey, House of Representatives, Washington, D.C., December 31, 1889; Carey to CO, Fort Apache, January 11, 1890, and Endorsements, AAG, WD, January 17, 1890, Captain William Davis, CO, B/10th Cavalry, January 31, 1890, and Lieutenant Colonel George G. Huntt, CO, Fort Apache, February 12, 1890, all in AGO, General Correspondence File, 1890–1917, NA, RG 94 (M-929, roll 3).

5. Colonel Jacob K. Mizner to AG, USA, January 19, 1891; AAG, USA, to Mizner, January 30, 1891; Baker, Fort Grant, Arizona, through Colonel Mizner, to AG, USA, January 30, 1891; First Endorsement to Memorandum, First Lieutenant G. W. Jones, Adjutant and CO, Regimental Noncommissioned Staff, AAG, USA, September 8, 1891, all

in AGO, General Correspondence File, 1890–1917, NA, RG 94 (M-929, roll 3).

6. Mizner to AG, USA, April 14, 1892, and AAG, USA, to CO, 10th Cavalry, April 27, 1892, AGO, General Correspondence File, 1890–1917, NA, RG 94 (M-929, roll 3).

7. See Baker, *Roster of Non-Commissioned Officers*.

8. Edward L. Baker, Jr., "The Environments of the Enlisted Man of the United States of To-Day," *Georgia Baptist* 19 (April 13, 1899): 1.

9. Schubert, *On the Trail of the Buffalo Soldier*, 23.

10. Major C. de Grandprey, Military Attaché to the French Embassy, to Baker, October 31, 1896, and Baker to Adjutant, 10th Cavalry, Fort Assiniboine, Montana, November 12, 1896, AGO, General Correspondence File, 1890–1917, NA, RG 94 (M-929, roll 3).

11. First Endorsement, First Lieutenant Malvern H. Barnum, Adjutant, 10th Cavalry, Fort Custer, Montana, November 12, 1896, to Baker to Adjutant, 10th Cavalry, Fort Assiniboine, Montana, November 12, 1896, AGO, General Correspondence File, 1890–1917, NA, RG 94 (M-929, roll 3).

12. Second Endorsement, Colonel Mizner, Fort Custer, November 13, 1896, to Baker to Adjutant, 10th Cavalry, Fort Assiniboine, Montana, November 12, 1896, AGO, General Correspondence File, 1890–1917, NA, RG 94 (M-929, roll 3).

13. Bateman, "Biographical Sketch of Edward L. Baker, Jr.," AGO, General Correspondence File, 1890–1917, NA, RG 94 (M-929, roll 3).

14. Fith Endorsement, Major General Nelson A. Miles, November 25, 1896, to Baker to Adjutant, 10th Cavalry, Fort Assiniboine, Montana, November 12, 1896, AGO, General Correspondence File, 1890–1917, NA, RG 94 (M-929, roll 3).

15. Sixth Endorsement, Assistant Secretary of War Joseph B. Doe, December 2, 1896, to Baker to Adjutant, 10th Cavalry, Fort Assiniboine, Montana, November 12, 1896, AGO, General Correspondence File, 1890–1917, NA, RG 94 (M-929, roll 3).

16. Memorandum, AAG, WD, May 19, 1897; Secretary of War to Secretary of State, May 27, 1897; AAG, WD, to CG, Department of Dakota, July 1, 1897, all in AGO, General Correspondence File, 1890–1917, NA, RG 94 (M-929, roll 3).

17. *Army and Navy Journal* 34 (July 3, 1897): 820.

18. Cosmas, *An Army for Empire*, 209, 214; Schubert, *On the Trail of the Buffalo Soldier*, 509; David F. Trask, *The War with Spain in 1898* (New York, 1981), 241.

19. "Diary of E. L. Baker," 264.

20. Ibid.; Glass, *History of the Tenth Cavalry*, 33.

21. Second Lieutenant Jacob C. Smith, 9th USV Infantry, Crista, Cuba, to General T. A. Baldwin, March 15, 1899; Brigadier General Joseph Wheeler to Senator Francis E. Warren, December 13, 1901; Descriptive List and Account of Pay, Edward L. Baker, 10th Cavalry, August 16, 1901;

Affidavit, Blacksmith Charles E. Parker, G/10th Cavalry, May 5, 1899, all in AGO, General Correspondence File, 1890–1917, NA, RG 94 (M-929, roll 3); "Diary of E. L. Baker," 264–66; Glass, *History of the Tenth Cavalry*, 33; Schubert, *On the Trail of the Buffalo Soldier*, 320; Rebecca Robbins Raines, *Getting the Message Through: A Branch History of the U.S. Army Signal Corps* (Washington, DC, 1996), 93–94.

22. Glass, *History of the Tenth Cavalry*, 34; "Diary of E. L. Baker," 266–67; Trask, *War with Spain in 1898*, 243–44.

23. GO 15, AGO, February 13, 1900, AGO, Orders and Circulars, 1797–1910, NA, RG 94 (M-929, roll 3); Marvin Fletcher, *The Black Soldier and Officer in the United States Army, 1891–1917* (Columbia, 1974), 45–46.

24. (Salt Lake City) *Deseret Evening News*, September 30 and October 1, 1898.

25. Garna L. Christian, *Black Soldiers in Jim Crow Texas, 1899–1917* (College Station, 1995), 3–15; Glass, *History of the Tenth Cavalry*, 39.

26. Baker, Fort Assiniboine, to AG, USA, September 3 and October 21, 1898; Memorandum, Acting Assistant Surgeon Carroll D. Buck, Fort Assiniboine, September 28, 1898; Telegram, Baldwin, Huntsville, Alabama, to AG, USA, October 26, 1898, all in AGO, General Correspondence File, 1890–1917, NA, RG 94 (M-929, roll 3); Steward, *Colored Regulars*, 291–92.

27. Gatewood, *"Smoked Yankees" and the Struggle for Empire*, 104–5; Telegram, AAG, USA, to CG, Augusta, Georgia, March 2, 1899, AGO, General Correspondence File, 1890–1917, NA, RG 94 (M-929, roll 3).

28. Second Lieutenant Jacob C. Smith, 9th USV Infantry, Crista, Cuba, to Baldwin, March 15, 1899, with Endorsements by Baldwin, CO, 7th Cavalry, late Lieutenant Colonel, 10th Cavalry, Camp Columbia, Cuba, July 11, 1899, and Colonel S. M. Whitside, CO, 10th Cavalry, Bayamo, Cuba, July 25, 1899, AGO, General Correspondence File, 1890–1917, NA, RG 94 (M-929, roll 3); Schubert, *On the Trail of the Buffalo Soldier*, 389.

29. Telegram, Captain Thaddeus W. Jones, 10th Cavalry, late Lieutenant Colonel, 10th USV Infantry, to AG, USA, August 30, 1899, AGO, Record and Pension Office, General Correspondence File, 1889–1904, NA, RG 94 (M-929, roll 3).

30. Steward to AG, USA, August 25, 1899, AGO, General Correspondence File, 1890–1917, NA, RG 94 (M-929, roll 3).

31. Bateman, Fort Wright, Washington, to AG, USA, September 6, 1899, AGO, General Correspondence File, 1890–1917, NA, RG 94 (M-929, roll 3).

32. SO 235, WD, October 9, 1899, AGO, Record and Pension Office, General Correspondence File, 1889–1904, NA, RG 94 (M-929, roll 3); SO 8, 49th Infantry, Jefferson Barracks, October 3, 1899, Order Book, 49th Infantry, NA, RG 94; Schubert, *On the Trail of the Buffalo Soldier*, 347, 365.

33. "Extracts from Official Documents for File with Efficiency Record of 2nd Lieut. Edward Lee Baker, Jr., Philippine Scouts, U.S. Army," AGO, General Correspondence File, 1890–1917, NA, RG 94 (M-929, roll 3); *Army and Navy Journal* 38 (October 13, 1900): 151; *Manila Times*, January 22 and February 1, 1900; Regimental Returns, 49th Infantry, January and June 1900 and January 1901, NA, RG 94; Company Returns, L/49th Infantry, USV, March 1900–May 1901, NA, RG 94; Muster Roll, L/49th Infantry, November–December 1899, NA, RG 94; Efficiency Report, Edward L. Baker, Jr., Captain, 49th Infantry, Claveria, PI, June 30, 1900, and Major Henry Wygant, 24th Infantry, Acting Inspector General, 2d District, Department of Northern Luzon, Report of Inspection of Claveria Post, March 11, 1901, AGO, General Correspondence File, 1890–1917, NA, RG 94 (M-929, roll 3).

34. Horace F. Wheaton, "A Feast with the Filipinos," *Colored American Magazine* 3 (June 1903): 154–55; Schubert, *On the Trail of the Buffalo Soldier*, 459, 485.

35. Telegram, CG, Division of the Philippines, to AG, USA, February 8, 1901, AGO File 355163, AGO Document Files, 1890–1917, NA, RG 94; Secretary of War, *Annual Report, 1902*, 1:289; Schubert, *On the Trail of the Buffalo Soldier*, 114, 173; Fletcher, *Black Soldier and Officer*, 74.

36. Baker to AG, Division of the Philippines, March 15, 1901, AGO, General Correspondence File, 1890–1917, NA, RG 94 (M-929, roll 3).

37. On black veterans who chose to seek their fortunes in the Philippines, see Era Bell Thompson, "Veterans Who Never Came Home," *Ebony* 27 (October 1972): 104–8, 112–15.

38. George M. Cortelyou, Secretary to the President, to Secretary of War Elihu Root, August 6, 1901; Secretary of War Root to Cortelyou, August 9, 1901; Brigadier General Joseph Wheeler to Senator Francis E. Warren, December 13, 1901; Baker to the President of the United States, January 2, 1902; Frederic Remington, New Rochelle, New York, to President Roosevelt, January 8, 1902; Baker, San Juan de BocBoc, Batangas, Philippines, to AG, USA, June 15, 1902; President Joshua H. Jones, Wilberforce University, to Military Secretary, WD, April 12, 1906, all in AGO, General Correspondence File, 1890–1917, NA, RG 94 (M-929, roll 3).

39. Senate Committee on Veterans' Affairs, *Medal of Honor Recipients*, 349; AAG, WD, to Second Lieutenant Edward L. Baker, Jr., Philippine Scouts, March 8, 1902, and Baker, Calamba, Laguna, Luzon, Philippines, to AG, USA, September 1, 1902, AGO, General Correspondence File, 1890–1917, NA, RG 94 (M-929, roll 3).

40. Baker, CO, 33d Company, Tabaco, Albay, to AG, 3d Brigade, Department of Luzon, Batangas, September 12, 1903, AGO, General Correspondence File, 1890–1917, NA, RG 94 (M-929, roll 3).

41. Individual Service Report, Baker, July 1, 1904–June 30, 1906, and Telegram, AG, USA, to Major General Leonard Wood, Manila, Sep-

tember 27, 1906, AGO, General Correspondence File, 1890–1917, NA, RG 94 (M-929, roll 3).

42. Proceedings of Examining Board, Case of First Lieutenant Edward L. Baker, 37th Co., Philippine Scouts, Camp Hayt, Samar, July 9, 1908, AGO, General Correspondence File, 1890–1917, NA, RG 94 (M-929, roll 3).

43. Proceedings of Examining Board, Case of First Lieutenant Edward L. Baker, July 9, 1908; Major General J. H. Maston, CG, Division of the Philippines, August 4, 1908; AG, USA, September 22, 1908, all in AGO, General Correspondence File, 1890–1917, NA, RG 94 (M-929, roll 3).

44. Appointment, Baker, November 11, 1908, AGO, General Correspondence File, 1890–1917, NA, RG 94 (M-929, roll 3).

45. VA Pension File XC 2715800, Edward L. Baker, Jr.

46. Baker to AG, USA, July 14, 1909, AGO, General Correspondence File, 1890–1917, NA, RG 94 (M-929, roll 3).

47. Endorsement, Major General William Duvall, CG, Division of the Philippines, to Baker to AG, USA, July 14, 1909, AGO, General Correspondence File, 1890–1917, NA, RG 94 (M-929, roll 3).

48. AG, USA, to QMG, USA, September 10, 1909, AGO, General Correspondence File, 1890–1917, NA, RG 94 (M-929, roll 3).

49. AG, USA, to CO, Recruiting Depot, Fort McDowell, California, September 24, 1909, and January 6, 1910; both in AGO, General Correspondence File, 1890–1917, NA, RG 94 (M-929, roll 3).

50. SO 4, WD, January 6, 1910; Telegram, CO, Fort McDowell, to AG, USA, January 12, 1910; Descriptive List and Pay Account, Baker, 1021 Sedora Street, Los Angeles; Major General Arthur Murray, CO, Western Department, San Francisco, to AG, USA, August 27, 1913; Report of Death and Disposal of Remains, August 29, 1913, all in AGO, General Correspondence File, 1890–1917, NA, RG 94 (M-929, roll 3).

Chapter 12, "The Recognition of Black Valor," pp. 163–73

1. Steward, *Colored Regulars*, 280.

2. See the cover story, "Military Injustice," *U.S. News & World Report* 120 (May 6, 1996), especially the article by Joseph L. Galloway entitled "Debt of Honor," on 28–31, 34, 36, 38–39.

3. Coffman, *Old Army*, 369.

4. Lee, *Fort Meade and the Black Hills*, 161.

5. John P. Langellier, *Men A-Marching: The African American Soldier in the West, 1866–1896* (Springfield, 1995), 27.

6. Dowling, "Intelligence in the Final Indian Wars, 1866–1887," 25.

7. Thomas D. Phillips, "The Black Regulars," in *The West of the American People*, ed. Allan G. Bogue et al. (Itasca, n.d.), 141. Phillips

breaks down the 141 engagements by regiment as follows: Ninth Cavalry, 68; Tenth Cavalry, 49; Twenty-fourth Infantry, 9; and Twenty-Fifth Infantry, 15.

8. Glass, *History of the Tenth Cavalry*, 22.

9. Schubert, *On the Trail of the Buffalo Soldier*, 116, 289, 371, 456–57.

10. Coffman, *Old Army*, 309; Schubert, *Buffalo Soldiers, Braves, and the Brass*, 61–63.

11. Regimental Returns, 10th Cavalry, February 1868, September 1870, and May 1879, NA, RG 393 (M-744, rolls 95 and 96).

12. GCMO 17, HQ, Department of the Platte, October 1, 1892, OJAG, Court Martial Case Files, 1809–1894, NA, RG 153 (M-929, roll 3).

13. Schubert, *On the Trail of the Buffalo Soldier*, 147.

14. Murray Kempton, "The Beat of War," *New York Review of Books* 43 (February 15, 1996): 40.

15. William W. Gwaltney, "The Making of *Buffalo Soldiers West*," *Colorado Heritage* (Spring 1996): 47.

16. M. Dion Thompson, "Visiting the World of Buffalo Soldiers," Baltimore *Sun*, April 21, 1996, travel section.

17. *New York Times*, May 15, 1994.

18. Patricia Erickson, "Buffalo Soldier Monument Planned," *Public History News* 12 (Fall 1991): 1; Sandra Griffin, "Silver City Paying Tribute to Buffalo Soldier," *New Mexico Magazine* (July 1992): 31.

19. Author's telephone conversation with Lorri Welsh, 90th Services Squadron, Warren Air Force Base, October 7, 1996.

20. Cincinnati *Enquirer*, October 28, 1984.

21. Hagerstown *Daily Mail*, May 22, 1988.

22. Program, Memorial Day, May 29, 1995, "A Celebration of America's Forgotten Heroes," First Sergeant Augustus Walley, St. Luke's United Methodist Church, Reisterstown, Maryland; author's personal notes on the proceedings.

23. Minneapolis *Star Tribune*, August 20, 1996.

24. Program, Memorial Day, May 27, 1996, " 'Lest We Forget,' A Celebration of America's Forgotten Heroes," Soldiers' and Airmen's Home National Cemetery, Washington, DC.

25. Program, Dedication of the African-American Medal of Honor Monument, Morgan State University, Baltimore, May 5, 1995; author's personal notes on the ceremony.

26. GO 15, HQ, Department of the Army, May 31, 1991.

27. Elliott V. Converse III et al., "The Medal of Honor and African Americans in the United States Army during World War II," unpublished study for the United States Army Military Awards Branch, Shaw University, 1995; Washington *Post*, April 28, 1996; Galloway, "Debt of Honor," 36. The Shaw study was published by McFarland and Company in 1996 as *The Exclusion of Black Soldiers from the Medal of Honor in World War II: The Study Commissioned by the United States Army to In-*

vestigate Racial Bias in the Awarding of the Nation's Highest Military Decoration.

28. Joseph L. Galloway, "The Last of the Buffalo Soldiers," *U.S. News & World Report* 120 (May 6, 1996): 45–46; Washington *Post*, April 29, 1996; *New York Times*, May 7 and 23, 1996.

Bibliography

Military Records in the National Archives

Adjutant General's Office, Document Files, 1890–1917. RG 94.
Documents Relating to the Military and Naval Service of Blacks
    Awarded the Congressional Medal of Honor from the Civil War
    to the Spanish-American War. Microcopy M-929, 3 rolls.
        Roll 2. Indian Campaigns—U.S. Regular Army.
        Roll 3. Spanish-American War—U.S. Regular Army.
Fort Robinson, Nebraska, Post Orders, 1886–1898. RG 393.
Judge Advocate General's Office, General Court Martial Case Files.
    RG 153.
Military Division of the Missouri, Special File, Seminole-Negro In-
    dians, 1872–1876. Entry 2547, RG 393.
Principal Record Division, Adjutant General's Office, Document
    Files. RG 94.
        File 5993 PRD 1890, Henry Johnson.
        File 12608 PRD 1890, Augustus Walley.
Record and Pension Office, General Correspondence File, 1889–
    1904. RG 94.
Register of Enlistments in the United States Army, 1798-1914.
    RG 94. Microcopy M-233.
        Roll 31, Volumes 62–63, 1866, A–O.
        Roll 32, Volume 64, 1866, P–Z.
Unit Records
    Ninth Cavalry. RG 391.
        Letters, Orders, and Reports Received from and Relating
            to Members of the Ninth Cavalry ("Name File"), 1867–
            1898.
        Special Orders & General Orders Issued, 1876–1878.
        Regimental Orders Issued, 1876–1881.
        Regimental Returns, 1866–1891. Microcopy M-744,
            Rolls 87–89.
    Tenth Cavalry. RG 391.
        Regimental Returns, 1887–1890. Microcopy M-744,
            Rolls 97–98.
    Twenty-fourth Infantry. RG 391.
        Regimental Returns, 1870–1889. Microcopy M-665,
            Rolls 245–47.

Forty-ninth Infantry. RG 94.
  Company Returns, L Company, 1900-1901.
  Descriptive Books, K Company and M Company.
  Muster Rolls, L Company, 1899-1901.
  Order Book.
  Regimental Returns, 1899-1901.
Veterans Administration Pension Files
  File XC 2715800, Edward L. Baker, Jr.
  File SC 441287, Thomas Boyne.
  File C 2577213, William Henry Bush.
  File C 922002, Clinton Greaves.
  File SO 1231751, Fitz Lee.
  File XC 2419213, William McBryar.

Published Works

Amos, Preston E. *Above and Beyond in the West: Black Medal of Honor
  Winners, 1870–1890.* Washington, DC: Potomac Corral, The West-
  erners, 1974.
———. " 'Augustus Walley Day' Observed in Maryland County,"
  *The Annals, Official Publication of the Medal of Honor Historical
  Society* 17, no. 1 (September 1995): 11–13.
———. "Buffalo Soldier Found," *The Annals, Official Publication of
  the Medal of Honor Historical Society* 16, no. 3 (March 1995): 57–
  59.
Baker, Edward L., Jr., "The Environments of the Enlisted Man of
  the United States of To-Day," *Georgia Baptist* 19 (April 13, 1899):
  1.
———. *Roster of Non-Commissioned Officers of the Tenth Cavalry with
  Some Regimental Reminiscences, Appendixes, etc., connected with the
  Early History of the Regiment.* St. Paul, MN: Wm. Kennedy Print-
  ing Company, 1897. Mattituck, NY: J. M. Carroll and Company,
  1983.
Ball, Eve. *In the Days of Victorio: Recollections of a Warm Springs
  Apache.* Tucson: University of Arizona Press, 1970.
Bennett, Lerone, Jr. *Before the Mayflower: A History of Black America.*
  New York: Penguin Books, 1989.
Beyer, W. F., and O. F. Keydel. *Deeds of Valor: How America's Heroes
  Won the Medal of Honor.* 2 vols. Detroit: Perrien-Keydel Company,
  1903.
Bogue, Allan G., Thomas D. Phillips, and James E. Wright, eds. *The
  West of the American People.* Itasca, IL: F. E. Peacock, n.d.
Brinsfield, John. "The Battle of New Market Heights," *Soldiers* 51
  (February 1996): 50–51.

Carroll, John M., ed. *The Black Military Experience in the American West*. New York: Liveright, 1969.

Cashin, Herschel V., Charles Alexander, William T. Anderson, Arthur M. Brown, and Horace W. Bivins. *Under Fire with the Tenth Cavalry*. London: F. Tennyson Neely, 1899.

Christian, Garna L. *Black Soldiers in Jim Crow Texas, 1899–1917*. College Station: Texas A & M University Press, 1995.

Clarke, Powhatan. "A Hot Trail," *Cosmopolitan* 22 (October 1894): 706–16.

Coffman, Edward M. *The Old Army: A Portrait of the American Army in Peacetime, 1784–1898*. New York: Oxford University Press, 1968.

Cornish, Dudley Taylor. *The Sable Arm: Black Troops in the Union Army, 1861–1865*. Lawrence: University Press of Kansas, 1987.

Cosmas, Graham A. *An Army for Empire: The United States Army in the Spanish-American War*. Columbia: University of Missouri Press, 1971.

Cox, Clinton. *The Forgotten Heroes: The Story of the Buffalo Soldiers*. New York: Scholastic, 1993.

Delgado, Deane G. *Historical Markers in New Mexico: A Traveler's Guide*. Santa Fe, NM: Ancient City Press, 1990.

DeSalvo, James. "The Home's Heroes Span 5 Wars," *United States Soldiers' and Airmen's Home* 11 (December 18, 1992): 14–15.

Downey, Fairfax D. *The Buffalo Soldiers in the Indian Wars*. New York: McGraw-Hill, 1969.

———. *Indian-Fighting Army*. New York: Charles Scribner's Sons, 1943.

Dunlay, Thomas W. *Wolves for the Blue Soldiers: Indian Scouts and Auxiliaries with the United States Army, 1860–1890*. Lincoln: University of Nebraska Press, 1982.

Emmitt, Robert. *The Last War Trail: The Utes and the Settlement of Colorado*. Norman: University of Oklahoma Press, 1954.

Erickson, Patricia. "Buffalo Soldier Monument Planned,"*Public History News* 12 (Fall 1991): 1.

Erisman, Fred, and Patricia L. Erisman. "Letters from the Field: John Sylvanus Loud and the Pine Ridge Campaign of 1890–1891," *South Dakota History* 26 (Spring 1996): 24–45.

Fletcher, Marvin. *The Black Soldier and Officer in the United States Army, 1891–1917*. Columbia: University of Missouri Press, 1974.

Foner, Jack D. *The United States Soldier between Two Wars: Army Life and Reforms, 1865–1898*. New York: Humanities Press, 1970.

Fowler, Arlen L. *The Black Infantry in the West, 1869–1891*. Westport, CT: Greenwood, 1971.

Galloway, Joseph L. "Debt of Honor," *U.S. News & World Report* 120 (May 6, 1996): 28–31, 34, 36, 38–39.

———. "The Last of the Buffalo Soldiers," *U.S. News & World Report* 120 (May 6, 1996): 45–46.

Gatewood, Willard B., Jr. "Negro Troops in Florida, 1898," *Florida Historical Quarterly* 49 (July 1970): 1–15.

———. *"Smoked Yankees" and the Struggle for Empire: Letters from Negro Soldiers, 1898–1902*. Urbana: University of Illinois Press, 1971.

"George Henry Wanton," *Negro History Bulletin* 4, no. 1 (January 1941): 87.

Giese, Dale F. *Echoes of the Bugle: Forts of New Mexico*. N.p., 1991.

Gladstone, William A. *United States Colored Troops, 1863–1867*. Gettysburg, PA: Thomas Publications, 1990.

Glass, Edward L. N. *The History of the Tenth Cavalry, 1866–1921*. Fort Collins, CO: Old Army Press, 1972.

Glathaar, Joseph T. *Forged in Battle: The Civil War Alliance of Black Soldiers and White Officers*. New York: Free Press, 1990.

Greene, A. C. *The Last Captive*. Austin, TX: Encino Press, 1972.

Griffin, Sandra. "Silver City Paying Tribute to Buffalo Soldier," *New Mexico Magazine* (July 1992): 31.

Gwaltney, William W. "The Making of *Buffalo Soldiers West*," *Colorado Heritage* (Spring 1996): 45–48.

Hamersley, L. R. *Records of Living Officers of the United States Army*. Philadelphia: L. R. Hamersley and Company, 1884.

Hargrove, Hondon B. *Black Union Soldiers in the Civil War*. Jefferson, NC: McFarland and Company, 1988.

Hart, Herbert M. *Old Forts of the Far West*. New York: Bonanza Books, 1965.

Heitman, Francis B. *Historical Register and Dictionary of the United States Army*. 2 volumes. Washington, DC: Government Printing Office, 1903.

Hollandsworth, James G., Jr. *The Louisiana Native Guards: The Black Military Experience during the Civil War*. Baton Rouge: Louisiana State University Press, 1995.

Illustrated Review, Ninth Cavalry, U.S.A., Fort D. A. Russell, Wyoming, 1910. Denver: Medley and Johnson, 1910.

Jamieson, Perry D. *Crossing the Deadly Ground: United States Army Tactics, 1865–1899*. Tuscaloosa: University of Alabama Press, 1994.

Jensen, Richard E., R. Eli Paul, and John E. Carter. *Eyewitness at Wounded Knee*. Lincoln: University of Nebraska Press, 1991.

Johnson, Edward A. *History of Negro Soldiers in the Spanish-American War*. Raleigh, NC: Capital Printing Company, 1899.

Johnson, John Allen. "The Medal of Honor and Sergeant John Ward and Private Pompey Factor," *Arkansas Historical Quarterly* 29 (1970): 361–75.

Johnson, Virginia W. *The Unregimented General: A Biography of Nelson A. Miles*. Boston: Houghton Mifflin, 1962.

Karnow, Stanley. *In Our Image: America's Empire in the Philippines*. New York: Random House, 1989.

Katz, William Loren. *Black Indians: A Hidden Heritage*. New York: Atheneum, 1986.

Kelley, William F. *Pine Ridge, 1890: An Eye Witness Account of the Events Surrounding the Fighting at Wounded Knee*. San Francisco: Pierre Bovis, 1971.

Kempton, Murray. "The Beat of War," *New York Review of Books* 43 (February 15, 1996): 35–40.

Kennedy, Frances, ed. *The Civil War Battlefield Guide*. Boston: Houghton Mifflin, 1990.

Kerrigan, Evans E. *American Medals and Decorations*. Noroton Heights, CT: Medallic Publishing Company, 1990.

Langellier, John P. *Men A-Marching: The African American Soldier in the West, 1866–1896*. Springfield, PA: Steven Wright, 1995.

Leckie, William H. *The Buffalo Soldiers: A Narrative of the Negro Cavalry in the West*. Norman: University of Oklahoma Press, 1967.

———. *The Military Conquest of the Southern Plains*. Norman: University of Oklahoma Press, 1963.

———, and Shirley A. Leckie. *Unlikely Warriors: General Benjamin H. Grierson and His Family*. Norman: University of Oklahoma Press, 1984.

Lee, Irwin H. *Negro Medal of Honor Men*. New York: Dodd, Mead, 1967.

Lee, Robert. *Fort Meade and the Black Hills*. Lincoln: University of Nebraska Press, 1991.

Logan, Rayford W. *The Betrayal of the Negro, from Rutherford B. Hayes to Woodrow Wilson*. New York: Collier Books, 1965.

McAndrews, Eugene V. "Sergeant Major Frederick Gerber: Engineer Legend," *The Military Engineer* 63 (July–August 1971): 240–41.

McMurray, John. *Recollections of a Colored Troop*. Randon W. Bartley, comp. Brookville, PA: McMurray Company, 1994.

Miller, Darlis A. *Soldiers and Settlers: Military Supply in the Southwest, 1861–1885*. Albuquerque: University of New Mexico Press, 1989.

Miller, Robert. *Buffalo Soldiers: The Story of Emanuel Stance*. Morristown, NJ: Silver Press, 1995.

Millis, Walter. *The Martial Spirit: A Study of Our War with Spain*. New York: Viking Press, 1965.

Mulroy, Kevin. *Freedom on the Border: The Seminole Maroons in Florida, the Indian Territory, Coahuila, and Texas*. Lubbock: Texas Tech University Press, 1993.

Nankivell, John H. *The History of the Twenty-fifth Regiment United States Infantry, 1869–1926.* Fort Collins, CO: Old Army Press, 1972.

Neihardt, John G. *Black Elk Speaks, Being the Life Story of a Holy Man of the Oglala Sioux.* Lincoln: University of Nebraska Press, 1961.

Parker, James. *The Old Army Memories, 1872–1918.* Philadelphia: Dorrance and Company, 1928.

Pohanka, Brian C., ed. *Nelson A. Miles, A Documentary Biography of His Military Career, 1861–1903.* Glendale: Arthur H. Clark, 1985.

Porter, Kenneth Wiggins. *The Negro on the American Frontier.* New York: Arno Press and the New York Times, 1971.

"Preventing Cotton-Press Damage," *United States Department of Agriculture Leaflet No. 241,* 1944: 2–8.

Price, Byron. "Mutiny at San Pedro Springs," *By Valor & Arms, The Journal of American Military History* 1 (Spring 1975): 31–34.

Raines, Rebecca Robbins. *Getting the Message Through: A Branch History of the U.S. Army Signal Corps.* Washington, DC: U.S. Army Center of Military History, 1996.

Rickey, Don, Jr. *Forty Miles a Day on Beans and Hay: The Enlisted Soldier Fighting the Indian Wars.* Norman: University of Oklahoma Press, 1963.

Robinson, Charles M., III. *Bad Hand: A Biography of General Ranald S. Mackenzie.* Austin, TX: State House Press, 1993.

Sanford, Joseph B. *Fighting Rebels and Redskins: Experiences in Army Life of Colonel George B. Sanford, 1861–1892,* ed. E. R. Hagemann. Norman: University of Oklahoma Press, 1969.

Santala, Russel D. *The Ute Campaign: A Study in the Use of the Military Instrument.* Fort Leavenworth, KS: U.S. Army Command and General Staff College, 1994.

Schubert, Frank N. *Buffalo Soldiers, Braves, and the Brass: The Story of Fort Robinson, Nebraska.* Shippensburg, PA: White Mane, 1993.

———. *On the Trail of the Buffalo Soldier: Biographies of African Americans in the U.S. Army, 1866–1917.* Wilmington, DE: Scholarly Resources, 1995.

———. "The Suggs Affray: The Black Cavalry in the Johnson County War," *Western Historical Quarterly* 4 (January 1973): 57–68.

———. *Vanguard of Expansion: Army Engineers in the Trans-Mississippi West, 1819–1879.* Washington, DC: Government Printing Office, 1980.

———. "The Violent World of Emanuel Stance, Fort Robinson, 1887," *Nebraska History* 55 (Summer 1974): 203–19.

Sommers, Richard J. *Richmond Redeemed: The Siege at Petersburg.* Garden City, NY: Doubleday and Company, 1981.

Sonnichsen, C. L. *The Mescalero Apaches.* Norman: University of Oklahoma Press, 1973.

Starobin, Robert S. *Industrial Slavery in the Old South*. New York: Oxford University Press, 1970.

Steward, Theophilus G. *The Colored Regulars in the United States Army*. Philadelphia: A.M.E. Book Concern, 1904.

Sullivan, Jerry M. *Fort McKavett: A Texas Frontier Post*. N.p.: Texas Parks and Wildlife Department, n.d. Originally published as *The Museum Journal* 20 (1981).

Swanson, Donald A. *Seminole, Lipan, Cherokee, Creek Indian Scouts: Enlistment Records, Ft. Clark*. Bronte, TX: Ames-American, n.d.

Thompson, Era Bell. "Veterans Who Never Came Home," *Ebony* 27 (October 1972): 104–8, 112–15.

Thrapp, Dan L. *Al Sieber, Chief of Scouts*. Norman: University of Oklahoma Press, 1964.

———. *The Conquest of Apacheria*. Norman: University of Oklahoma Press, 1967.

———. *Victorio and the Mimbres Apaches*. Norman: University of Oklahoma Press, 1974.

Thweatt, Hiram. *What the Newspapers Say of the Negro Soldier in the Spanish-American War*. Thomasville, GA: N.p., n.d.

Thybony, Scott. "Against All Odds, Black Seminoles Won Their Freedom," *Smithsonian* 22 (August 1991): 90–101.

Trask, David F. *The War with Spain in 1898*. New York: Macmillan, 1981.

U.S. Army. Adjutant General's Office. *Correspondence Relating to the War with Spain, including the Insurrection in the Philippine Islands and the China Relief Expedition, April 15, 1898, to July 30, 1902*. 2 volumes. Washington, DC: Center of Military History, United States Army, 1993.

———. Headquarters, Military Division of the Missouri. *Record of Engagements with Hostile Indians within the Military Division of the Missouri from 1868 to 1882, Lieutenant General P. H. Sheridan, Commanding*. Washington, DC: Government Printing Office, 1882.

———. Public Information Division. *The Medal of Honor of the United States Army*. Washington, DC: Government Printing Office, 1948.

U.S. Congress. *Congressional Globe*, 39th Cong., 1st sess., 1866.

———. Senate. Committee on Veterans' Affairs. *Medal of Honor Recipients, 1863–1978*. 96th Cong., 1st sess., Senate Committee Print No. 3, February 14, 1979. Washington, DC: Government Printing Office, 1979.

U.S. Department of War. *Annual Report of the Secretary of War*. Washington, DC: Government Printing Office, 1870–1902.

U.S. Navy. *Dictionary of American Naval Fighting Ships*. Volume 5. Washington, DC: Navy Department, 1970.

Utley, Robert M. *Frontier Regulars: The United States Army and the Indian, 1866–1890*. New York: Macmillan, 1973.

————. *The Last Days of the Sioux Nation*. New Haven: Yale University Press, 1963.

Wade, Richard C. *Slavery in the Cities: The South, 1820–1860*. New York: Oxford University Press, 1964.

Wallace, Edward S. "General John Lapham Bullis, Thunderbolt of the Texas Frontier, I," *Southwestern Historical Quarterly* 54 (April 1951): 452–61.

————. "General John Lapham Bullis, Thunderbolt of the Texas Frontier, II," *Southwestern Historical Quarterly* 55 (July 1951): 77–85.

Watson, James W. "Scouting in Arizona," *Journal of the U.S. Cavalry Association* 10 (June 1897): 128–35.

Wheaton, Horace F. "A Feast with the Filipinos," *Colored American Magazine* 3 (June 1903): 154–55.

Williams, George Washington. *A History of the Negro Troops in the War of the Rebellion, 1861–1865*. New York: Bergman Publishers, 1968.

Wilson, Joseph T. *The Black Phalanx: African American Soldiers in the War of Independence, the War of 1812, and the Civil War*. New York: Da Capo Press, 1994.

Woodhull, Frost. "The Seminole Indian Scouts on the Border," *Frontier Times* 15 (December 1937): 118–27.

Wooster, Robert A. *The Military and the United States Indian Policy, 1865–1903*. New Haven: Yale University Press, 1988.

Newspapers

Army and Navy Journal, 1886–1900.
Baltimore *Sun*, 1938, 1995–96.
Chicago *Inter-Ocean*, 1890.
Cincinnati *Enquirer*, 1984.
(Crawford) *Northwest Nebraska News*, 1934.
Crawford (Nebraska) *Tribune*, 1904.
Fort Worth *Star Telegram*, 1990.
Hagerstown (Maryland) *Daily Mail*, 1988.
Manila Times, 1900.
Minneapolis *Star Tribune*, 1996.
New York Times, 1994, 1996.
Paterson (New Jersey) *Morning Call*, 1899.
Richmond *Planet*, 1898.
(Salt Lake City) *Deseret Evening News*, 1898.
Sidney (Nebraska) *Telegraph*, 1885.
Washington *Post*, 1996.
Washington *Times*, 1995.

Other

Converse, Elliott V., III, Robert K. Griffith, Daniel K. Gibran, Richard H. Kohn, and John A. Cash. "The Medal of Honor and African Americans in the United States Army during World War II." Unpublished study for the United States Army Military Awards Branch, Shaw University, 1995.

Dowling, Thomas E. "Intelligence in the Final Indian Wars, 1866–1887." Master of Science of Strategic Intelligence thesis, Joint Military Intelligence College, 1996.

Fletcher, Marvin E. "The Negro Soldier and the United States Army, 1891–1917." Ph.D. diss., University of Wisconsin, 1968.

Hamilton, Colonel George F. "History of the Ninth Regiment U.S. Cavalry, 1866–1906." Unpublished manuscript. Copy from United States Military Academy Library, West Point.

Hubener, Hal. "Lakeland Jubilee: The African-American Experience, 1882–1954." Unpublished manuscript, Lakeland, Florida, Public Library, n.d.

Johnson, Harry E., Sr. "The Formation of the Ninth Cavalry Regiment, July 1866 to March 1867." Master of Military Art and Science thesis, U.S. Army Command and General Staff College, 1991.

McMiller, Anita Williams. "Buffalo Soldiers: The Formation of the Tenth Cavalry Regiment from September 1866 to August 1867." Master of Military Art and Science thesis, U.S. Army Command and General Staff College, 1990.

Program, Dedication of the African-American Medal of Honor Monument, Morgan State University, Baltimore, Maryland, May 5, 1995.

Program, Memorial Day, May 29, 1995, "A Celebration of America's Forgotten Heroes," First Sergeant Augustus Walley, St. Luke's United Methodist Church, Reisterstown, Maryland.

Program, Memorial Day, May 27, 1996, " 'Lest We Forget,' A Celebration of America's Forgotten Heroes," Soldiers' and Airmen's Home National Cemetery, Washington, DC.

Index

Adams, John Q. (Ninth Cavalry), 46, 63
Ahern, George P., 136, 137
Albay Province, Philippines, 159
Alexander, John, 110
Alexandria, Louisiana, 9
Alexandria, Virginia, 141
American Legion, 144
Anderson, Marian, 110
Anderson, William T., 88
Apache Indians, 15, 20, 31, 41–42, 48, 56–57, 61, 68, 102, 129, 153, 166; Chiricahua band, 44; Mescalero band, 17, 44, 77; origin of name, 48; Warm Springs band, 44, 49
Apache wars, 49, 67, 73, 76–77, 165
Apacheria, 48
Appomattox Court House, Virginia, 18, 48
Arapaho Indians, 15, 32
Arlington National Cemetery, Virginia, 71, 114, 115, 144
Army and Navy Journal, 26, 126, 131
Arrington, George, 93, 95, 98
Arthur, George G., 113

Bacon, John M., 18
Badge of Military Merit, 1
Badie, David, 78, 83
Bailey, Albert, 14
Baker, Dexter Murat, 159
Baker, Edward L., Jr., 111, 114, 145–61, 166, 169; applies for commission in Philippine Scouts, 158; applies for French cavalry school, 148–50; appointed sergeant major of Tenth Cavalry, 148; background, 147–48; in Cuba, 145, 150–52; Medal

of Honor, 154, 159; in Philippines, 155–57, 159–60; quoted, 151, 159; retirement and death, 160–61
Baker, Eugenia Sheridan, 159
Baker, Mary Elizabeth Hawley, 147, 158
Baker, Vernon, 172, 173
Baldwin, Theodore A., 151, 155
Baltimore, Maryland, 57, 109
Banks, Frank, 133, 134
Barnes, William E., 3
Barnum, Malvern Hill, 149
Barongan, Samar, Philippines, 160
Bateman, Cephas C., 147, 149, 155
Beaty, Powhatan, 3
Beck, William H., 157
Belknap, William W., 28
Bell, Arthur, 137
Bell, Dennis, 137, 141, 142
Bell, James M., 87
Bellevue, Nebraska, 130
Bennett, Lerone: quoted, 23
Benson, Caleb, 64, 68, 69
Berry, George, 152
Bettens, Philip A., 123
Beyer, Charles D., 41, 44–45, 49–52, 54–56
Biddle, James, 56–57
Big Flats, New York, 54
Big Foot (Sioux), 121
Black Hills, Dakota Territory, 59
Black officers, 5, 110–11, 158
Black Range, New Mexico, 53–54, 79
Bliss, Zenas R., 28, 29, 96
Boca Grande Mountains: battle (1877), 45
Boston, Massachusetts, 144
Bowen, Thomas. *See* Boyne, Thomas
Bowers, Edward, 17

221